Why the Middle Ages Matter

The word "medieval" is often used in a negative way when talking about contemporary issues. *Why the Middle Ages Matter* refreshes our thinking about this historical era, and our own, by looking at some pressing concerns from today's world, asking how these issues were really handled in the medieval period, and showing why the past matters now. The contributors here cover topics such as torture, marriage, sexuality, imprisonment, refugees, poverty, work, the status of women, disability, race, political leadership, and end of life care. They focus on a variety of regions, from North Africa and the Middle East, through Western and Central Europe, to the British Isles.

This collection challenges many negative stereotypes relating to medieval people, revealing a world from which, for instance, much could be learned about looking after the spiritual needs of the dying, and about integrating prisoners into the wider community through an emphasis on reconciliation between victim and criminal. It represents a new level of engagement with issues of social justice by medievalists and provides a highly engaging way into studying the middle ages. All the essays are written so as to be accessible to students, and each is accompanied by a list of further readings.

Celia Chazelle is Professor of History and co-director of the Center for Prison Outreach and Education at the College of New Jersey, **Simon Doubleday** is Professor of History at Hofstra University, **Felice Lifshitz** is Professor of Women's Studies, with a joint appointment to the Campus St. Jean, at the University of Alberta, and **Amy G. Remensnyder** is Associate Professor of History and Director of the Program in Medieval Studies at Brown University.

Why the Middle Ages Matter

Medieval light on modern injustice

Edited by
Celia Chazelle, Simon Doubleday, Felice
Lifshitz, and Amy G. Remensnyder

Routledge
Taylor & Francis Group

LONDON AND NEW YORK

First published 2012
by Routledge
2 Park Square, Milton Park, Abingdon, Oxon OX14 4RN

Simultaneously published in the USA and Canada
by Routledge
711 Third Avenue, New York, NY 10017

Routledge is an imprint of the Taylor & Francis Group, an informa business

British Library Cataloguing in Publication Data
A catalogue record for this book is available from the British Library

Library of Congress Cataloging-in-Publication Data
Why the Middle Ages matter: medieval light on modern injustice/edited
by Celia Chazelle ... [et al.].
p. cm.
1. Social justice. 2. Social justice--History--To 1500. 3. Social problems--
History--To 1500. 4. Social history--Medieval, 500–1500. I. Chazelle, Celia
Martin.
HM671.W49 2011
303.3'720940902--dc22
2011010784

ISBN: 978-0-415-78064-3 (hbk)
ISBN: 978-0-415-78065-0 (pbk)
ISBN: 978-0-203-80386-8 (ebk)

Typeset in Bembo
by Taylor & Francis Books

MIX
Paper from
responsible sources
FSC® C004839
www.fsc.org

Printed and bound in Great Britain by
CPI Antony Rowe, Chippenham, Wiltshire

John Boswell (1947–94)
Howard Zinn (1922–2010)
In memoriam

Contents

Contributors

Megan Cassidy-Welch is Australian Research Council Future Fellow in the School of Philosophical, Historical & International Studies at Monash University. She is the author of *Imprisonment in the Medieval Religious Imagination, c. 1150–1400* (2011) and *Monastic Spaces and their Meanings: Thirteenth-century English Cistercian Monasteries* (2001), and co-editor of *Practices of Gender in Late Medieval and Early Modern Europe* (2008, with Peter Sherlock). More details can be found on her website: http://arts. monash.edu.au/history/staff/mcassidy-welch.php.

Celia Chazelle is Professor of History and Department Chair at The College of New Jersey. She is the co-director of the College's Center for Prison Outreach and Education and a board member of the Center for Environmental Transformation in Camden New Jersey. Author of *The Crucified God in the Carolingian Era: Theology and Art of Christ's Passion* (2001), she has also co-edited several essay collections, including *Paradigms and Methods in Early Medieval Studies: A Reconsideration* (2007, with Felice Lifshitz) and *The Crisis of the Oikoumene: The Three Chapters and the Failed Quest for Unity in the Sixth-Century Mediterranean* (2007, with Catherine Cubitt). More details can be found on her website: http://www.tcnj.edu/~chazelle/.

Simon Doubleday is Professor of History at Hofstra University. He is a board member of the Edeyo Foundation, an NGO – based in New York – dedicated to the renewal of Port-au-Prince (Haiti) through education. His books include *The Lara Family: Crown and Nobility in Medieval Spain* (2001); he is co-editor of *Border Interrogations: Crossing and Questioning the Spanish Frontier* (2008, with Benita Sampedro Vizcaya) and *In the Light of Medieval Spain: Islam, the West, and the Relevance of the Past* (2008, with David Coleman). He is also Executive Editor of the *Journal of Medieval Iberian Studies*. For more details, see the website of the Hofstra history department: http://www.hofstra.edu/Academics/Colleges/Hclas/HIS/his_faculty.html

Dyan Elliott is Peter B. Ritzma Professor of the Humanities and Professor of History at Northwestern University. Her books include *Spiritual Marriage: Sexual Abstinence in Medieval Wedlock* (1993); *Fallen Bodies: Pollution, Sexuality, and Demonology in the Middle Ages* (1999); *Proving Woman: Female Spirituality and Inquisitional Culture in the Later Middle Ages* (2004), and *The Bride of Christ Goes to Hell: Metaphor and Embodiment in the Lives of Pious Women, 200 – 1500* (2011). More details can be found on her website: http://www.history.northwestern.edu/people/elliott.html.

G. Geltner is Professor of Medieval History and Director of the Center for Medieval Studies at the University of Amsterdam. His books include *The Medieval Prison: A Social History* (2008). He is also co-editor of *Defenders and Critics of Franciscan Life* (2009, with Michael F. Cusato). More details can be found on his website: http://home.medewerker.uva.nl/g.geltner/.

Ruth Mazo Karras is Professor of History and Director of the Center for Medieval Studies at the University of Minnesota. Her books include *Sexuality in Medieval Europe: Doing Unto Others* (2005), and *From Boys to Men: Formations of Masculinity in Late Medieval Europe* (2003). She is co-editor of *Law and the Illicit in Medieval Europe* (2008, with Joel Kaye and E. Ann Matter), and of the journal *Gender and History*. More details can be found on her website: http://www.hist.umn.edu/~rmk/.

Maghan Keita is Professor of History and Director of the Institute for Global Interdisciplinary Studies at Villanova University. His books include *A Political Economy of Health Care in Senegal* (2007) and *Race and the Writing of History: Riddling the Sphinx (2000)*. He is also editor of *Conceptualizing/Re-conceptualizing Africa: The Construction of African Historical Identity* (2002). More details can be found on his website: http://www86.homepage.villanova.edu/maghan.keita/.

Geoffrey Koziol is Professor of History at the University of California-Berkeley. He is the author of *The Politics of Memory and Identity in Carolingian Royal Diplomas: The West Frankish Kingdom (840–987)* (forthcoming, Brepols, 2011) and *Begging Pardon and Favor: Ritual and Political Order in Early Medieval France* (1992). More details can be found on his website: http://history.berkeley.edu/faculty/Koziol/.

Mathew Kuefler is Professor of History at San Diego State University. He is the author of *The Manly Eunuch: Masculinity, Gender Ambiguity, and Christian Ideology in Late Antiquity* (2001) and editor of *The Boswell Thesis: Essays on Christianity, Social Tolerance, and Homosexuality* (2006). He is also the editor of *Journal of the History of Sexuality*. More details can be found on his website: http://www-rohan.sdsu.edu/~mkuefler/.

Felice Lifshitz is Professor of Women's Studies, with a joint appointment to the Campus St. Jean, at the University of Alberta. She is the author of *The Name of the Saint: The Martyrology of Jerome and Access to the Sacred in Francia (627–827)* (2005),

The Norman Conquest of Pious Neustria: Historiographic Discourse and Saintly Relics (684–1090) (1995), and co-editor of *Gender and Christianity in Medieval Europe: New Perspectives* (2008, with Lisa Bitel). She is also the editor of *History Compass*. More details can be found on her website: http://www.womensstudies.ualberta.ca/FacultyandStaff/FacultyLifshitz.aspx.

Peter Linebaugh is Professor of History at the University of Toledo. His books include *The London Hanged* (1991) and *The Magna Carta Manifesto: Liberties and Commons for All* (2008). He is also co-author of *The Many-Headed Hydra: Sailors, Slaves, Commoners and the Hidden History of the Revolutionary Atlantic* (2000, with Marcus Rediker). More details can be found on his website: http://www.utoledo.edu/as/history/faculty/plinebaugh.html.

Martha G. Newman is Associate Professor of History and Religious Studies, and Chair of the Department of Religious Studies at the University of Texas–Austin. She is the author of *Boundaries of Charity: Cistercian Culture and Ecclesiastical Reform, 1098–1180* (1996). More details can be found on her website: http://www.utexas.edu/cola/depts/rs/faculty/newmanmg.

Frederick S. Paxton is Brigida Pacchiani Ardenghi Professor of History at Connecticut College. His books include *Christianizing Death: The Creation of a Ritual Process in Early Medieval Europe* (1990) and *Anchoress and Abbess in Ninth-Century Saxony: The Lives of Liutbirg of Wendhausen and Hathumoda of Gandersheim* (2009). More details can be found on his website: http://www.conncoll.edu/Academics/web_profiles/paxton.html.

Amy G. Remensnyder is Associate Professor of History and Director of the Program in Medieval Studies at Brown University, and a regular participant in the Brown Education Lecture Link Series at the Rhode Island Adult Correctional Institution. She is the author of *La Conquistadora: Muslims, Christians, Jews, Native Americans, and the Virgin Mary* (forthcoming, Oxford University Press, 2012) and of *Remembering Kings Past: Monastic Foundation Legends in Medieval Southern France* (1995). More details can be found on her website: http://www.brown.edu/Departments/History/people/facultypage.php?id=10097.

Kristina Richardson is Assistant Professor of History at Queens College, CUNY. She is the author of *Blighted Bodies: Difference and Disability in the Medieval Islamic World* (forthcoming, Manchester University Press, 2012). More details can be found on her website: http://qcpages.qc.edu/~krichardson/.

Acknowledgments

The dedication of this book to John Boswell and Howard Zinn reflects the inspiration that we have drawn from two historians, a medievalist and an Americanist, whose lives and careers synthesized graceful scholarship, social activism, and commitment to students. Along with their countless readers and students, within and beyond the university, we have become convinced that history matters in urgent and immediate ways. We hope this volume makes some small contribution to efforts to combat injustice throughout the world, both by bringing history to bear through the influence of its chapters and through the direct donation of all royalties to a number of NGOs that really matter: the Center for Environmental Transformation, dedicated to combating social and environmental injustice in Camden New Jersey; the Center for Prison Outreach and Education, dedicated to providing educational opportunities to inmates in New Jersey state prisons; the Edeyo Foundation, an independent, non-profit organization based in New York City, dedicated to improving the future for young children in Haiti through education; the Rhode Island Community Food Bank; Changing Together – A Center for Immigrant Women in Edmonton; and the American Friends Service Committee, working across the globe for social justice and peace.

We have accumulated many debts of gratitude along the way, not only to colleagues, friends, and relatives who share our devotion to fusing historical awareness with the search for justice, but also to those who were, at least at first, skeptical, and thereby strengthened the book. It would be impossible to name all the audience members who offered perceptive comments and criticisms during the panels on medieval studies and modern social justice we organized over the past five years, at meetings of the International Congress of Medieval Studies, the American Historical Association, the Distinguished Lecture Series of the Medieval and Renaissance Center, New York University, and the Babel Working Group. The lively discussions at these events encouraged us to refine and sharpen many of our arguments. We are grateful to all the speakers whose presentations provided insights that have further stimulated our thoughts, and of course to our contributors, for their commitment to this intellectual project and for their patience with our requests for revisions. A special thank you to Leah DeVun, who was a speaker and also co-organized two sessions on "The Historian as Activist" for the annual meeting of the American Historical Association in 2009, which brought together several of the authors of essays here. We extend our warm appreciation, as well, to Gabrielle Spiegel and Jack Censer, who helped us find our way to Routledge; to Vicky Peters, who welcomed us once we found our way there; and to Emily Kindleysides and Laura Mothersole, who worked so hard to smooth the path to publication.

Celia is grateful to The College of New Jersey for release time from teaching through regular "SOSA" awards; and to Princeton Theological Seminary for a Visiting Scholar position in Spring 2009 that provided a welcome opportunity for sustained research and writing. Her deep appreciation also to Meg Ayers, Program Assistant, Carol Bresnahan, Provost and Executive Vice President, Mark Kiselica, Vice Provost, and Ben Rifkin, Dean of Humanities and Social Sciences at the College of New Jersey for their enthusiastic support of causes that matter, to her inmate students for their intellectual passion, and to the remarkable people of Camden New Jersey, whose warmth and capacity for joy are constantly inspiring. At Hofstra University, Simon thanks Herman Berliner, Provost, Bernard J. Firestone, Dean of the College of Liberal Arts and Sciences, Athelene Collins, Senior Associate Director of the Hofstra Cultural Center, and all the faculty and students who generated and energized the Hofstra for Haiti alliance, for their extraordinary commitment to making the campus a hub for advancing social justice and civic engagement. He is deeply appreciative of the efforts made by Doris Pradieu, Michael Pradieu, and Unik Ernest, to transform the fate of Bel-Air, one of the poorest communities of Port-au-Prince, and their enthusiasm for engaging Hofstra University in this process. Simon would also like to acknowledge the perceptive remarks of the students enrolled in History 177B (The Berbers), who – in the spring semester of 2011 – provided helpful and constructive criticism of the introduction.

Felice is indebted to Rabbi Jody Cohen, formerly of the Union for Reform Judaism and now the spiritual leader of Temple Israel of Greater Miami, for teaching her that *Tzedakah* (צדקה) is better translated as "justice" or "fairness" than as "charity," and to the Wissenschaftskolleg zu Berlin (including the Fellows of *Jahrgang* 2008–09), for providing the ideal atmosphere in which to work on this volume. Amy, too, thanks a warmly hospitable German institution for a year-long fellowship that gave her time to think about new ways of being a medievalist: the Internationale Kolleg für Geisteswissenschaftliche Forschung at the Ruhr-Universität in Bochum. She is grateful as well to Margaret Malamud, who has always encouraged her to follow new paths in scholarship and life; to Shana Klinger, founding member of the Listening to Rhode Island Project, who ever since 11 September 2001 has been a constant source of activist inspiration and leadership; and, as always, to Linda Heuman, partner in life and all new adventures, including this one. Amy also acknowledges her great debt to Kerrissa Heffernan, Director of Faculty Engagement and the Royce Fellowship at

Brown University's Swearer Center for Public Service, who for years has believed that medievalists really can become engaged scholars.

Heartfelt thanks to our families for stimulating discussions of current events, social injustice, and their historical background, and for sharing with us the stress as well as the excitement of scholarly work. Above all, we would all like to express our gratitude to our undergraduate students, for reinforcing our conviction that history matters, and that it is still, always, possible – as it was for the Fabians depicted (on the cover of our book) in George Bernard Shaw's post-medieval stained-glass window – to forge a new world.

A note to readers

In the interests of readability, footnotes have been kept to a minimum in this volume and used only to provide references for direct quotations or for specific points of factual information. The "Suggestions for Further Reading" section following each article contains references both to the works that have influenced the author's argument and to those that provide further context for it.

INTRODUCTION

Celia Chazelle, Simon Doubleday, Felice Lifshitz, and Amy G. Remensnyder

Some time in the 1930s, as the world was about to explode into war, a young French boy, Étienne, asked his father, the medievalist Marc Bloch, a hauntingly simple question: "Tell me, Papa. What is the use of history?" Bloch had no doubt about the importance of the problem. "The question far transcends the minor scruples of a professional conscience," he would write. "Indeed, our entire Western civilization is concerned in it."[1] The observation soon took on a particular poignancy. In 1940, Bloch – a professor at the University of Paris-Sorbonne – would be called for military service to resist the Nazi onslaught, and soon, like his son, joined the French resistance. Under these circumstances, he wrestled with the question that Étienne had posed, and began to write a searching defense of the study of history. Bloch would die without finishing *The Historian's Craft*, as the work would be known in its English translation. He was captured by the Germans, tortured, and – on 16 June 1944 – executed. His meditation on historical studies and their use for the contemporary world would be published four years after the war's end.

The presence of war in *The Historian's Craft* is unmistakable, tinging its first pages with sadness: Bloch apologizes to readers, explaining that because he no longer has access to a library and has lost his books, he must rely only "upon my notes and upon memory." Yet in the wake of the terrifying, disorienting fall of France to the Nazis, he was concerned that his compatriots, searching the historical past to illumine the social and political horrors of the present, might find their knowledge of history to be "useless." "Are we to believe that history has betrayed us?" one of his fellow soldiers evidently cried as the Germans entered Paris. "A long-standing penchant," Bloch explains, "prompts us, almost by instinct, to demand of [history] the means to direct our actions and, therefore, as in the case of the conquered soldier mentioned above, we become indignant if, perchance, it seems incapable of giving us guidance." On the contrary, Bloch himself was optimistic that historical studies could illumine the present, even in Nazi-occupied France.

"Misunderstanding the present," he wrote, "is the inevitable consequence of ignorance of the past."[2]

Historians and the "real world"

Today, we find ourselves in a new period of ethical and political urgency, as our world order, too, is radically – often violently – recast. One has only to pick up a newspaper or magazine to find journalists, political leaders, social theorists, activists, and other members of the educated public looking to the past for help with the challenges of the present. Sometimes, people draw lessons from historical situations that seem analogous to present circumstances, or dissect the origins of modern predicaments in order to clarify where responsibility lies, and the direction in which change should proceed. The physician–anthropologist Paul Farmer's passionate advocacy on behalf of the millions in Haiti who lack adequate health care is just one of many possible telling examples. Farmer, who has devoted much of his career to providing medical services in Haiti (as well as Rwanda), has written vehemently about the suffering this country has experienced as a direct result of colonial policies in the Caribbean since the sixteenth century.[3] In citing this historical record, he urges readers seeking solutions to Haiti's continuing state of crisis to advocate for a change in US policy. Others in pursuit of social justice seek explanations and solutions in a still more distant historical past: a quest to which the Fabian window – designed by George Bernard Shaw in 1910 – pays homage. This window, which appears as the cover image of this volume, depicts the struggle of progressive thinkers and activists in the modern age to forge the world anew, and reflects the inspiration that many have drawn from the middle ages.

Yet the public desire to look to history to elucidate "real world" problems and concerns is not always shared by those men and women who devote their lives to investigating materials from the past. Today in the twenty-first century, professional historians are often among the people *most* reluctant to invoke history to combat modern injustice. From history's professionalization as an academic discipline in the nineteenth century through much of the twentieth century, most historians were taught to examine the past as if it should be essentially disconnected from present day concerns. History, they thought, should try to emulate the positivist methods of inquiry associated with the physical sciences. According to this view, historians were supposed to be neutral, dispassionate observers of empirical evidence. They should not take sides, display emotions in their analysis, or allow passion to color their research; their task was solely the disinterested recovery of historical facts as if these were fixed, certain, and accessible to modern researchers, and as if historical texts and other sources were open windows through which to view these facts. Already for Marc Bloch, this specter of scientific history had to be exorcised. Bloch paid homage to the achievements of such scholarship – it "has taught us to analyze more profoundly, to grasp our problems more firmly, and even, I dare say, to think less shoddily" – but simultaneously stressed its limitations for the overwhelming ethical and political crisis of his own time: he insisted on the "solidarity" of past and present.[4]

In the generations since Bloch's death, and more specifically since the 1970s, philosophical movements emphasizing the power of linguistic structures to shape reality, and to dictate the form in which it is narrated, have further shaken the belief of most academic historians that the past so readily offers itself up for observation. The majority of historians now are keenly aware that history "as it really was" is, ultimately, inaccessible. Most people in the past have left no traces for us to follow, and even those tracks that remain are difficult for us to interpret: it is impossible to observe the past without one's own perspective coloring the view. Yet many professional historians have found it hard to awaken from the spell of what has been called the "noble dream" of objectivity. They continue to assert that they should conduct their investigations *as if* neutrality were possible. Any reading of the past through the lens of modern concerns, they maintain, jeopardizes this pretense of detachment. They argue that it encourages simplification or distortion of the historical record in service of a partisan agenda – and thus risks undermining the integrity of their research.

In recent years, though, a small but growing number of scholars have argued that *precisely* because genuine historical neutrality does not exist, historians can no longer claim that the remembrance of the past is ever disassociated from the present. These scholars do not dismiss the necessity of seeking as deep and accurate knowledge of the past as possible; they indeed believe that only by understanding the past can we lay the foundation for serious reflection on history's relation to the present. Yet they contend that since the researcher's personal situation necessarily shapes his or her work on the past, it is legitimate to conduct the search for historical understanding with an overt commitment to today's world. Historians, they argue, rightly offer their expertise alongside journalists, activists, policy makers, and members of the wider public who seek to respond to the modern problems that *should* worry all of us. Questioning the ideal of objective, dispassionate historical research can thus encourage historians to take ethical stances with regards to their own world – which is exactly what the contributors to this volume do. The essays here bear witness to the so-called "ethical turn," the recognition that all academic disciplines have an inescapable ethical dimension, not least because knowledge brings the ability to influence, to deceive, to control. "Knowledge is a form of power," one historian has written, "that can be used, as traditionally, to maintain the status quo … or to change it."[5]

Participating in the "ethical turn" faces historians with some particular challenges. Many of the sources that survive to illuminate the past come from those small fractions of the population that possessed fortune, prestige, and authority. Relatively few sources remaining from the past give direct voice to the countless people who, although they constituted the bulk of the population, had little access to power. Too often, historians themselves – whether consciously or unconsciously – have colluded in this "silencing of the past." Ignoring the power dynamic that produced the very sources they use, they have taken these traces of the past at face value and composed stirring accounts of the rise of empires and the victories of armies, celebrating the political, cultural, and intellectual achievements of powerful religious and political leaders belonging to the "great" civilizations. Such historians unintentionally convey the message that power is a good thing, whether in the past or the present, and that the oppression it inflicts on ordinary populations is less worthy of our attention.

Narratives about the rich and powerful do have their place. But historians have a moral obligation to recall the silenced victims of the past and to think about how this knowledge might assist in empowering disenfranchised, persecuted, and impoverished people of the present. In 2006, historians were even urged to do so by the president of their own professional organization in the United States, the American Historical Association. "We are all historians of human rights," declared the president of this association, Linda Kerber. All historians, she wrote, seek a "complex understanding of events" that necessarily engages ethical issues. Because historians gather the evidence "on which large moral choices can be made" in the future, Kerber argued, they must "think with care about the physical, social, political, and moral contexts in which human choices have been made" in the past.[6] Another prominent historian, Afsaneh Najmabadi, has issued a stark warning to those of her colleagues who think they adhere to a noble professional ideal by pursuing "neutral" historical scholarship without concern for the ethical implications of their work. Such scholars, she writes, need to understand that silence can itself be an ethical position, one that can verge on tacit collusion in the injustices of the present.[7]

It is no accident that both Kerber and Najmabadi are historians who work on the modern world. Most academic historians who produce socially and ethically engaged history are in fact specialists of the modern era, as was the single most famous exemplar of such historical writing in the United States: Howard Zinn, author of the best-selling *A People's History of the United States*. Zinn's radically engaged approach to history deeply influenced the thinking of several editors and authors represented in this volume. From the 1950s right up until his death in January 2010, Zinn wrote prolifically and spoke vigorously about the social and political injustices of past and present, whether committed in the US or in countries over which the US has extended its influence. He actively struggled on behalf of his ideals, leading protests for civil rights and against US wars, imperialism, and militarism.

In his *The Politics of History* (1970), Zinn made an eloquent case for engaged history. His arguments still resonate today, four decades after he first published them. All knowledge is "open to doubt and all truths partial," Zinn wrote. While he granted that historical research concerned only with the past had its place, he argued that it was never disinterested. Since powerful groups continually use historical and pseudo-historical information to shape oppressive policies and thought, Zinn continued, it is critical to make room in the historical profession for scholarship guided by compassion for the victims of oppression. He urged historians to acknowledge the reality of injustice and to show empathy for those who have suffered not only in the past but also in our modern age. Scholars should "deliberately seek to focus [historical] knowledge, not by random choice of past facts, or from simple curiosity, or with a desire to show the glories of America, but through the prism of a present urgency, whether it be starvation or war or race prejudice or something else."[8] The effort to maintain neutrality "is a disservice to the very ideals we teach about as history, and a betrayal to the victims of an un-neutral world."[9]

Medievalists and the ethical turn

While some historians who work on the same era as Zinn – modernity – have taken his words to heart, the potential for socially engaged history of the distant past has not yet been fully realized. The one partial exception is classical antiquity: popular perceptions of ancient Greece and Rome as the harbinger of modern Western culture, values, and institutions encourage people to believe that the classical heritage can inspire and guide us as we face the pressing issues of our day. Medieval history, in contrast, receives at best passing interest and is frequently dismissed as both backward and irrelevant.

The two conceptions of the middle ages that dominate modern popular culture themselves suggest that an unbridgeable cultural and intellectual chasm severs the medieval from us. On the one hand, the word "medieval" conjures images of a romanticized space, where we can flee modern life and indulge in fantasies of castles, heroic knights, ravishing damsels, and the occasional dragon. Needless to say, this escapist fantasy of the middle ages represents the antithesis of engagement with the social problems of the present. On the other hand, in popular culture, the word evokes an unredeemable Dark Age rife with barbarism and savagery – and serves as a convenient foil for our own self-proclaimed "enlightenment." The intellectuals who, centuries ago, coined the terms "Middle Age" and "Dark Age" in fact intended them in just this way. These men were convinced that the light of classical culture had been doused by the descent of medieval barbarism, only to blaze forth in its "rebirth" (renaissance) in fourteenth-century Italy, which they saw as the beginnings of civilized modernity. No wonder that many pundits today stigmatize acts of contemporary barbarism or savagery as "medieval." In the wake of the terrorist attacks of 11 September 2001, journalists have deployed the term as shorthand for everything that the US-led "war on terror" seeks to eradicate – or, conversely (as Amy G. Remensnyder discusses in this volume), to describe the US government's own support for the use of torture. Whether romantic or barbaric, the medieval is wrongly perceived as something disconnected from – and irrelevant to – the modern.

Medieval historians rightly complain about these flawed and fantastic images of the period they study. They rarely venture, though, to suggest concrete and credible ways in which knowledge about the middle ages might be relevant, as we seek to meet the social and political challenges of our own world. Predictably, some medievalists today contend that all professional historians, regardless of period or region of specialization, should steer clear of ethically engaged scholarship. They argue that while it may be appropriate to criticize and correct modern social commentary that misuses historical references, historians should otherwise confine their research and teaching to their areas of scholarly expertise.

Why are medievalists now, in general, more resistant to socially engaged history than modern historians or even classicists? It is perhaps safe to say that, for many medievalists, the technical skills they have to master and the types of sources they use in their research actively foster a sense of the radical distance of the medieval past from the modern present. Medievalists commonly receive kinds of training not shared by modern historians or classicists. Like classicists, they learn how to read "dead" languages such as Latin and classical Greek, but in addition they often study vernacular languages in forms no longer spoken today: Frisian, Old English, Old Norse, Old Russian, and Old French among them. Again like many classicists, they familiarize themselves with archaeology, epigraphy (the study of inscriptions), and numismatics (the study of coins), but while classicists typically work with modern printed editions of textual sources, medievalists frequently rely on trips to European archives and libraries in order to consult manuscripts. To decipher handwritten texts dating from centuries ago recorded by scribes and notaries using scripts illegible to the untrained modern eye, medievalists need to master paleography (the study of ancient writing). They also need to understand the principles of codicology, the science of gleaning information about manuscripts' circumstances of production from these texts' physical features. Wielding these specialized tools in order to forge their visions of the past, medievalists naturally can feel that the era they study is disconnected from the modern world.

Acquiring the skills of a professional medievalist is both time-consuming and difficult. It can become an all-consuming endeavor that leaves little room for attention to less traditional approaches to the past. Many medievalists thus continue to embrace the positivist forms of analysis on which disciplines like codicology rest, and show little concern for philosophical critiques of the ideas of scholarly objectivity and disengagement. Even those medievalists who have employed categories of analysis whose roots lie in the political awakenings of the modern world – gender theory, ethnic studies, queer studies, and so on – have all too often used them to paint an image of the middle ages as intrinsically foreign, strange, or even grotesque. In their work, the medieval once again emerges as isolated from modern, real world concerns: those of women, the gay community, or other marginalized and oppressed social groups.

This volume of essays asks how the work of medieval historians today can speak directly to our present. In posing this question and seeking to answer it, the contributors and editors are mindful of their debt both to Marc Bloch and to other, more recent, predecessors. Foremost among these pioneers was John Boswell, a professor of history at Yale University, who died of AIDS in 1994 at the age of 47. Boswell's studies of homosexuality in medieval Europe and the Mediterranean remain prized today by gays and lesbians both in the US and abroad: texts to which these men and women return again and again as they fight against homophobia and for full civil rights. "I often think of myself as a weapons-maker," Boswell once wrote; "that is, I'm trying to produce the knowledge that people can then use in social struggles."[10] Boswell's words live on, quite directly, in the words of several of his former graduate students whose work is included in this volume: Celia Chazelle, Ruth Karras, and Mathew Kuefler. Not only did his example inspire their own social commitment, but his fight for the human rights of gay people also finds its echo in the articles here by Kuefler and Karras, as well as by Dyan Elliott, all of which address the impact of medieval conventions on modern issues of sexuality.

Perhaps more surprising for non-medievalists, the feminist medieval historian Judith Bennett has produced a large body of work exploring the role that knowledge of the medieval past can play in resisting modern sexism and gender discrimination. In this volume, Felice Lifshitz makes a similar argument, though on different grounds. Bennett believes that disseminating information about what she sees as the pervasive reality of medieval women's low status relative to men will assist in ending discrimination against women in our own time. As Lifshitz's essay indicates, however, the history of women in medieval Europe offers not only evidence of women's repression but also stories of saintly and merely mortal women who behaved in notably "feminist" ways, sometimes with the full support of male-dominated institutions. Their experiences, too, can inspire our continued struggles to achieve gender equality today.

Boswell and Bennett entered the path of engaged scholarship in part impelled by their personal identities and political situations, as Bennett herself explains. Remembering her years in graduate school in the 1970s, she writes of how engaged scholarship helped her resolve the urgent conflict she felt between her "two full but contrary identities." "In one," she writes, "I was a lesbian feminist absorbed by activism at home and in the streets. In the other, I was a studious medievalist, training under the guidance of male professors, most of them priests. ... Radical feminist by night; medievalist by day; feminist history brought my two selves together."[11]

A less personal but no less urgent spur that incited some other medieval historians to activism in their scholarly work was the cataclysm of 11 September 2001. In the wake of the terrorist attacks on the US and the resulting rhetoric about the "clash of civilizations," some medievalists (among them one editor of this volume, Simon Doubleday) who study medieval Spain – a place where Muslims, Christians, and Jews co-existed from the eighth century until 1492 – drew on their knowledge of the historical relationship between Islam and the West to speak out. Indeed, it may be appropriate to talk of a new "9/11 Generation" of historians fully committed to engagement in public debate about the complex, overlapping relationships between "the West" and "the non-West" – the latter often encompassing, in modern media representations, Africans and Muslims wherever they happen to live.

The 2008 volume of essays co-edited by Doubleday and entitled *In the Light of Medieval Spain: Islam, the West, and the Relevance of the Past* was catalyzed by his first-hand experience of witnessing the destruction of the World Trade Center, and by subsequent debates about how scholars should respond to the wars in first Afghanistan and then Iraq. This ethical impulse also shaped Maria Menocal's evocative book, *The Ornament of the World: How Muslims, Jews, and Christians Created a Society of Tolerance in Medieval Spain*. Published in the immediate wake of the terrorist attacks of 2001, this book quickly became a *New York Times* bestseller. Academic historians were divided about Menocal's conclusions. Still, the value of her book in widely publicizing the important, long-standing presence of Muslims within Europe – not Islam *versus* the West but Islam *as part of the West* – is indisputable. It presents a significant challenge to current prejudices that impede cooperation and understanding. Maghan Keita's essay in this volume has a similar aim, calling attention to the centuries-old, largely unrecognized presence of Africans in Europe: the medieval political origins of Europe were neither exclusively Christian nor exclusively white.

If the essays here represent the radically new approach to medieval history exemplified by Bennett, Boswell, and the "9/11 Generation," it is also important to recognize that this volume's call for socially engaged medieval history in some ways represents a return to much earlier practices. The notion that historical studies should try to emulate the neutrality, detachment, and objectivity identified with the natural sciences only really emerged in the nineteenth century. Before the eighteenth-century Enlightenment, the study of history was widely regarded as, by definition, responsive to issues of the historian's present. For hundreds of years, historians had been fully conscious that their writings, teachings, and other actions constituted a form of social engagement nourished by ethical concerns.

Indeed, the text often considered *the origin of modern historical method*, the *Treatise on the Donation of Constantine* written in 1440 by the Italian Renaissance historian Lorenzo Valla, sprang from such concerns. There is no trace of "ivory tower" detachment in Valla's demonstration that the "Donation of Constantine," an early medieval document that claimed Emperor Constantine I transferred Roman imperial territories to papal control, was a forgery. At the time Valla prepared his text, he was in the service of the king of Aragon, Sicily, and Naples, who was embroiled in conflict with Pope Eugenius IV over some of the same territories. As Valla emphatically stated: "I am writing against not only the dead, but the living also." Fueled by moral outrage, he utilized his knowledge of Roman imperial and medieval history to construct a profound indictment of popes up to his own day, an indictment that he hoped would provoke similar passion in his contemporaries. "The slaughter and devastation of all Italy and of many of the provinces," he wrote, "has flowed from this single source [the papacy]. ... Can we justify the principle of papal power when we perceive it to be the cause of such great crimes and of such great and varied evils?"[12]

A tale of two bishops

If we look before Valla, all the way back to some of the foundational texts written by early medieval historians, we again find a commitment to rectifying the injustices of the present through appeal to the past. Gregory of Tours, bishop of Tours in Gaul (modern-day France) from 573 until his death around 594, is probably best remembered for his *Histories*. Commonly titled today the *History of the Franks*, Gregory's book is not at all a coherent tale of the glories of Frankish beginnings or Frankish kings. In his opening words, Gregory famously reported: "A great many things keep happening, some of them good, some of them bad."[13] Airing every piece of dirty laundry he could find, and inventing others, he energetically assaulted the reputation of the powerful in his age – kings, queens, and fellow bishops.

A seemingly interminable parade of villains and their only marginally less nasty victims traipses across the stage, garroting brothers and throttling sons. The reader is led through a historical house of horrors; we rejoice with Gregory, breathing a sigh of relief when at last he reports the brief respite of a "good" thing – a miracle. We side with him on behalf of St. Injuriosus, an earlier bishop of Tours, when the saint refuses to agree to King Lothar's demands that all churches pay a third of their revenues to the royal treasury and miraculously prevails with the help of an even earlier (deceased) bishop, St. Martin. Calling into question the basic legitimacy of royal power, Gregory's saints liberate prisoners, breaking their chains, with no explanation of why rulers and lords had incarcerated those people in the first place. For Gregory, rulers and institutions that forcibly marginalize, segregate, or imprison a portion of their society's population can raise serious ethical concerns. He was also clearly disturbed by the ravages of war. Throughout the *Histories* he draws a sharp distinction between "the holy deeds of the Saints and the way in which whole races of people were butchered," between "the wars waged by kings and the holy deeds of martyrs."[14] In the words of two modern historians, Gregory's accounts of military violence were designed to convince readers of "the grotesque seaminess of secular affairs" and to curb the "aggressiveness and militarism" of his day.[15]

But Gregory of Tours was by no means representative of all historians living in early medieval Europe or even all churchmen. Some of his peers wrote history not to critique power but instead to serve it. In the 620s, for example, Isidore (d. 636), bishop of the Spanish city of Seville, made a conscious decision to align his pen with the interests of his royal lords, the Visigothic kings Sisebut (d. 621) and Suinthila (d. 625), at whose behest he wrote his *History of the Goths, Sueves, and Vandals*. Isidore's loyalty to power was near-absolute and his praise of military adventures vociferous. In 621, he recounts, the "most glorious" Suinthila "ascended to the summit of royal dignity" and, "with amazing fortune, triumphed even more gloriously than had the other kings." Suinthila "launched an expedition against the Basques who … promised to be obedient to [his] rule and dominion and to carry out whatever they were ordered to do."[16] Equally telling is Isidore's view of the entire historical landscape:

> The Goths … waged such great wars … that Rome itself … submitted to the yoke of captivity and yielded to the Gothic triumphs: the mistress of all nations served them like a handmaid. All of the peoples of Europe feared them. … While most peoples are scarcely permitted to rule through entreaties and gifts, the liberty of the Goths has come about more through battle than petitions for peace. … In the arts of war they are quite spectacular. … They love to exercise themselves with weapons and compete in battle. … Subjected, the Roman soldier serves the Goths, whom he sees being served by many people and by Spain itself.[17]

The bishop of Seville was more than happy to proclaim that God approved of these wars. In Isidore's historical writing, fear is good and peace is bad, in clear contrast to Gregory, who did not hesitate to denounce kings and nobles who waged war and loved butchery.

The professional historians who today study the middle ages must decide whether to stand with Gregory or with Isidore – and then they must speak, write, and act in light of that decision. They should be aware that even as medieval historians in recent years have emphasized the need for objectivity and neutrality, some – like Isidore in the seventh century – have succumbed to the lure of powerful allegiances. The eminent historian of the medieval state, Joseph Strayer, for example, worked in the 1960s with a group of other academics as a high-level consultant for the CIA. The knowledge of state formation that Strayer and other scholars fed the agency supported its covert operations during this decade, which included the toppling of numerous democratically elected and constitutional governments around the world judged antithetical to American interests.[18]

Other medievalists have instead chosen to walk Gregory's path, as Ienaga Saburō (d. 2002), an expert on medieval Japan, eventually did. In 1965, he sued the Japanese government for having censored his high school textbook, *New Japanese History*. The government objected to the book because of its negative portrayal of Japan's role in the Second World War. Saburō wrote his textbook – and fought against its censorship – for two reasons: his desire to expose wartime atrocities and his guilt at having glorified Japan and its emperor to the high school students whom he had taught more than two decades earlier. Inculcated in this mythic imagery of imperial greatness, his young male students then went off to the battlefront to kill and die. During the war, Saburō did not speak out for fear of retribution; instead, he retreated to the safe refuge offered by the study of the history and art of medieval Japan. It was only after the war that he rejected his earlier passivity and took up the history of modern Japan.[19] A product of the knowledge he had gradually acquired of both the distant past and his present, his textbook was meant to help assure that his country never engaged in war again.

The editors of and contributors to this volume share a comparable sense of pressing ethical responsibility. In our view, every historian must resist the magnetic attraction of power, refuse to be seduced by its allure, and combat, as the French philosopher-historian, Michel Foucault (d. 1984) urged, "the fascism that causes us to love power."[20] We cannot all sue governments as did Saburō, or join a formalized resistance as did Marc Bloch, but we can think deeply about what we teach, write, and study, and about the many positive contributions that knowledge of the medieval past can make to responding to the urgent problems of today.

Weapons-makers

This book aims to illustrate a variety of ways in which medieval historians can use their knowledge to cast a distinctive new light on contemporary social and political concerns. The authors of the essays here adopt diverse approaches based on their different areas of scholarly expertise and attention to different modern issues. Some are specialists in the high or late middle ages, the twelfth through fifteenth centuries CE, while others mainly study the early medieval period of the fifth through eleventh centuries. While most focus their research on Europe, one is a historian of the Middle East and another of Africa. Yet all are *medieval* historians united by their interest in that era, their committed engagement with the modern world, and their conviction that medieval history can assist in addressing important issues of our age. The middle ages do matter.

This is not to say that this volume presents medieval history as more important than other historical fields, or proposes that information about the history of any era or region can by itself incite the changes needed today. Knowledge of the past can enhance and expand the basis for social action in the present, but from the perspective of communities in real crisis – a tent city in Port-au-Prince, Haiti, the ravaged city-scape of Camden New Jersey, or US prisons, to mention some places where editors of this book have recently worked – what is most essential is *action*. But knowing about medieval history does carry some particular benefits; its intermediate location, "in the middle," provides grounds for the positive *use* of history. Properly under-standing the relationship between this not-so-distant past and our present can clarify modern debates and provide ammunition for action, both when people today act too "medieval" and when, perhaps, they fail to act "medieval" enough.

On the one hand, the middle ages are close enough to us to mean that a fairly large quantity of sources survives to fuel research, and that we can easily discern many of the ways in which the period mirrored and shaped – for better or for worse – the development of our modern world. Several essays in this volume discuss medieval modes of thought and behavior that directly foreshadowed some of our modern issues concerning sexuality. Ruth Karras examines the parallels between the modern rhetoric denouncing gay marriage and the arguments of medieval writers who con-demned clerical marriage; Dyan Elliott discusses the concept of "scandal" as it developed in medieval Christian thought, a concept that has had a major impact in the recent clerical sex abuse crisis. And Mathew Kuefler casts a new spotlight on modern Christian leaders who denounce homosexual activity in public while en-gaging in it in private: he shows how their deceit parallels the struggle St. Augustine of Hippo (d. 430) seems to have endured.

On the other hand, the middle ages are sufficiently remote from the contemporary world to stimulate our ability to envisage positive alternatives to current practices and attitudes. In some respects, the period's "alien" qualities make it much more useful in this regard than either antiquity or the early modern period. Somewhat counter-intuitively, as illustrated by Frederick Paxton's article, medieval monastic practices have inspired innovative new approaches to modern palliative and end-of-life care; study of the middle ages in this case has provided not an ivory tower escape, but a therapeutic mode of refuge from suffering. Other contemporary problems, too, might be better resolved and justice better served if we took inspiration from the middle ages – if, in other words, we were to become *more* medieval. What if modern government leaders were to heed the warnings of medieval writers regarding the unreliability of confessions extracted through torture, discussed here by Amy G. Remensnyder, or the medieval insights on the plight of refugees and the dignity of labor, examined by Megan Cassidy-Welch and Martha Newman? What if, as Geoffrey Koziol suggests, we were to demand that our political leaders display the political virtue of wisdom, a major theme of the medieval "mirrors for princes" genre? What if – as Celia Chazelle discusses – our penal system were to incorporate some practices of early medieval communities aimed toward the rehabilitation of wrongdoers; or if we gave thought to the ways later medieval governments sought not to hide social deviants and the disabled but to integrate them at least partially into the public sphere, as discussed by G. Geltner and Kristina Richardson? What if we were to honor even a fraction of Wat Tyler's egalitarian vision of society, recalled by Peter Linebaugh? All the essays in this volume suggest how we might usefully direct attention both to those modern social and political problems that continue to be sidelined in public discussions, and to concerns already prominent on the national and international agenda.

Of course, this book does not come close to exhausting the possibilities for socially engaged medieval history. One area for future work is environmental history, where – again – knowledge of the medieval past will surely illuminate the present in new ways. In *The Fall of Rome and the End of Civilization*, published in 2005, Brian Ward-Perkins observes that in the early middle ages, the use of pottery ware for kitchens and tables diminished in every social class. Before then, under the Roman Empire, people used innumerable pottery vessels as containers for transport and then discarded them. "Like us," he notes, "the Romans enjoy the dubious distinction of creating a mountain of good-quality rubbish." Not only was there less trash in the early middle ages than in the Roman era, but the pollution caused by smelting lead, copper, and silver also declined – Ward-Perkins points out that it did not return to the levels found in the Roman Empire until the sixteenth century.[21]

For Ward-Perkins, the trash heaps, along with the damage to the environment caused by mining and metallurgy, are markers of Roman "civilization"; medieval Europe produced nothing comparable. One does not have to see the hit animated film "Wall-E" (2008) to consider it suspect for a historian today to be so apparently blithe about garbage mountains and other pollution. It might make a lot more sense for those who study the past to celebrate instead the early medieval retreat from Roman practices. The gradual replacement of long-distance trade by more local patterns of production, consumption, and exchange, and diminished mining and smelting – all visible in the early middle ages – are just the sort of changes the modern environmental movement hopes for today. There is a sense in which we sabotage that movement if we bemoan the early medieval developments as a "decline" and "the end of civilization."

If we want a different world, we might think further about the benefits of the disappearance of Roman exploitation of the environment and the rise of medieval, smaller-scale farming and industry; refuse to be cheerleaders for industrial revolutions; revisit how we measure "standard of living" in view of the rampant consumerism creating Roman-style garbage mountains today.[22] To re-engage with the distant past with modern needs in mind can help us understand more fully the societies in which we live, illuminating precedents for – and sometimes the origins of – our customs, ideas, and institutions. To study the medieval period from this perspective reveals some surprising analogues for current situations: analogues that, while never perfect and sometimes facile, always lend themselves to fresh debate and renewed reflection on the relation between the past and our world. It underscores the perseverance of certain elements of human experience over the centuries, but also the radical changes that remind us how beliefs and practices we might today think are unalterable or

<u>universal are neither.</u> Seeing the continuities and the transformations of societies and cultures over time and space can help us imagine alternatives to the present state of affairs, and discern where our efforts to change modern patterns of thought or behavior are likely to succeed. Most fundamentally, our recollection of distant historical events, however seemingly unrelated to our own situations, can encourage our optimism that change is always possible.

Notes

1 M. Bloch, *The Historian's Craft*, trans. P. Putnam, Manchester: Manchester University Press, 1954, repr. 1984, p. 4.
2 Bloch, *Historian's Craft*, pp. 6, 11, 43.
3 P. Farmer, *The Uses of Haiti*, 3rd rev. ed., Monroe, ME: Common Courage Press, Part I, pp. 49–213. Also see N. Chomsky, "Introduction," in ibid., pp. 15–40.
4 Bloch, *Historian's Craft*, pp. 15, 43.
5 H. Zinn, *The Politics of History*, Boston, MA: Beacon Press, 1970, pp. 5–14, esp. pp. 6–7; also see *Mapping the Ethical Turn: A Reader in Ethics, Culture, and Literary Theory*, ed. T.F. Davis and K. Wormack, Charlottesville, VA: University of Virginia Press, 2001.
6 L. Kerber, "We are all Historians of Human Rights." Online. Available HTTP: <www.historians.org/perspectives/issues/2006/0610/0610pre1.cfm> (accessed 7 March 2011).
7 A. Najmabadi, "Must We Always Non-Intervene?" Online. Available HTTP: <www.barnard.edu/bcrw/respondingtoviolence/najmabad.htm> (accessed 7 March 2011).
8 Zinn, *Politics of History*, pp. 293, 297.
9 Zinn, *Politics of History*, p. 8.
10 B. Schlager, "Reading *CSTH* as a Call to Action: Boswell and Gay-Affirming Movements in American Christianity," in *The Boswell Thesis: Essays on Christianity, Social Tolerance and Homosexuality*, ed. M. Kuefler, Chicago: University of Chicago Press, 2006, pp. 74–87, at pp. 75–76.
11 J. Bennett, *History Matters: Patriarchy and the Challenge of Feminism*, Philadelphia: University of Pennsylvania Press, 2006, p. 1.
12 *The Treatise of Lorenzo Valla on the Donation of Constantine*, trans. C. B. Coleman, New Haven, CT: Yale University Press, 1922; repr. Toronto: University of Toronto Press, 1993, pp. 177–79.
13 Gregory of Tours, *History of the Franks*, trans. L. Thorpe, London: Penguin, 1974, p. 63.
14 Gregory, *History of the Franks*, p. 103.
15 B.S. Bachrach, "Gregory of Tours as a Military Historian," in *The World of Gregory of Tours*, ed. K. Mitchell and I.N. Wood, Leiden: Brill, 2002, pp. 351–63, at p. 352; W. Goffart, "Conspicuously Absent: Martial Heroism in the Histories of Gregory of Tours and its Likes," in ibid., pp. 365–93, at p. 366.
16 Isidore of Seville, "History of the Goths," in *Conquerors and Chroniclers of Early Medieval Spain*, trans. K.B. Wolf, Liverpool: Liverpool University Press, 1990, p. 108.
17 Isidore, "History of the Goths," pp. 108–10.
18 J. Cavanagh, "Dulles Papers Reveal CIA Consulting Network." Online. Available HTTP: <www.cia-on-campus.org/princeton.edu/consult.html> (accessed 7 March 2011).
19 T. Yoshida, *The Making of the "Rape of Nanking:" History and Memory in Japan, China and the United States*, Oxford: Oxford University Press, 2006, p. 58.
20 Cited by J. Bourg, *From Revolution to Ethics: May 1968 and Contemporary French Thought*, Montreal: McGill-Queen's University Press, 2007, p. 171.
21 B. Ward-Perkins, *The Fall of Rome and the End of Civilization*, Oxford: Oxford University Press, 2005, pp. 92, 95.
22 Cf. B. Southgate, "'*Humani nil alienum*': The Quest for 'Human Nature'," in *Manifestos for History*, ed. K. Jenkins, S. Morgan, and A. Munslow, London: Routledge, 2007, pp. 67–76. Although he never mentions medievalists, Southgate lauds signs of a

"pre-scientific" attitude as part of the "greener movement" and suggests that historians can play a major role here, "not least by laying bare the traces of earlier emphases as an alternative to current values, and by presenting an alternative model of humans' relationship with 'nature'" (p. 72).

Suggestions for further reading

Rethinking history

Clark, E., *History, Theory, Text: Historians and the Linguistic Turn*, Cambridge, MA: Harvard University Press, 2004.

Davis, T.F. and Wormack, K., *Mapping the Ethical Turn: A Reader in Ethics, Culture, and Literary Theory*, Charlottesville, VA: University of Virginia Press, 2001.

History and Theory, Theme Issue 43 ("Historians and Ethics"), 2004.

Novick, P., *That Noble Dream: The "Objectivity Question" and the American Historical Profession*, Cambridge: Cambridge University Press, 1988.

Southgate, B., *What is History For?* London: Routledge, 2005.

Trouillot, M.-R., *Silencing the Past: Power and the Production of History*, Boston, MA: Beacon Press, 1995.

Zinn, H., *The Politics of History*, 2nd ed., Chicago: University of Illinois Press, 1990.

Engaging with the Middle Ages

Altschul, N., "Postcolonialism and the Study of the Middle Ages," *History Compass* 6, 2008, 588–606.

Bennett, J., *History Matters: Patriarchy and the Challenge of Feminism*, Philadelphia: University of Pennsylvania Press, 2006.

Boswell, J., *Christianity, Social Tolerance, and Homosexuality: Gay People in Western Europe from the Beginning of the Christian Era to the Fourteenth Century*, Chicago: University of Chicago Press, 1980.

Bull, M., *Thinking Medieval: An Introduction to the Study of the Middle Ages*, New York: Palgrave Macmillan, 2005.

Doubleday, S., and Coleman, D. (eds) *In the Light of Medieval Spain: Islam, the West, and the Relevance of the Past*, New York: Palgrave, 2008.

Holsinger, B., *Neomedievalism, Neoconservatism, and the War on Terror*, Chicago: Prickly Paradigm Press, 2007.

Menocal, M.R., *The Ornament of the World. How Muslims, Jews and Christians Created a Culture of Tolerance in Medieval Spain*, Boston, MA: Little Brown, 2002.

Ortenberg, V., *In Search of the Holy Grail: The Quest for the Middle Ages*, London: Hambledon Continuum, 2007.

1

CRIME AND PUNISHMENT

Penalizing without prisons

Celia Chazelle

With an incarcerated population of over 2.3 million, the US has more people and a higher percentage of its population behind bars than any other country.[1] If we add those on probation and parole, over seven million – more than 90 percent male – are under American penal supervision. In 1970, fewer than 200,000 Americans were incarcerated. Since then, crime rates have fluctuated and are now roughly where they were in 1973, yet our prison population has steadily grown. Much of the growth stems from tougher drug legislation passed during the last three decades; about one-third of incarcerations today are for drug offenses, mostly nonviolent.[2] These policies affect more middle class white Americans than we may realize, yet the impact on them is tiny compared with that on minorities – especially black men – from poor urban neighborhoods and our inner cities.[3] If present trends continue, one-third of African-American men will go to prison during their lives; of those who do not finish high school, almost 60 percent serve prison sentences by the age of 40.[4] Many black urban children grow up thinking of prison as a normal part of adult male life and barely knowing incarcerated fathers, partly because the facilities to which most inmates are sent lie more than a hundred miles from their home communities. The prisons support the economies of those largely rural white locales, while the inner cities bearing the brunt of crime remain impoverished.

Experts who study prisons today know that history is valuable if we are to solve the problems of our penal system. Numerous studies draw comparisons between modern American prison policies and earlier penal customs in Europe and the US, or trace the evolution of prisons from the past to the present. Like Michel Foucault's classic 1975 work, *Discipline and Punish: The Birth of the Prison*, however, most of this scholarship pays little attention to the European middle ages and even less to the early medieval centuries, the so-called Dark Ages of *c.* 500–1100. True, incarceration was rare in early medieval Europe. Yet precisely for this reason, it is useful to examine

16 Celia Chazelle

some of the very different penal practices of that era as we think about how we might improve those of today. In the following pages, I first review the common judicial penalties of early medieval Europe in light of recent scholarship and the textual and archaeological record. I then look at the intersection of poverty, crime, race, and incarceration in American inner cities, focusing on Camden, New Jersey. Here the sources are both studies in sociology and criminology, and my own experiences working in a Camden neighborhood and teaching in a New Jersey state prison. At the end of the essay, I consider how this juxtaposition of early medieval to modern suggests policy changes that might lessen the negative effects of American prisons, in particular on minority urban neighborhoods.

The principles of community and reparative justice and their analogies to recorded early medieval procedures for handling disputes lie at the heart of the reforms I discuss. Despite all our lip service to rehabilitation as a penal goal, early medieval people were more concerned than we are about reintegrating wrongdoers into society. In traditional criminal justice in the modern US, the accused is compelled to appear before a formal judicial apparatus that listens to representations from the different parties – defendants, victims, witnesses, lawyers – but then reaches a supposedly disinterested decision about guilt or innocence and, in the former case, about punishment, often incarceration. In contrast, early medieval sources report many acts – sometimes even murder – that we would classify as criminal, yet are presented there as disputes. To resolve them, offenders negotiated settlements with their victims, victims' representatives, and community members. Settlements typically hinged on the payment of reparations or compensation along with, frequently, the performance of penance or other rituals of humiliation that ideally reestablished – according to reports – friendship or "love" between the antagonists and community peace.

Similarly, modern community justice programs sometimes encourage reparative sanctions as alternatives to incarceration. Usually in these programs, governments yield partial jurisdiction to community residents, who work with municipal police to address the conditions encouraging crime and to deal with incidents in ways that limit the resort to prisons. When crimes occur, community panels may mediate among the different parties; taking individual circumstances into account, they devise responses intended to assist both the victim and the neighborhood as a whole. A guiding concern is the damage that wrongdoing inevitably does to social bonds throughout the community. The hope is that the penalty – reparations, perhaps in the form of work service – will compensate for damages and heal the divisions between offenders, victims, and other residents. Observing that offenders undertake "a species of secular penance" for the harm done not just to one person but to many, one expert in this field unknowingly echoes early medieval ideas. The penalty, he explains, offers "an apology" to victims and the wider public.[5]

Early medieval practices underscore the value of community and reparative justice for responding to nonviolent offenders in cities like Camden and, further, point toward initiatives that could provide similar benefits when dealing with violent offenders. Among the advantages of looking at modern penal policies through the lens of early medieval justice, one is that it reveals the particular importance of family and social networks to community wellbeing.

Early medieval justice

The best known medieval European judicial punishments are no doubt the spectacularly dramatic, painful torments seen in Hollywood films and *Far Side* cartoons: bodies broken on wheels and hanging from public gallows, beheadings, burnings, tortures like the thumbscrew and the rack. Foucault famously begins *Discipline and Punish* with a lurid account of the torture and drawing and quartering of Damiens, the would-be regicide (king-killer), in Paris in 1757. For Foucault, this scene harked back to a medieval emphasis on punishing the body, an approach to crime for which, he asserts, modernity has substituted the equally coercive punishment of prison. We now realize physical torture is still with us; but most Americans would agree that prisons illustrate our modernity, and most – unlike Foucault – believe these institutions are far more humane than any penalties of the middle ages.

Medieval records, however, reveal a more nuanced situation. The majority of the sources for studying medieval penalties date from the twelfth and later centuries. The evidence is sparser for the early middle ages, yet people then, too, were familiar with a host of painful practices. Early medieval lawcodes enjoin execution for offenses ranging from homicide to adultery to relapsing into paganism. Narrative sources tell of kings and aristocrats who condemned enemies to exile or death, and of lords who commanded that dependents be branded, blinded, or lose noses or ears. Courts ordered torture and ordeals – such as trial by fire, where the suspect walked on burning coals, or trial by water where he or she picked an object out of boiling water. Skeletons unearthed from burial grounds show the effects of decapitation, amputation, and limbs bound possibly for hanging.[6] Furthermore, while imprisonment was unusual, it was not absent, and again the experience must have been decidedly unpleasant. Nobles who rebelled against kings, priests who disobeyed bishops, and slaves or serfs (people of servile or unfree status) who tried to escape were sometimes confined in monasteries; some religious houses had a special room called a *carcer* – the origin of our term, incarceration – where misbehaving monks were kept until they repented. Probably worse off were those offenders confined by secular authorities, often with chains, in dungeons or other dismal spaces. Many were evidently locked up only until they could be brought before lords or courts and another penalty like a fine or execution imposed. But some people clearly died in those places.

All these practices would seem to confirm popular ideas about Dark Age barbarism and to prove we have done well to leave that era behind us. Frequently omitted from this picture, though, is an array of early medieval penal customs rooted in the dearth of centralized government and, accordingly, in the importance of small-scale, local, and regional networks. Most early medieval European kingdoms were much smaller than those of the later middle ages, and in general, the governing elites – rulers and high-level nobility – were politically weaker than at any other point in Western history. Even in the Carolingian Empire, which covered most of western continental

Europe in the ninth century, it was hard for emperors, kings, or aristocrats to exercise authority much beyond their courts or at the lowest social levels. A corollary is that common people had exceptional autonomy relative to other historical periods. Countless non-elite minor nobles and peasants lived in more or less independent agrarian households and communities that managed their affairs locally, with little outside interference. In modern American cities, the poor live under significantly more "state" control than they did in early medieval Europe. Medieval church authority was equally patchy. Bishops of minor dioceses, monks and nuns of small religious houses, priests overseeing local saints' shrines, and village clergy distant from the main centers of wealth and privilege were often left on their own, not bothered by the higher echelon of bishops, archbishops, and the pope.

At the lowest social ranks as at the top of these hierarchies, personal connections were critical to the work of justice. Much as today, when the famous and well connected are the least likely to be imprisoned or executed, knowing the right people counted for a lot. Some ties that made a difference were familial: extended, overlapping, shifting associations of "kinship" that could encompass parents, children, and varied relations by blood, marriage, godparentage, adoption, and friendship. Additionally, just about everyone was conscious of their social class and of legal or customary responsibilities binding them to those higher and lower on the social ladder. Serfs were subject to lords, women to husbands and brothers, peasants to the local nobles, priests to bishops, and so on. Overall, the severest judicial reprisals were suffered by individuals who, when they ran afoul of more powerful people, lacked relatives, friends, lords, or patrons with sufficient clout to resist *and* the desire to do so. For them, penalties could be harshly punitive: death, maiming, flogging, and the like. Such unfortunates might include women punished by male relatives because of their sexual offenses; men abandoned by allies to face powerful enemies alone because their reckless behavior endangered the group; homeless exiles cut off from families and entangled in other villages' strife; and doubtless huge numbers of slaves, serfs, and free but poor peasants whom lords decided, whatever the reason, not to spare when they got into trouble.

Many times, however, social disturbances were handled as disputes without any "big men" around to wield power unilaterally. Either the disputants possessed roughly equal status and influence, so no side was strong enough simply to impose its will; or if one party was weaker, it still had enough power to defend its interests, and the opposing side had to negotiate to end the conflict. Most recorded early medieval disputes were between nobles, monasteries, or clergy over property; but violent offenses such as rape, kidnapping, and homicide, at all social levels, could be addressed in this manner. Feud, we should bear in mind, was widespread in this period. Cycles of tit-for-tat vengeance, sometimes low intensity with sporadic violence, might persist for years before adversaries stopped fighting and started talking. When they did so, knowledge of law mixed with local custom might play a role; yet typically, the driving concern was less to follow specific laws than to make peace. To the extent that the conflict was treated as a dispute, the settlement had to be accepted by every party involved.

Just as neighbors today can end their quarrels peacefully without calling police or lawyers, early medieval disputants might resolve their differences alone or with help from only a few supporters. Other disputes were brought for mediation or arbitration before larger groups of relatives and neighbors or external courts convened by aristocrats, bishops, or royal representatives. More often, though, if disputes were not settled extra-judicially, assistance came from local courts somewhat akin to modern community justice panels: assemblies led by clergy, landowners, or other influential men of the neighborhood. It is important not to underestimate the frequent messiness of these proceedings. Local "bosses" could manipulate an affair to their personal benefit, throwing support to one side in exchange for loyalty in other matters. Multiple powerbrokers might take opposing sides and intensify the conflict, with tensions spilling into new violence. Courts could demand ordeals, and the poor and powerless mixed up in their lords' disputes might be tortured. Gaining help from relatives and friends required negotiations and jockeying for position, with promises of future recompense. If the bartering failed and allies turned against disputants, the latter might encounter unanticipated retribution. When harvests were bad, communities may have been more likely than on other occasions to "settle" disputes by banishing or executing some participants. If nothing else, the punishments decreased the number to feed, and troublemakers could be blamed for bringing God's wrath on others.

Yet a notable feature of reported early medieval dispute settlements is how often they depend not on a physically severe penalty such as exile or execution, but on reparations. Although historians sometimes associate the reparative sanctions mentioned in our sources with the early medieval term, *wergeld*, meaning "man money" or the price for killing someone, payments could compensate for other wrongs besides murder. Early medieval lawcodes list precise amounts for many offenses, but like other aspects of settlements, and like the penalties in modern community justice, what was owed depended in practice on the circumstances. The basic concept underlying the bargaining in early medieval disputes is the same as that underlying modern community justice deliberations: reciprocity. This principle was implicit in feud as well: every injury should induce equivalent hardship in return. The factors weighed in determining reparations, however, could be quite complicated. The penalty might need to measure up not only to the nature of the offense but to demands by big men trying to direct the affair to their advantage and, almost invariably, to the factors informing the disputants' own sense of honor and outrage, such as the gender or rank of victims and offenders. Feelings of honor and shame were as important in early medieval relations as they are among modern urban street gangs.[7] To be the victim of an offense was degrading; it hurt one's social standing and that of family and allies. For the victim or victim's circle to give up the right to retaliation, the recompense had to outweigh not simply the loss of goods or life but also the humiliation.

Offenders, too, worried about their honor and that of family and friends. Those who thought a proposed resolution was too shameful and had the capacity to resist would do so. Still, some recorded dispute settlements were very large, perhaps because the offenders' side was unable to strike a good deal. The settlement for the murder of the seventh-century Kentish princes, Aethelred and Aethelbert, for example, required the murderers' side to hand over a massive amount of land to endow a new monastery.[8] Family and supporters might scramble to gather resources or installment payments could be spread over years, a guarantee, possibly, of the loser's long-term good behavior. Wrongdoers might flee, take sanctuary in churches, or be confined while supporters collected funds. Assisting with reparations was an obligation of kinship, one of the many ties holding family networks together; but if the required amount was so great that relatives and allies could not or chose not to pay, a free person might be forced into servitude or slavery. Or the settlement itself could involve loss of freedom: a seventh-century Irish text tells of a wealthy kinsman who paid for the release of a murderer caught by the victim's family; the murderer then became his relative's servant.[9] Besides money and land, reparations could include gifts of people already in bondage, like the serfs sent to the monastery of Redon when one of its serfs was killed and cattle were stolen, or gifts of objects or women in marriage.[10] Additionally, offenders might try to calm opponents through acts of supplication or "begging pardon," such as prostration and the kissing of feet; or they could submit to humiliating public rituals like riding backwards on an ass. Bishops, local clergy, and abbots sometimes served as peacemakers during disputes in which they were not participants. The shaming rituals they could impose on offenders – excommunication and public penances like fasts, the wearing of sackcloth and ashes, floggings, alms-giving, and pilgrimages – also helped reconcile disputants and restore peace, at least in theory. The settlement in the eleventh-century feud between the Anglo-Saxon (English) earl Ealdred and the Dane Carl, for example, included a brotherhood ritual and the promise (never fulfilled) of a joint pilgrimage to Rome to atone for the disturbance.[11]

Pilgrims had to leave their homes, but excommunication, reparations, and rituals of humiliation did not necessarily separate offenders from their social groups. Since former enemies might continue to live near one another, this must have meant that even after settlements were reached, conflict frequently started up again. The fragility of these situations may have encouraged everyone to tread carefully for awhile; if someone broke the settlement, that person might then receive harsher treatment, such as execution or permanent exile. Yet as long as the penalized stayed within their communities, there was at least the possibility they would join in everyday tasks alongside relatives and neighbors, work essential to others' survival. Social ties might thus be preserved without further loss to the labor force. Implicitly recognized in this system – if we can use that term for such diverse customs – was that an offense carried consequences for the perpetrator's family and neighbors as well as for the victim and victim's family. The offense affected all these groups. All were harmed by the wrongful action, whether they suffered physically, suffered economically from paying reparations, felt shame, lost work time due to the disruption, or for another reason. Thus everyone in a sense needed compensation for harmony to be restored. Excommunication and public rituals of penitence, supplication, and humiliation marked offenders for shunning, by not only victims and their families but the offenders' own kin and neighbors. Remaining in the community, marginalized but not invisible as are the inmates of our prisons, the wrongdoers would provide an ongoing reminder to all of the boundaries of acceptable behavior and what happened when they were transgressed. Yet even as relatives and community members might ostracize them, excluding them from feasts or other celebrations, the penalized could share in farming, nurturing children, and other collective tasks that might appease both their enemies and supporters angry at the trouble. To the extent any of this occurred in specific situations (it is impossible to judge the actual success of most dispute settlements from our sources), such actions assisted the offenders' reintegration into social networks. At the same time, penances atoned God as well, smoothing the way to reconciliation between the earthly community and heaven.

Prisons, Camden, and American inner cities

If the history of early medieval penal practices has any relevance for rethinking modern policies, the lessons must be applicable in those disadvantaged urban communities where the impact of our prison system is most apparent. Camden, New Jersey epitomizes this issue. A city in one of the richest states of the US, it is situated a ten-minute drive from Philadelphia on the potentially beautiful Delaware River shoreline. In spite of its proximity to a vital business center and in spite of New Jersey's overall wealth, Camden is now ranked the poorest and one of the most crime-ridden cities in the country.[12]

Until the mid-twentieth century, Camden was a prosperous industrial center with a primarily European immigrant, middle class population.[13] Decline set in during the decade after the Second World War, as African-Americans migrated to the city from the South in search of work in the city's industries, and white residents and businesses began to leave for the suburbs. Over the next two decades, the loss of jobs and the growing poverty of an increasingly minority population contributed to the stagnation of the housing market and drop in property tax revenue. Public services decreased, and racial tensions rose. A series of bad decisions in urban planning hastened the transformation, among them the construction of a highway cutting residential areas in half, completed in the 1980s, and a county sewage treatment plant that brought few jobs yet massive air pollution. Demonstrations and riots broke out in the late 1960s and early 1970s; in their wake, crime soared, leading more white-owned businesses to close and white residents to leave. The city's population fell from a peak of 124,500 in 1950 to 79,318 in 2006. Fifty-three percent of inhabitants are now African-American and 39 percent Hispanic (of any race). Over one-third live in poverty, with unemployment at roughly 17 percent (2009 figures).[14] Urban blight is visible everywhere. Giant metal heaps sit along the southern waterfront, blocking the view of the river; one of Camden's few presently successful businesses is scrap metal recycling. More than a thousand derelict buildings stand boarded up, fire hazards for those living next door. Empty houses and vacant lots lining pot-holed streets attract drug users, prostitutes, trash, roaches, and rodents.

Camden residents who find employment and affordable housing in other places continue to move away, whereas many who stay seem trapped in a vortex of poverty, unemployment, substance abuse, and crime. For many children, especially boys, the principal adult role models are drug dealers and gang members who entice them to follow the same path. The annual violent crime rate in Camden is more than five times the US average and almost ten times that of Glasgow, the "murder capital" of western Europe.[15] There were 32 homicides in 2009 and again in 2010; 52 homicides occurred in 2008.[16] (Remember, this is in a population of less than 80,000.) Most murder victims are men under 30 killed by guns, often as part of gang vengeance – the ancient tradition of feud, far deadlier than its early medieval counterparts. As in early medieval Europe, however, the human toll extends well beyond the victims. A mass held in Camden's Sacred Heart Church each November, to commemorate those killed in the previous 12 months, starkly illumines the riptide of sorrow sweeping yearly through the city. Most of the parishioners are white and from nearby suburbs, but on this day they sit squeezed into pews between as many black and Hispanic Camden residents – friends and relatives of the deceased who come just for this mass. As the priest calls out each name with the age and cause of death – "Tyson Jones, 16, death by gunshot; Jesse Baylor, 40, death by gunshot; Daryl Cole, 17, death by gunshot"[17] – a family member, friend, or representative steps forward to stand near the altar holding a candle. Empty spaces gradually widen in the pews while the list is read and the line beside the altar grows longer. The sound of quiet weeping mingles with the rythmic recitation of names and ages, punctuated over and over by the word "gunshot," as mothers, wives, fathers, children, other relatives, friends, and parishioners bear witness to the accumulated loss of life the city endures every year.

My prison students, who are incarcerated in a facility located in a more rural part of New Jersey, are mostly black and (fewer) Latino men in their twenties from cities such as Camden. Most have been convicted of gang violence, frequently homicide; in this regard they represent the culture of violent death mourned in Sacred Heart's November mass. The people still living in Camden whom I know best, mainly women, have all had friends and relatives killed, sometimes their sons or children's fathers. Although the women seem resilient, they yearn for safe streets as much as do middle class suburbanites. Some believe the violence persists because local authorities have little real concern for their security. The police drive along the streets, stopping to frisk young men, yet I have listened to numerous complaints about police collaboration in the drug trade and slowness to respond to disturbances. The one occasion I was near a gun battle, sirens were not heard until twenty minutes after shots were fired. This estrangement from law enforcement reinforces law-abiding residents' sense of solidarity; though generally ignored in news reports, the strength of their social networks is a major positive feature of community life in Camden unmatched in many suburban areas. Disadvantaged minority urban households tend to be loosely organized around several generations of relatives and sometimes unrelated members. In Camden, women predominate, partly because violent death claims so many men and others cycle in and out of prison. But aside from the gender imbalance, the households recall early medieval kin groups more than the nuclear families of middle class suburbs. Despite large and shifting memberships, they tend to be close knit. The women care for each other's biological, adoptive, step, and foster children, and sometimes for abandoned children brought in from the streets. They exchange clothes and share groceries, cars, cash, cell phones, and food stamps. Low-level conflicts over stolen TV cables, vandalism, and drug dealing between nearby homes are often resolved through informal "dispute settlements," without police intervention, and occasionally the women protect male relatives from the police. But they vehemently denounce the drug trade and gang violence, express little sympathy for violent offenders whom the police arrest, and worry about the safety of children. As in early medieval Europe, and as Carol Stack discussed in *All Our Kin*, her classic 1974 study of poor African-American urban family structures, Camden is a place where "family" is critical to coping with the demands of daily life.

The desire for public safety in Camden deserves the same respect it receives in middle class suburbs. Penal reform must take into account the right of inner city people to feel safe, and under present conditions it is impossible to imagine this without prisons for those who commit serious crimes. But let us be clear about the negative effects, in places like Camden, of a justice system that offers so few alternatives to prison and so thoroughly isolates inmates. Like executions and exile, but unlike numerous reparative sanctions in early medieval Europe, modern prisons deprive neighborhoods of the labor and income – legally or illegally acquired – that offenders used to contribute. Resources are further drained when relatives must supplement inmates' meager wages from prison jobs so they can buy incidentals, or pay for collect phone calls and transportation for visits. Imprisonment also impedes productivity after release, partly because education and job training in American prisons have been steadily cut over the last decades, and because government control remains pervasive for ex-felons, sometimes for life: laws prevent them from holding certain jobs, strip them of certain civil rights, such as the right to vote or serve on juries, and deny them certain types of government assistance. Exacerbating all this is the huge emotional toll of incarceration on inmates as well as their families and friends. The stress of arrest, trial, conviction, and sentencing, and then the years locked up in distant facilities erode prisoners' ties to their children and law-abiding adult relatives, friends, and neighbors – the people who raise their kids while they are gone and could help them get back on their feet after prison. Phone calls, letters, and visits dwindle and sometimes end entirely; one of my prison students told me his family had moved out of state without giving him the new address. If former prisoners return to their old neighborhoods, normal social relations are hard to develop; studies show, for instance, that ex-felons are less likely than other men to marry. As connections to law-abiding people on the outside weaken, those to gangs grow stronger. A quasi-substitute for family while convicts are inside, providing protection and emotional support, gangs are frequently the main avenue of employment (drug dealing) when they get out.[18]

Possible reforms

Problems of this magnitude cannot be truly resolved without comprehensive changes to government policies in multiple areas. But as a start, we could do worse than adapt to our needs practices that early medieval people got right. It is extraordinarily difficult for those incarcerated in the US today ever fully to re-enter society. There are obviously many attributes of early medieval justice we do not want to replicate; but one good feature meriting attention is the various penalties that allowed offenders to continue to live and work alongside relatives and neighbors, and thus facilitated their eventual restoration to full social membership in their communities.

Prison policy often recycles old ideas while presenting them as new. A partial recycling of early medieval practices is found in modern community justice measures, especially those that stress reparative sanctions. Unfortunately, most such programs are for nonviolent offenders from white middle class areas. Like the early medieval poor who lacked powerful patrons to negotiate advantageous settlements, poor minority offenders today have much less recourse to reparative justice, even for nonviolent crimes like drug-dealing. New Jersey spends about $39,000 per year per prisoner; the annual bill for both prisons and jails nationwide is $60 billion.[19] Yet even with the economic crisis (imagine the social programs this money could finance!), tough-on-crime policies emphasizing incarceration enjoy strong support; most Americans still think of prison as the best means to assure safe streets and diminish crime. Unlike in early medieval Europe, where state structures were weak and limited in power, centralized government largely directs penal practices today; despite a few hopeful rumblings on the horizon,[20] there remains little political will to alter them on a widespread scale, in particular for poor minorities.

Nonetheless, we should push for change, especially in regard to nonviolent offenders, not only to save money but for the social benefits. Just as renewed conflict could easily disrupt fragile early medieval dispute settlements, modern community justice advocates recognize that if we reduce our use of prisons, some offenders sentenced to reparative sanctions that keep them in their neighborhoods will commit new wrongs. Crime will not necessarily decline in the short term. But in the long run, community justice programs focused on reparations can respond effectively to offenses, and they address the urban problems that foster crime. The money saved by decreasing prison expenditures can be put toward the great need in inner cities for better government services, improved schools, and rebuilt infrastructure; and any service work done by penalized offenders would add to these improvements. Perhaps the most significant consequence, though, is the opportunity, through reparative sanctions, to repair the broken bonds of trust between offenders, victims, and neighbors. As in early medieval Europe, the work of inner city wrongdoers who are living in − rather than excluded from − their communities can resonate with other inhabitants' sense of injured honor and heal the divisions the offenses created.

Political support for moving away from incarceration for violent offenders would be harder to obtain. Yet for them, too, prison terms could be shortened and alternative sentencing expanded without jeopardy to public safety. Moreover, other more politically palatable measures might lessen the degree to which imprisoned offenders – whether convicted of violent or nonviolent crimes – are cut off from families and communities. Here too, policy changes would be especially beneficial for disadvantaged urban areas. Greater effort could be made, for one, to place prisoners from the inner cities in facilities close to their homes so relatives can visit without onerous transportation expenses. Further, many incarcerated for violent crimes are not so dangerous that they cannot be safely brought into their neighborhoods to work under supervision. The image of the chain gang has distorted the popular understanding of such work and obscured its potential value. Like the reparative sanctions imposed on nonviolent offenders and the labor and rituals of early medieval wrongdoers, this work can be directed toward helping the inmates' home communities and strengthening social bonds in those areas.

Regardless of their skills, prisoners could accomplish an enormous amount of good in their neighborhoods while serving sentences. Have them work under police supervision to fix sidewalks, fill potholes, pick up trash, gut derelict buildings, and plant trees and gardens in empty lots. Teach them construction techniques so they can build new homes. Some of them are incredible artists; prison walls are covered with artwork invisible to the outside world. Assign them to paint murals for victims' homes, their children's homes, or public spaces, restoring beauty to places made ugly partly through their offenses. Some know how to cook and could prepare meals for soup kitchens or schools. Many are athletes and musicians who, with supervision, could assist sports and music programs for local youth. The list of possible projects is long. Undertaken in public view and, conceivably, a source of shame – as were the humiliating rituals imposed on early medieval offenders – the work would provide some compensation to victims and the community for the harmful acts. The vocational skills the prisoners would learn might reduce recidivism and would certainly make their neighborhoods better places to live. Equally if not more important, lessening isolation would reduce the destructive impact of prison on the inmates' ties to neighbors and family, including children, who might learn to associate their fathers with caring for the community rather than detrimental activities.

Certain of these suggested reforms are doubtless more feasible than others, but the basic point is this: let's have a penal system that does not force so many disadvantaged, minority urban men to waste years in exile. Early medieval Europeans often executed or banished wrongdoers; but they also developed penalties that, in theory, safeguarded their connections to kin and allowed them to work in ways useful to their households and communities. As early medieval people seem to have understood, offenses spread damage widely; in addition to victims and victims' families, they hurt the perpetrators' own families, friends, and neighbors. All these people suffer from the crimes and the crimes' impact on the places where they live. All of them deserve reparations for the injury to the entire social web. Penal policies like those suggested here, inspired in part by customs of the deep past, would by no means solve every problem we face. But they would surely achieve greater healing of the emotional – as well as physical – devastation that crime brings to our inner cities than does our current obsession with prisons.

Notes

I am grateful to many friends and colleagues for helpful comments on previous drafts of this article. Thanks especially to my co-editors Simon Doubleday, Felice Lifshitz, and Amy Remensnyder; to G. Geltner and Geoff Koziol, contributors to this volume; to my husband Bernard Chazelle; and to my friends Joseph Hlubik, who gave me the idea for the slant this essay has taken, Eileen Borland, and Bruce Stout.

1 By the end of 2008, the total incarcerated population in the US was 2,424,279: W.J. Sabol, H.C., West, and M. Cooper, *Bureau of Justice Statistics Bulletin: Prisoners in 2008*, Washington, DC: US Department of Justice, 2009, p. 8. Online. Available HTTP: <http://bjs.ojp.usdoj.gov/content/pub/pdf/p08.pdf> (accessed 13 January 2011). American jails are generally run by counties; they incarcerate suspects awaiting trial and convicts with sentences of less than one year. Prisons are state and federal institutions holding convicts with longer sentences. The population total cited here also includes military and juvenile facilities. The numbers have slightly declined since 2008.
2 Bureau of Justice Statistics. Online. Available HTTP: <http://bjs.ojp.usdoj.gov/content/glance/corrtyp.cfm> (accessed 13 January 2011).
3 D. Garland, "Introduction: The Meaning of Mass Imprisonment," *Punishment and Society* 3, 2001, 5–7. Online. Available HTTP: <http://pun.sagepub.com/content/3/1/5.full.pdf+html> (accessed 13 January 2011).
4 B. Western, *Punishment and Inequality in America*, New York: Russell Sage, 2006, p. 33 (with B. Pettit).
5 R.A. Duff, *Punishment, Communication, and Community*, Oxford: Oxford University Press, 2001, pp. 106, 112–14; see T.R. Clear, *Imprisoning Communities: How Mass Incarceration Makes Disadvantaged Neighborhoods Worse*, Oxford: Oxford University Press, 2007, pp. 191–93.
6 A. Reynolds, *Anglo-Saxon Deviant Burial Customs*, Oxford: Oxford University Press, 2009, pp. 34–69.
7 C. Adamson, "Tribute, Turf, Honor and the American Street Gang Since 1820," *Theoretical Criminology* 2, 1998, 57–84. Online. Available HTTP: <http://tcr.sagepub.com/content/2/1/57.full.pdf+html > (accessed 13 January 2011).
8 P. Hyams, *Rancor and Reconciliation in Early Medieval England*, Ithaca, NY: Cornell University Press, 2003, p. 89.
9 J.M.H. Smith, *Europe After Rome: A New Cultural History, 500–1000*, Oxford: Oxford University Press, 2005, p. 109.
10 W. Davies, "People and Places in Dispute in Ninth-Century Brittany," in *The Settlement of Disputes in Early Medieval Europe*, ed. W. Davies and P. Fouracre, Cambridge: Cambridge University Press, 1986, pp. 65–84, at p. 77.
11 Hyams, *Rancor and Reconciliation*, pp. 76, 278.
12 2006 data shows Camden as the poorest city in the US measured by median household income and percentage living in poverty: CAMConnect, "Poverty in Camden: Camden Quick Facts." Online. Available HTTP: <www.camconnect.org/documents/poverty_handout.pdf > (accessed 13 January 2011). In 2008, the median household income estimate for New Jersey was the second highest in the nation, at $70,347. Maryland was the highest ($70,482) and West Virginia the lowest ($37,528): US Census Bureau, *Small Area Income and Poverty Estimates*. Online. Available HTTP: <www.census.gov/did/www/saipe/data/highlights/2008.html> (accessed 13 January 2011).
13 H. Gillette, *Camden After the Fall: Decline and Renewal in a Post-Industrial City*, Philadelphia: University of Pennsylvania Press, 2005.
14 US Census Bureau, *State and County QuickFacts: Camden (city), New Jersey*. Online. Available HTTP: <http://quickfacts.census.gov/qfd/states/34/3410000.html> (accessed 13 January 2011); "Camden, New Jersey," *Wikipedia*. Online. Available HTTP: <http://en.wikipedia.org/wiki/Camden,_New_Jersey > (accessed 13 January 2011).
15 Glasgow had a murder rate of fifty-five per one million population in 2005; Camden's rate in 2009 and 2010, with thirty-two homicides each year, was 437.5 per one million

population: see "Report Ranks Camden Most Dangerous US City," *Courier-Post*, 24 November 2009. Online. Available HTTP: <www.courierpostonline.com/apps/pbcs. dll/artikkel?NoCache=1&Dato=20091124&Kategori=NEWS01&Lopenr=911240338& Ref=AR> (accessed 13 January 2011). On Glasgow: "Homicide Rate Hits 10-Year High," *BBC News*, 14 December 2005. Online. Available HTTP: <http://news.bbc.co. uk/2/hi/uk_news/scotland/4527570.stm> (accessed 13 January 2011).
16 "Camden Resources." Online. Available HTTP: <http://www.camdenresources.org/ murders/> (accessed 13 June 2011). Also see "Camden, New Jersey: Crime," *Wikipedia*. Online. Available HTTP: <http://en.wikipedia.org/wiki/Camden,_New_Jersey> (accessed 7 March 2011).
17 Names have been changed to protect anonymity.
18 J.M. Hagedorn, *A World of Gangs: Armed Young Men and Gangsta Culture*, Minneapolis: University of Minnesota Press, 2008, pp. 11–22.
19 C. Dela Cruz, "Proposed Bill Would Charge NJ Prisoners for Cost of Incarceration," *The Star-Ledger*, 14 May 2009. Online. Available HTTP: <www.nj.com/news/index.ssf/ 2009/05/proposed_bill_would_charge_pri.html> (accessed 13 January 2011); D. Cole, "Can Our Shameful Prisons Be Reformed?" *The New York Review of Books*, 19 November 2009. Online. Available HTTP: <www.nybooks.com/articles/archives/ 2009/nov/19/can-our-shameful-prisons-be-reformed/> (accessed 13 January 2011).
20 N. Gingrich and P. Nolan, "Prison Reform: A Smart Way for States to Save Money and Lives," *The Washington Post*, 7 January 2011. Online. Available HTTP: <www. washingtonpost.com/wp-dyn/content/article/2011/01/06/AR2011010604386.html> (accessed 12 January 2011).

Suggestions for further reading

Early medieval justice

Brown, W., *Unjust Seizure: Conflict, Interest, and Authority in an Early Medieval Society*, Ithaca, NY: Cornell University Press, 2001.
Davies, W. and Fouracre, P. (eds) *The Settlement of Disputes in Early Medieval Europe*, Cambridge: Cambridge University Press, 1986.
Geary, P., "Extra-Judicial Means of Conflict Resolution," in *La Giustizia nell'alto medioevo (secoli IX-XI) 11–17 aprile 1996*, 2 vols, Spoleto: Presso la sede del Centro, 1997, Volume 2, pp. 569–601.
Hyams, P., *Rancor and Reconciliation in Early Medieval England*, Ithaca, NY: Cornell University Press, 2003.
Koziol, G., *Begging Pardon and Favor: Ritual and Political Order in Early Medieval France*, Ithaca, NY: Cornell University Press, 1992.
Smith, J.M.H., *Europe After Rome: A New Cultural History, 500–1000*, Oxford: Oxford University Press, 2005.

Ancient, medieval, and modern crime and punishment

Braithwaite, J., *Crime, Shame and Reintegration*, Cambridge: Cambridge University Press, 1989.
Cassidy-Welch, M., "Incarceration and Liberation: Prisons in the Cistercian Monastery," *Viator* 32 (2001), 23–42.
Clear, T.R., *Imprisoning Communities: How Mass Incarceration Makes Disadvantaged Neighborhoods Worse*, Oxford: Oxford University Press, 2007.
Coss, P. (ed.) *The Moral World of the Law*, Cambridge: Cambridge University Press, 2000.
Duff, R.A., *Punishment, Communication and Community*, Oxford: Oxford University Press, 2001.

Foucault, M., *Discipline and Punish: The Birth of the Prison*, trans. A. Sheridan, New York: Vintage Books, 1979, c. 1977.

Garland, D., *The Culture of Control: Crime and Social Order in Contemporary Society*, Chicago: University of Chicago Press, 2002.

Geltner, G., *The Medieval Prison: A Social History*, Princeton, NJ: Princeton University Press, 2008.

Gottschalk, M., *The Prison and the Gallows: The Politics of Mass Incarceration in America*, Cambridge: Cambridge University Press, 2006.

Jewkes, Y. (ed.) *Handbook on Prisons*, Portland, OR: Willan, 2007.

Morris, N. and Rothman, D.J. (eds) *The Oxford History of the Prison: The Practice of Punishment in Western Society*, New York: Oxford University Press, 1995.

Stout, B.D., "The Case for Rational Reform," *New Jersey Reporter* 34 (2006), pp. 36–43.

Wacquant, L., "The Body, the Ghetto and the Penal State," *Qualitative Sociology* 32 (2009), 101–29.

Western, B., *Punishment and Inequality in America*, New York: Russell Sage, 2006.

Camden and American inner cities

Anderson, E., *Code of the Street: Decency, Violence, and the Moral Life of the Inner City*, New York: W.W. Norton, 1999.

Gillette, H., *Camden After the Fall: Decline and Renewal in a Post-Industrial City*, Philadelphia: University of Pennsylvania Press, 2005.

Hagedorn, J. M., *A World of Gangs: Armed Young Men and Gangsta Culture*, Minneapolis: University of Minnesota Press, 2008.

Katz, M., "Camden Rebirth: A Promise Still Unfulfilled," *Philadelphia Inquirer*, 8 November, 2009. Online. Available HTTP: <http://articles.philly.com/2009-11-08/news/24987941_1_state-takeover-sewer-sewage> (accessed 12 January 2011).

Stack, C.B., *All Our Kin: Strategies for Survival in a Black Community*, New York: Harper and Row, 1974.

2

SOCIAL DEVIANCY

A medieval approach

G. Geltner

The moral test of a government is how it treats those who are at the dawn of life, the children; those who are in the twilight of life, the aged; and those who are in the shadow of life, the sick, and the needy, and the handicapped.

Hubert H. Humphrey

NIMBY (Acronym: not in my backyard). Opposition to the locating of something considered undesirable (as a prison or incinerator) in one's neighborhood.

Merriam-Webster Dictionary

"Harm Reduction" refers to policies, programmes and practices that aim primarily to reduce the adverse health, social and economic consequences of the use of legal and illegal psychoactive drugs without necessarily reducing drug consumption. Harm reduction benefits people who use drugs, their families and the community.

International Harm Reduction Association

Between the twelfth and fourteenth centuries, European cities witnessed a growth of what are sometimes called marginalizing institutions and spaces – hospitals, brothels, leper-houses, prisons, and Jewish quarters. Historians have often cited this development in order to illustrate the persecuting mentality that allegedly characterized a Europe coming into its own: an increasingly introspective society seeking self-definition and, so the argument runs, closing its ranks to religious outsiders, such as Jews and heretics, as well as to internal Others, from homosexuals and lepers, to prostitutes, to the physically and mentally ill. Seen in this light, medieval society appears to have failed yet another moral test set to it by its modern heirs.

The available evidence supports a different reading, however, one that stresses the social semi-inclusiveness of institutions benefiting those at the dawn, twilight, and shadow of life. From this revised perspective, the choice to create facilities such as brothels and prisons within cities and to govern them responsibly constitutes a high – rather than low – benchmark of medieval adaptation to social and religious heterogeneity and the growing presence of at-risk populations. In the parlance of modern public health, medieval city councils adopted a strategy of harm reduction. For this particular, spatial form of othering did not merely create stigmatized groups from disparate individuals; it also enabled their monitored social inclusion. Given the abrasive and generally intolerant environment in which urban magistrates operated, the choice raises an important question: Why bother with the weakest members of society by allocating substantial resources for keeping them alive and well in designated spaces?

The answer lies partly in medieval urban society's increasing social, economic, ethnic, and religious heterogeneity, and partly in local governments' desire to control their populations more effectively and reduce disorder. The creative tension between these two developments produced some new centralized facilities for deviants (prisons, brothels, and "red-light" districts), and revised approaches towards existing institutions and spaces (hospitals, leper-houses, Jewish quarters). Jointly these places underscored the presence of threatening Others while normalizing their presence; born of a need to organize a diverse population, such spaces integrated some deviants further into society and expanded the boundaries of civic responsibility towards others. On a theoretical scale between the absolute reception of deviants and their total ejection, so-called marginalizing institutions offered a middle ground of semi-inclusiveness.

The durability of harm-reducing, semi-inclusive institutions runs up against modern quests for manicured cities, as attested, among other phenomena, by the rise of not-in-my-backyard (NIMBY) organizations. Across Europe, numerous prisons, hospitals, asylums for the mentally ill, and even leprosaria (leper houses) continued to function in mildly revised forms in urban areas well into the nineteenth century, even as their rationales gradually fell out of favor and as time and neglect rendered their fabrics obsolete. By the end of the twentieth century, it was the institutions themselves that came to be seen as undesirable constituents of the urban landscape, although their roles and activities had been substantially rethought. From symbols of central power and civic responsibility they have come to epitomize social despair and civic shame, which in turn rendered them easy targets for the juggernaut of urban real-estate development.

In light, however, of the massive erosion of the social welfare state and its role in addressing deviancy, tailoring semi-inclusiveness to modern needs may have considerable benefits. For one, it would reverse the dangerous trend towards warehousing the underprivileged and the dispossessed in violent, mammoth, underfunded, and often remote prison facilities. Second, it would prevent societies from slipping further into a narrow, self-indulgent form of solipsistic politics which values good housekeeping over good citizenship, or, even more alarming, confuses the former with the latter.[1]

The present essay introduces medieval semi-inclusiveness and explores its relevance to present-day debates on urban social justice. It is divided into two sections. The first begins by describing and analyzing the key marginalizing institutions of medieval urban Europe, and then explains their proliferation as a process reflecting a shift in attitudes towards certain stigmatized groups, from flat rejection to partial, structured acceptance. The second section suggests how an adapted form of semi-inclusiveness can benefit modern cities, spaces increasingly threatened by homogeneity under a veneer of diversity and by widespread ignorance about social groups tagged as undesirable.

Semi-inclusiveness in the medieval urban context

Several years ago I wrote a book on late-medieval urban prisons. Reflecting on how best to conclude the work, it seemed useful to me to juxtapose these facilities with other so-called marginalizing institutions that were thriving in that period: the brothel, the leper house, the Jewish quarter, and the hospital. My working hypothesis – or, to call a spade a spade – my superficial impression was that what distinguished the prison from other facilities for other socially stigmatized groups was its central location and physical prominence in the urban landscape, which contrasted with the physical marginality of institutions for non-criminal deviants.

Delving deeper into the topic challenged my assumptions on three counts. First, the scale of medieval cities was generally rather modest. Crossing even the largest among them (Paris, Florence, Granada) would have been a feat lasting little more than 20 minutes on foot – the equivalent of two subway stops in a modern North American city. Thus physical proximity worked against any attempt (medieval or modern) to equate spatial with social marginality. The observation is especially true when a deviant community (such as Jews) or an institution (such as a brothel) existed within a city's walls – structures that were continuously expanded until the onset of the Black Death in 1348.

Second, even when a marginalizing institution was located beyond a city's walls, as in the case of most leper houses and some hospitals, the social disjuncture was more apparent than real. Leprosaria were founded outside medieval cities ostensibly to prevent contamination, but lepers themselves were never wholly barred from interacting with urban residents so long as they followed certain dress and behavioral codes that communicated their presence and approach. Likewise, the inmates of hospitals, especially the poorer among them, relied for their livelihood on begging for alms outside the hospital, and so came into constant touch with urban residents who in any case were never far away.

It was not only inmates who sought proximity to the city and its residents. Urban regimes too were expanding their walls as well as their jurisdictions, a process that integrated leper houses and hospitals even further into society. Driven perhaps more by greed and a desire for control than by compassion, by the fourteenth century, urban magistrates in France stressed the location of leprosaria "near the city" (*iuxta civitatem*) in contrast to their earlier designation "outside the city" (*extra civitatem*); and English municipalities became increasingly invested in securing their jurisdiction over hospitals and leprosaria, despite their lack of active involvement in these institutions.[2]

Third and most importantly, being both visible and accessible, most marginalizing institutions, much like contemporaneous prisons, never severed their inhabitants from free society. Their routine functioning depended on and was variously shaped by external interventions. For instance, hospital, leprosaria, and prison inmates were fed daily by their families or charity officials, and they were often allowed to leave their respective compounds to beg for alms or plead with creditors to resolve debts. Moreover, external social and economic hierarchies were frequently grafted onto the space and routine of these institutions, as is apparent from the classification of inmates into wards according to their ability to pay rather than the crimes they committed (in the case of prisons) or their physical condition (in hospitals).[3] Physically, legally, and socially, then, such compounds reflect an approach to urban undesirables perched between integration and marginalization.

After recovering from these three strikes, I could no longer justify branding the medieval prison an anomalous, semi-inclusive space in an urban landscape otherwise characterized by a blanket rejection of socially stigmatized groups. Instead, I began to understand it as exemplifying a quest – however uncoordinated – by different governments, organizations, and individuals to accept the presence of such groups, on the one hand, and to regulate social interaction with them, on the other. The approach enabled governments to identify urban Others but at the same time offered the latter a place of their own within the urban panorama. Identifying this harm-reducing, semi-inclusive approach towards socially stigmatized groups and individuals did not convince me that medieval cities suddenly or even gradually became progressive havens of tolerance and cultural relativism. Yet it did suggest that the foundation of marginalizing institutions can be seen in a new light, one that qualifies some historians' belief that facilities and their residents were indeed marginal, their proliferation ill-omened, and their routines inhumane and typical of a brutal culture.

A generation ago, influential medievalists such as Norman Cohn, John Boswell, and R. I. Moore observed how medieval society gradually closed its ranks through a process of identifying "Europe's inner demons" (Jews, heretics, homosexuals, lepers, etc.).[4] Stigmatization and the ubiquitous profiling of dangerous Others precipitated their persecution by various religious and secular powers, a process that culminated at length with their attempted destruction. Like many scholars with a social conscience at the time, Cohn, Boswell, and Moore were pondering a looming question in post-Second World War historiography, partly exacerbated by the Civil Rights movement in the 1950s and 1960s, namely, where and how were the seeds sown for the systematic annihilation of minorities and deviants in twentieth-century Europe. From these scholars' perspective, the foundation of leprosaria and brothels and, perhaps more ominously, the creation of Jewish quarters, signaled the "formation of a persecuting society" – an introspective reflex within Latin (Western) Christian Europe as it began defining its eventual geopolitical borders during the Crusading Era.

While minorities such as Jews, lepers, and prostitutes suffered greatly and almost constantly throughout the middle ages, the proliferation of marginalizing institutions did not epitomize their agony. Instead, the foundation of Jewish quarters, leprosaria, and brothels can be seen as a way to address a broader shift in attitudes toward integrating stigmatized groups, not eradicating them, in the increasingly heterogeneous cities of later medieval Europe. Much had changed since Rome's western provinces had entered a phase of accelerated political fragmentation in the early fifth century.

Lack of effective centralized rule encouraged the kind of paralegal alternatives for punishment described by Celia Chazelle elsewhere in this volume. By contrast, later medieval urban governments were operating in far more ambitious and highly centralized environments, rendering earlier ideas about dispute settlement (even if they were never fully realized) antithetical to contemporary political endeavors.

The available alternatives differed in each case for urban magistrates. Take prisons, for instance. From a penal perspective, incarceration represented a marked departure from routine measures that were (at least from a post-Enlightenment perspective) violent and socially destructive: exile, execution, and a variety of corporal punishments. Medieval prisons, by contrast, maintained culprits in a reasonable state of health and allowed for frequent social contact with the outside world. If such facilities were not yet envisioned as rehabilitative institutions (though certain elements of such an approach certainly can be detected), they nonetheless differed from many of the socially destructive measures that contemporary penal law sanctioned.

We, witnessing the incarceration binge of the late twentieth century, are loath to imagine an expansion of the penal state that was actually accompanied by a growing focus on inmate conditions and the social integration of deviants. Yet precisely such concerns for the welfare of stigmatized groups are attested across thirteenth- and fourteenth-century Europe, even as other crises (for instance, incessant wars and the Black Death) could have justified their neglect. Seemingly minor problems such as corruption among prison staff and inmate hygiene genuinely occupied urban magistrates, who rather than excusing deteriorating conditions as collateral damage for "getting tough on crime," rolled up their sleeves: they founded effective supervisory committees and devised mechanisms to reduce overcrowding and improve living conditions and access to water and health care. The modern solution to rising inmate numbers is – at best – to build more cells for less money, by privatizing prisons and moving them to remote locations, far from the public eye and often inaccessible to convicts' friends and families. By contrast, for some pre-industrial cultures, including medieval Europe, severing culprits from their social world would have been the epitome of barbarity.[5] For they were following, in practice if not in theory, the path of socially integrative harm reduction.

Jewish quarters offer another striking example of a semi-inclusive approach to urban marginals. The clustering of Jews in and within cities had various religious, economic, and social roots, yet their periodic enclosure by urban magistrates formed part of a complex strategy to *maintain* these communities, not eradicate them.[6] Furthermore, it is often forgotten that, when the Venetian Council designated the first Jewish ghetto, in 1516, its action in fact "marked the *abandonment* of the traditional policy of excluding Jews from the city."[7] True, the founding of Venice's ghetto, much like the occasional enclosure of Jews in previous centuries, was hardly an act of Christian charity. Cities, like kings, had much to gain from regulating and protecting "their" Jews, since the latter's presence enabled credit-based activities to expand in a mainly Christian society theoretically forbidden from lending at interest. And, to be sure, throughout medieval history Jews were rarely free from persecution, oppression, or expulsion, whatever regime they lived under. But pointing to the foundation of Jewish quarters and, later, ghettos, as the quintessence of a medieval persecuting mentality, one, moreover, that foreshadowed the violent extermination of European Jewry in the twentieth century, is fundamentally flawed. Jewish quarters were not heavens and often not even havens, but their designation or formation addressed real safety concerns and offered their residents a modicum of coexistence alongside a large Christian majority, hostile, friendly, or simply apathetic. Such a solution may be unacceptable today, not least due to its *twentieth-century* connotations, but its origins lie in a semi-inclusive approach to rather than a rejection of urban marginals.

Municipal brothels furnish us with a final and palpable example of urban magistrates' attempt to provide for a traditionally undesirable population, namely sex workers. From the thirteenth century on, and often in the face of ecclesiastical resistance, urban governments across Europe organized and regularized the activities of sex workers under their jurisdictions.[8] Much as in modern metropolises, there were diverse forms of paid sex in medieval cities and various solutions for accommodating it: from turning a blind eye, to imposing non-deterrent fines, to founding municipally run brothels. But whatever the solution, the underlying trend towards tolerance and regulation became increasingly noticeable.

Medieval sex workers, like Jews, were beneficial even if not essential for local economies. Both groups were periodically ejected from their cities and regions, and yet they gradually emerged as constant fixtures of the urban landscape. As cities grew and trade routes spread, sex workers became conspicuous with rising demand by locals and foreigners. Paid sex offered local but especially non-local, working-class women a way to augment their salaries or altogether break out of low-paid and often precarious employment situations such as domestic servitude. Over time, and despite unequivocal resentment by Church authorities, attempts to ban sex workers from cities, or even relocate them beyond their walls, had all but ceased. Like modern advocates of harm reduction, what late-medieval urban magistrates began to look for was a way to accept the inevitability of such activities, on the one hand, and yet regulate them, make them safer, and even profit from them, on the other.[9]

In this way brothels or designated areas where paid sex was licit (prototypical red-light districts) became increasingly integral to a city's social and economic fabric. Throughout urban Europe brothels were joined by other institutions and spaces — prisons, hospitals, leper-houses, alms-houses, and Jewish quarters — which, in the name of social control, reflected and promoted a trend towards acceptance, coexistence, and structured tolerance. In short, the growth of so-called marginalizing institutions suggests more than a clumsy attempt by municipalities to index Others or isolate them from mainstream society. Indeed, these institutions served to acquaint city dwellers with and teach them how to address key consequences of rapid urban-ization. Semi-inclusiveness offered no panacea for the myriad social problems afflicting medieval cities, but at the very least it promoted and reflected contemporaries' aware-ness of them. In this way, learning how to live alongside traditionally undesirable populations became part of a practical civic education.

Semi-inclusiveness and the just city

Since the 1980s, urban policy makers inspired by the theory of Broken Windows have repeatedly stressed a correlation between manicured downtowns and low crime rates: "if a window in a building is broken *and is left unrepaired,* all the rest of the windows will soon be broken."[10] In other words, allow minor rules to be bent, and soon even the most affluent neighborhood could turn into a lawless no-man's land. Conversely, acting swiftly and decisively to counter deviancy, especially in its minor and seemingly harmless forms, will prevent crime from daring to raise its ugly head.

Accordingly, physical as well as social clean-up operations have become widely accepted as instrumental for expanding a city's tax-base, attracting businesses, middle- and upper-middle-class families, and of course tourists. Rudolph Giuliani's term as Mayor of New York City (1994–2001) is often cited in this connection as a striking demonstration of the doctrine's efficacy, as crime rates dropped below national averages and the city's quality of life indicators improved. Despite widespread critiques of Broken Windows, its particular implementation in New York, and its dubious relation to Giuliani's proclaimed success, the methods associated with his administration have been celebrated and emulated far and wide.[11]

In the gentrified urban landscape that the proponents of Broken Windows envisaged, there is little room for modern total institutions such as prisons and mental asylums. Equally unwelcome are facilities, such as methadone clinics, psychiatric halfway houses, brothels (at least where these are legal), or even homes for developmentally disabled people, which rendered visible certain communities deemed undesirable. Variously citing safety issues, property values, space shortages, the presence of children, and (this is not a joke) the inhumane state of existing facilities, governments and NIMBY organizations have begun clearing these blemishes (at least where these are legal) and exporting them to the countryside. Widely supportive of this move has been a cynical form of "IMBYism," by which under-employed rural communities seek to harvest the fruits of inner-city poverty and disenfranchisement by lobbying for such institutions to be transferred nearer to them.

In this way, after centuries of activity among urban communities, marginalizing institutions are finally being themselves marginalized, indeed blotted out of city centers, residential neighborhoods, and social memory. Disregarding inmates has become progressively easier, their presence outside impoverished neighborhoods disturbingly rare. In 2007, for example, Harding Village, an affordable housing scheme for the homeless situated in Miami Beach, adjacent to the affluent town of Surfside, was finally completed after complaints from a local PTA froze the project. Tellingly, the eventual go ahead was given only after the contractors agreed to erect a six-foot wall around the compound – a former hotel – in order to give it the veneer of an enclosed space.[12] The architectural gesture to the prison clearly had a calming effect on the residents. Yet elsewhere, especially in city centers, such facilities that remained *in situ* have been camouflaged as hotels and office buildings. In downtown Los Angeles, by the early 1990s tourists were unknowingly ogling drug lords from their hotel windows – a reality now common among a number of US cities, including San Diego, Chicago, Philadelphia, and New York.[13]

The disappearance of institutions for undesirables such as prisons from US cityscapes both attests and furthers the ignorance of many regarding the scale, composition, and social needs of their inmates, who are predominantly urban African-Americans and Latinos of lower socio-economic strata. Prisoners, let alone their families, greatly benefit from the vicinity and accessibility of prisons and jails. Yet their welfare is hardly of interest for those seeking to increase local property value. For instance, Stop BHOD, an advocacy group founded in 2008 to oppose the reopening of the Brooklyn House of Detention (BHOD), argued that reactivating the prison, located in downtown Brooklyn, undermined "economics and the best interests of the community and city as a whole."[14] Exploiting popular unease about living near convicts (who are mostly non-violent offenders), NIMBY organizations such as Stop BHOD imply that inmates are not people but environmental hazards, like incinerators or open sewers. The BHOD is a "dinosaur," State Senator Marty Connor commented in June 2008. "*People live here now.* It (the Brooklyn neighborhood) has the fabric of a real community. A jail doesn't fit – it makes no sense."[15] Stop BHOD offered an alternative, "progressive vision" for the site of "mixed income housing" and a "public middle school," and stressed its alliance with other "community organizations."[16] As an alternative to reopening BHOD, it argued that reallocating funds to renovate the penal complex on Rikers Island was "the humane thing to do," given that some of its 16,680 beds were empty. Coincidentally, the organization's chief legal advisor, Randy M. Mastro, was former Deputy Mayor of Operations in the Giuliani administration. The attitude toward inmates illustrated by Connor's remark is as telling as it is troubling at a time when prisoners are becoming more numerous than ever before: there are currently about 2.4 million people in US custody – the largest documented per capita population in the world and the largest in absolute numbers; Justice Department officials estimate that one of every 15 US citizens born in 2001 will spend time behind bars during his or her lifetime.[17]

Scholarly discussions of the relations between urban planning and social justice have underscored the dangers of striving for a manicured modern city that bears no trace of the social problems it continues to breed.[18] Although they are not prominent in these discussions, the fantasies of predominantly white, middle-class anti-prison NIMBYists precisely epitomize the many dangers of this out-of-sight, out-of-mind approach, especially in the absence of clear boundaries between cleaning and cleansing.

The success of NIMBYists' myopic endeavor should concern us all. For how will we promote respect for the needs and rights of the homeless, the physically handicapped, substance abusers, or the mentally ill if we never see them? How will the welfare of sex workers be defended and the abuses they suffer be avoided if they are forced to operate in unprotected environments? What can we do to improve our understanding of the relations between unequal access to housing and education and crime and disease, if most of our exposure to these genuine social problems is – at best – through televised fiction? And how can we, as citizens, critically monitor our expansive criminal justice system, the most powerful arm of the executive, when zoning boards and public transportation authorities successfully conspire to make prisons and their inmates virtually invisible?

For those interested in integrating social justice and urban planning, such questions highlight the advantages of a medieval semi-inclusive approach to stigmatized urban residents, especially institutionalized or semi-institutionalized inmates. Consider, once again, medieval municipal prisons: they were doubtless imperfect institutions, and yet, largely thanks to their visibility and accessibility, they avoided being used as drainpipes for deviants. Their daily operation afforded inmates face-to-face interaction with the outside world, whether for legal and financial affairs, labor, religious worship, or nourishment. Unlike today, inmates' major contact with free society was not through TVs; their spouses did not lose precious wages while traveling far and in scarce public transportation for visits cut ever shorter by oversized and understaffed facilities; and they did not accrue debts in order to pay ghastly collect-call fees – a common practice today, even in non-privatized facilities.

Accessibility and visibility helped medieval inmates avoid what modern social psychologists call prisonization, or the process of conforming to prison subculture.[19] Increasing contact between prisoners and free society nowadays would counteract prisonization, which many experts agree inhibits successful re-entry. And, assuming we still believe that imprisonment's fundamental role is to keep offenders at arm's length – but no more – from free society, then allowing prisons to remain accessible and visible would also help curb corruption and mitigate some major pains of modern incarceration, including violence, substance abuse, material poverty, the deprivation of autonomy and security, and, crucially, the severing of social ties to the outside world, which have come almost to substitute for the prison's original penal role. Today's prisons present inmates of whatever stripe with fewer chances of surviving imprisonment unscathed, let alone emerging from it prepared for life at large. Small wonder that recidivism rates for adult male prisoners in the US approach 70 percent.[20] Frequent and structured contact with free society, by contrast, may help reduce some of these pains, avoid others altogether, and reaffirm for convicts what normative expectations they will face upon release. In fine, it will remind them that the prison is *not* their home, primary or surrogate.

Medieval prisons' openness and visibility, like that of other marginalizing institutions at the time, meant that they expanded the boundaries of civic responsibility. While not all local residents were pleased about living or working near criminals, prostitutes, or Jews, these groups' presence in population centers reminded everyone that society is a complex beast, and that governing it inclusively ought to benefit everyone. There would have been no obstacle to exiling such groups permanently or building prisons, brothels, or Jewish quarters outside the city walls. And yet few polities chose that path until the early modern period. Mostly for reasons of efficiency and political expedience, medieval urban regimes built marginalizing institutions within city centers and in plain view of passers-by, whose joint action or mere presence often benefited inhabitants' welfare. Locals cared and acted because undesirable institutions *were* in their backyards, and never did it seem that they wished to alter that basic situation.

Few modern cities can truly pride themselves on being tolerant and heterogeneous places, open-minded about religion, race, and sexual orientation. Reality is more than meets the eye even in places like Amsterdam, Barcelona, San Francisco, and

Brooklyn. Genuine diversity is not defined by the number of "ethnic" restaurants along Main Street, but by the range of people who can afford eating and living there without harm. Instead, real estate developers keep us on an artificial diet of normality, and municipalities hasten to remove any social blemishes from our parks, train stations, and shopping malls. In this way, under a veneer of diversity, we grow accustomed to a certain kind of cookie-cutter social landscape and, still worse, expect to find it wherever we go. But the greater danger attending this type of gentrification is that it leads us to blame social undesirables for their undesirability rather than search for a solution in our own manicured backyards.

One way to avoid slipping into social NIMBYism is to really "get medieval" on certain stigmatized groups: not by planting mammoth rural prisons and mental asylums back in population centers as-is, but by downsizing and then re-establishing them in cities, where most inmates originate. Ditto for facilities that cater to socially and developmentally disabled groups, who are finding it increasingly difficult to rent or purchase properties in their original residential areas. It may sound counterintuitive, even scary, but re-urbanizing (and de-camouflaging) some prisons, halfway homes, and other institutions for socially stigmatized groups may not only improve their residents' quality of life, but ours as well. A semi-inclusive approach towards deviants, through the monitored presence of modest-scale institutions, can teach us important lessons in civic responsibility and distributive justice: we will be less likely, indeed unable, to cast weaker members away. Loving all of our neighbors may be too much to ask, but we have much to gain from remembering that their plight is really, not just potentially, our own.

Notes

For their inspiring initiative and insights, I wish to thank the volume's editors and reviewers. Anne E. Lester and Shelly Makleff read, commented on, and improved earlier drafts.

1 A. De-Shalit, *The Environment: Between Theory and Practice*, Oxford: Oxford University Press, 2000, pp. 123–25.

2 A.E. Lester, "Cares Beyond the Walls: Cistercians Nuns and the Care of Lepers in Twelfth- and Thirteenth-Century Northern France," in *Religious and Laity in Western Europe, 1000–1400: Interaction, Negotiation, and Power*, ed. E. Jamroziak and J. Burton, Turnholt: Brepols, 2006, pp. 197–224; P.H. Cullum, "Leper Houses and Borough Status in the Thirteenth Century," in *Thirteenth Century England* 3, eds P.R. Coss and S.D. Lloyd, Woodbridge, Suffolk: Boydell, 1991, pp. 37–46.

3 See e.g. C. Rawcliffe, *Leprosy in Medieval England*, Rochester, NY: Boydell & Brewer, 2006, pp. 252–343.

4 N. Cohn, *Europe's Inner Demons: The Demonization of Christians in Medieval Christendom*, St. Albans: Paladin, 1976; J. Boswell, *Christianity, Social Tolerance, and Homosexuality: Gay People in Western Europe from the Beginning of the Christian Era to the Fourteenth Century*, Chicago: University of Chicago Press, 1981; R.I. Moore, *The Formation of a Persecuting Society: Power and Deviance in Western Europe, 950–1250*, Oxford: Basil Blackwell, 1987.

5 V. Elwin, *Maria Murder and Suicide*, 2nd ed., London: Oxford University Press, 1950, pp. xv–xvii, 196–200, 208–12; S.C. Dube, *The Kamar*, New Delhi: Oxford University Press, 2004, pp. 130–47. A similar argument underlies Celia Chazelle's essay in this volume.

6 See A. Haverkamp, "The Jewish Quarters in German Towns During the Late Middle Ages," in *In and Out of the Ghetto: Jewish–Gentile Relations in Late Medieval and Early*

Modern Germany, ed. R. Po-chia Hsia and H. Lehman, Cambridge: Cambridge University Press, 1995, pp. 13–28.

7 R. Bonfil, *Jewish Life in Renaissance Italy*, trans. A. Oldcorn, Berkeley: University of California Press, 1994, p. 70 (emphasis added).

8 See e.g. C.E. Meek, *The Commune of Lucca under Pisan Rule, 1342–1369*, Cambridge, MA: The Mediaeval Academy of America, 1980, pp. 41–42. R.M. Karras, "The Regulation of Brothels in Later Medieval England," *Signs* 14, 1989, 399–433.

9 M.L. Rekart, "Sex-Work Harm Reduction," *The Lancet* 366, 2006, 2123–34.

10 G.L. Kelling and J.Q. Wilson, "Broken Windows: The Police and Neighborhood Safety," *The Atlantic Monthly*, March 1982. Online. Available HTTP: <www.theatlantic. com/magazine/archive/1982/03/broken-windows/4465/> (italics in original; accessed 5 December 2010).

11 For critiques see B.E. Harcourt and J. Ludwig, "Broken Windows: New Evidence from New York City and a Five-City Social Experiment," *University of Chicago Law Review* 73, 2006, 271–320; D. Macallair and K. Taqi-Eddin, "Shattering 'Broken Windows': An Analysis of San Francisco's Alternative Crime Policies." Online. Available HTTP: <www.cjcj.org/files/shattering.pdf> (accessed 3 May 2010).

12 See B. Anderson, "Carrfour Beats Rising Costs, NIMBY," *Affordable Housing Finance*, February 2007. Online. Available HTTP: <www.housingfinance.com/ahf/articles/ 2007/feb/CARRFOUR0207.htm> (accessed 6 May 2010).

13 M. Davis, *City of Quartz: Excavating the Future of Los Angeles*, New York: Vintage, 1992, pp. 253–57.

14 Columbia Commons, Brooklyn, "Organized Opposition to House of D Plan Grows." Online. Available HTTP: <www.brownstoner.com/brownstoner/archives/2008/06/ organized_oppos.php > (accessed 22 December 2010).

15 "Officials at Brooklyn Jail Protest: 'People Live Here Now'," *The New York Observer*, 26 June 2008. Online. Available HTTP: <www.observer.com/2008/officials-brooklyn-jail-protest-people-live-now> (accessed 9 December 2010).

16 Stop BHOD. Online. Available HTTP: <www.idealist.org/view/asset/ xwFj3GGJ832D/> (accessed 9 December 2010). The quoted phrases were taken from <www.stopbhod.org> accessed 3 May 2010 (website no longer in service).

17 US Department of Justice, Bureau of Justice Statistics, "Prison Statistics." Online. Available HTTP: <http://bjs.ojp.usdoj.gov/index.cfm?ty=tp&tid=131> (accessed 3 May 2010).

18 E.g. A. Madanipour, G. Cars, and J. Allen (eds) *Social Exclusion in European Cities: Processes, Experiences, and Responses*, London: Jessica Kingsley, 1998.

19 "Prisonization" was a term originally coined by D. Clemmer, *The Prison Community*, Boston, MA: Christopher Publishing House, 1940, p. 300. Also see S. Wheeler, "Socialization in Correctional Communities," *American Sociological Review* 26, 1961, 697–712.

20 C.A. Visher and J. Travis, "Transitions From Prison to Community: Understanding Individual Pathways," *Annual Review of Sociology* 29, 2003, 89–113.

Suggestions for further reading

Medieval to modern institutions

Benevolo, L., *The European City*, trans. C. Ipsen, Oxford: Blackwell, 1993.

Braunfels, W., *Urban Design in Western Europe: Regime and Architecture, 900–1900*, trans. K.J. Northcott, Chicago: University of Chicago Press, 1988.

Elukin, J., *Living Together, Living Apart: Rethinking Jewish–Christian Relations in the Middle Ages*, Princeton, NJ: Princeton University Press, 2007.

Geltner, G., "Coping in Medieval Prisons," *Continuity & Change* 23, 2008, 151–72.

——, *The Medieval Prison: A Social History*, Princeton, NJ: Princeton University Press, 2008.

Henderson, J., *The Renaissance Hospital*, New Haven, CT: Yale University Press, 2006.

Karras, R.M., "The Regulation of Brothels in Later Medieval England," *Signs* 14, 1989, 399–433.

——, "Women's Labors: Reproduction and Sex Work in Medieval Europe," *Journal of Women's History* 15, 2004, 153–58.

Lester, A.E., "Lost But Not Yet Found: Medieval Foundlings and their Care in Northern France, 1200–1500," *Proceedings of the Western Society for French History* 35, 2007, 1–17.

Mengel, D.C., "From Venice to Jerusalem and Beyond: Milíč of Kromof Kroměříž and the Topography of Prostitution in Fourteenth-Century Prague," *Speculum* 70, 2004, 407–42.

Nirenberg, D., *Communities of Violence: Persecution of Minorities in the Middle Ages*, Princeton, NJ: Princeton University Press, 1996.

Orme, N. and Webster, M., *The English Hospital, 1070–1570*, New Haven, CT: Yale University Press, 1995.

Otis, L.L., *Prostitution in Medieval Society: The History of an Urban Institution in Languedoc*, Chicago: University of Chicago Press, 1985.

Reyerson, K.L., "Prostitution in Medieval Montpellier: The Ladies of Campus Polverel," *Medieval Prosopography* 18, 1997, 209–28.

Rossiaud, J., *Medieval Prostitution*, trans. L.G. Cochrane, Oxford: Basil Blackwell, 1988.

Shahar, S., *Childhood in the Middle Ages*, London: Routledge, 1990.

——, *Growing Old in the Middle Ages*, London: Routledge, 1997.

Stow, K., *Alienated Minority: The Jews of Medieval Latin Europe*, Cambridge, MA: Harvard University Press, 1992.

Sweetinburgh, S., *The Role of the Hospital in Medieval England*, Portland, OR: Four Courts Press, 2004.

Modern conditions

Cohen, S., *The Evolution of Women's Asylums Since 1500: From Refuges for Ex-Prostitutes to Shelters for Women*, Oxford: Oxford University Press, 1992.

Goffman, E., *Asylums: Essays on the Social Situation of Mental Patients and Other Inmates*, Garden City, NY: Anchor Books, 1961.

Great Britain Home Office, *New Directions in Prison Design: Report of a Study of New Generation Prisons in the U.S.A.*, London: Stationery Office Books, 1985.

Harcourt, B.E., *Illusion of Order: The False Promise of Broken Windows Policing*, Cambridge, MA: Harvard University Press, 2001.

Kelling, G.L., and Coles, C.M., *Fixing Broken Windows: Restoring Order and Reducing Crime in Our Communities*, New York: Free Press, 1996.

Marlett, G.A., *Harm Reduction: Pragmatic Strategies for Managing High-Risk Behaviors*, New York: Guilford Press, 2002.

Nagel, W.G., *The New Red Barn: A Critical Look at the Modern American Prison*, New York: Walker, 1973.

Marcuse, P., *et al.* (eds) *Searching for the Just City: Debates in Urban Theory and Practice*, London: Routledge, 2009.

Wacquant, L., *Deadly Symbiosis: The Rise of Neoliberal Penalty*, Oxford: Polity Press, 2003.

Weitzer, R., "The Sociology of Sex Work," *Annual Review of Sociology* 13, 2009, 213–34.

3

END OF LIFE

Listening to the monks of Cluny

Frederick S. Paxton

The rise of modern industrialized civilization profoundly transformed the experience of dying for most people in Europe and the West. In the pre-modern world, death was primarily a family event, whether or not attended by clerics or doctors. In medieval Europe, the dominant Christian world view embedded death, dying, and the care of the dead within layers of ritual.[1] Modernity changed all that. Scientific progress weakened religious belief, which led to the loss of the comfort provided by ritual behavior. The place of dying shifted from the home to the hospital, from a familial to a medical environment. More and more people died in a setting defined by the model of the clinic, rather than the family or the church. Death was hidden away, seldom witnessed or even discussed. As the French scholar Philippe Ariès put it, the modern West became "a society where death has lost the prominent place which custom had granted it over the millennia, a society where the interdiction of death paralyzes and inhibits the reactions of the medical staff and family involved."[2]

The most famous response to this situation is the hospice movement, whose medieval roots exemplify how the middle ages can matter in the modern world. A less well known example is music-thanatology, which seeks to ease the pain and distress of dying with music, whether at home or in a hospice, nursing facility, or intensive care unit. Much to my surprise, my research on death and dying in the middle ages came to play a significant role in the development of this new profession, and I have taught the history of death and dying to most of those practicing music-thanatology today. In what follows, I consider what my personal experience of music-thanatology suggests about the complexities of drawing on the medieval past to address the problems of the present.

Music-thanatology and the middle ages

As a young scholar just finishing a doctoral dissertation on Christian death rituals in early medieval Europe, I never imagined that such specialized research could inform contemporary responses to death and dying. But someone else did, and her interest initiated a collaboration that spanned some 20 years and took me back and forth between my home in Connecticut and a school in Montana for the last eight of them. Music-thanatology (from the Greek *Thanatos*, the god of death) is related to thanatology, the formal study of death and dying, but it is not just, or primarily, an academic or scientific pursuit. Like other medical fields, such as radiology or oncology, music-thanatology blends knowing with doing. Unlike them, however, it is a self-consciously spiritual discipline. It is the creation of Therese Schroeder-Sheker, a gifted harpist, singer, and composer who currently resides in Oregon, where she is a lay oblate at Mount Angel Abbey.

Ms. Schroeder-Sheker began working with medieval music and care for the dying in Denver, Colorado, in the 1980s, laying the foundations of a curriculum in music-thanatology while teaching at a Catholic university and seminary. Her work caught the attention of Dr. Lawrence White Jr., the president and CEO of St. Patrick Hospital, Missoula, Montana, who invited her, in 1992, to open a school of music-thanatology there, promising office and classroom space, clinical training and supervision, and ongoing institutional support. Therese's pilot program, "The Chalice of Repose Project" (CORP), was incorporated as a 501(c)(3) non-profit organization; Dr. White became a member of its board of directors; and a class of 15 students was enrolled in a two-year training program that would lead, after an additional year of clinical practice and a scholarly paper, to certification in the field.

On the home page of the Chalice of Repose Project's website, Therese defines music-thanatology as "a sub-specialty of palliative medicine." The field of palliative medicine owes its existence to Dame Cicely Saunders, the founder of the modern hospice movement, who wanted to treat the physical pain of the dying with drugs, no matter how potentially addictive they might be, while also responding to the psychic pain experienced by the dying and their loved ones. Palliative medicine's allowance for alternatives to drug therapies provided a foothold in contemporary end-of-life care for the new profession of music-thanatology. Therese also writes, however, that music-thanatology "derives profound spiritual inspiration and meaning from the Benedictine Cluniac tradition of monastic medicine." The link to the medieval monastery of Cluny (in modern France) is, as her statement implies, less direct than the one to palliative medicine, but it signifies how central a particular cultural product of the European middle ages has been to the identity of this new profession. Medieval monks practiced a form of medicine based on Greek and Roman medical science and on practical experience, and some monastic communities were known for their medical expertise. But the health of the soul was always more important to them than the health of the body, and the Cluniacs were almost universally regarded as the most perfect representatives of the care of souls, both in this life and the next.[3] More importantly for Therese, the monks of Cluny left detailed records of the spiritual care they provided to the dying. My work on those records was the reason she wanted me to join the faculty at the school in Missoula.

Therese has always conceived of music-thanatologists as "contemplative musicians."[4] Invoking the Christian notion of death (current at medieval Cluny) as birth into eternal life, she describes their work as "musical-sacramental midwifery." They are people who pursue "a contemplative practice with clinical applications." Thus, as Therese defined it, music-thanatology is as dependent for its efficacy on the spiritual discipline of its practitioners as on their medical knowledge, clinical experience, and skill as musicians. They are meant to be midwives of souls, helping to deliver them into the afterlife, whatever it may hold.

Singly or in pairs, music-thanatologists deliver prescriptive music, with voice and harp, in a setting called a vigil. Vigils can take place anywhere someone is dying, in a hospital, hospice, nursing home, or private home, and usually last about an hour. The description of the music as "prescriptive" is quite deliberate, for music-thanatologists adjust what they play to meet each dying person's specific needs. Thus there is no set repertoire and practitioners avoid playing recognizable songs or themes, which could raise memories or otherwise engage patients with thoughts of this world. The goal is to help the dying let go, unbind, even in the most mechanized of settings. In pursuit of that goal, the music is modal rather than tonal. That is, it is sung and played in the modes of medieval Gregorian chant (and ancient and medieval music in general) rather than in the major and minor keys that predominate today. Therese's decision to use modal music was not "out of allegiance to a religious tradition," she writes, but because she "found the ecclesiastical modes to be highly effective when people were extremely vulnerable."[5] Nevertheless that decision, like her highlighting of the Cluniac way of death, reflects the degree to which music-thanatology is grounded in the Christian traditions of the medieval Latin Church.

The other constitutive elements of music-thanatology derive from the confluence of Therese's career as a historical harpist, singer, composer, and performer with her experience of volunteer work in a nursing home in Denver in the mid-1970s. As she tells the story, she first conceived of music-thanatology after finding herself alone one night with a bitter and friendless old man struggling through his final agony. She got into his bed, held him, and began to sing hymns and chants of the medieval Latin liturgy. As she sang, the man calmed down. His breathing fell into rhythm with hers and he eventually died peacefully in her arms. Getting into bed with that dying man and turning to sung prayer was a deeply personal response to the loneliness and alienation of death he was facing. It was also a gesture toward the medieval past.

In the rest of this essay, I explain more fully how my research came to play a part in the development of music-thanatology, how teaching in the School of Music-Thanatology in Missoula challenged and altered my approach to the sources at the focus of my research, and, finally, how the challenges of building a professional community in the wake of the school's success led to its demise. For, just as members of the first four classes of graduates were starting to make a real impact outside of Missoula, the tightly knit community of some 75 students, graduates, faculty and board members began to unravel. After graduating one last class, in the autumn of 2002, the School of Music-Thanatology closed and my collaboration with Therese came to an end.

Music-thanatology and medieval monasticism

My side of the story begins in a graduate research seminar under the direction of Caroline Walker Bynum, whose presence at the University of Washington had drawn me into a master's program in history in the same year Therese encountered that dying man in the Denver nursing home. Each student in the seminar had to report on a different genre of twelfth-century spiritual literature, like guides for hermits or sermons on the contemplative life. I ended up with monastic customaries: books describing aspects of the institutional life and daily round of services that had become "customary" to particular houses of Benedictine monks. I worked with the only example available in English translation, Archbishop Lanfranc's customs for the monastic community at Canterbury, England.[6] As I read what seemed like an endless list of prayers, chants, and services for nearly every day of the year, I began to wonder what I could possibly report back to the seminar.

Near the end, the text turned to the care of the sick and dying. No way of life is more regimented than a medieval monastery, and death upset the routines of monastic life like no other event. Yet, the monks went to extraordinary lengths to help the dying prepare for their transition from this world to the next. Every step of the process by which a monk passed from the community of the living to the community of the dead was accompanied by ritual, prayer, and chant. I was fascinated. That initial interest led to a master's thesis on the death rituals at Cluny, the source of many of Lanfranc's customs. The study, which included translations of the Latin death ritual recorded by two monks of Cluny in the late eleventh century, was eventually published for use in the curriculum of the School of Music-Thanatology.[7]

After leaving Seattle, I pursued a doctorate at the University of California, Berkeley, where I developed my understanding of the medieval Cluniac death rites within the broader context of "rites of passage," that is, rituals such as baptism, coming of age, or marriage that accompany a change of status and thus both mark and shape key transformational moments in the human life cycle.[8] This anthropological approach to ritual provided a way of seeing death at Cluny not just in terms of Christianity and medieval monastic spirituality, but as a feature of something more universal.

In the spring of 1984, for my first professional paper, delivered at the International Congress on Medieval Studies in Kalamazoo, Michigan, I argued that, when viewed from an anthropological perspective, the elaborate play of gestures, prayers, and chants that accompanied the death and burial of a Cluniac monk appeared not just as a highlight of Benedictine monastic history, but as a particular expression of a universal human urge to structure and give meaning to the experience of death.[9]

At breakfast the next morning, Therese Schroeder-Sheker introduced herself and asked if we could talk about my presentation. She said that she wanted me to hear something. As we sat down to eat, she leaned over and sang in my ear two alternating lines in Latin and Middle Irish:

Deus meus, adiuva me.
Tuc dam do sheirc, a meic mo dé.
Tuc dam do sheirc, a meic mo dé.
Deus meus, adiuva me.

It was beautiful, and very moving. I understood the Latin, which means "My God, help me," but not the Irish for "Give me love of thee, O son of my God." The lines (I have since learned) are the first stanza of a poem by an Irish monk, Máel Isu Úa Brolchán, who died in 1086, although the melody known today is probably late medieval.[10] Therese said that she thought it might be a deathbed chant, like the ones I had spoken about in my paper. She asked if I realized that the Cluniac monks were actually singing people through the transition from this life to the next. I knew that the monks chanted psalms and antiphons during much of the ritual process, of course, but I had to admit I had not really *heard* those chants as music, nor understood their essential contribution to the rites, which drew, like the monastic liturgy as a whole, as heavily on chant as on spoken prayer.

The next year, Therese and I returned to Kalamazoo as co-organizers of a session on death in the middle ages. She performed some of the music with which she had been experimenting, using voice, harp and bells, and I reported on the progress of my dissertation research. However, our intense collaboration did not begin for another seven years, when Therese contacted me with the news about her move to Missoula and an invitation to come teach at the school. She had no intention of recreating the Cluniac death ritual, she said, but she saw it as a historical model of the kind of response to death that she was seeking, and wanted the students to understand what it was and what it represented. She also regarded my work as a model of the type of scholarship she expected from the students in the program, who would all have to produce a rigorous academic paper before achieving certification. She hoped that such academic research would give the students something of a graduate school experience. She also hoped, I think, that rooting music-thanatology in the particular sacred tradition of Cluniac monasticism would stand as a historical precedent for her ultimate goal, which was to help people experience a "blessed death in the modern world."[11]

Teaching the medieval in music-thanatology

Teaching the students in Missoula was the most challenging work I had ever done. The people who were drawn to the program came from widely diverse backgrounds. Some had extensive musical training; some almost none. Some were former nurses or nuns; others lawyers and businesspeople. They ranged in age from 20-somethings to people in their fifties. They came from all over the US, from Canada, and from abroad. One sold his furniture store in Australia and moved his whole family to Missoula just to pursue certification as a music-thanatologist. One was from Holland, one from Spain, another from Israel. Some were Catholics but others were Protestants, Jews, or Buddhists; some had no religious identity at all or drew inspiration from various new-age spiritualities. Most had undergraduate degrees and a few had done graduate work, but almost no one knew anything about the European middle ages or medieval monasticism, not to mention Cluny or the particulars of its responses to death and dying. The curriculum was equally diverse and challenging, including intensive vocal and harp training (provided by the resident faculty); basic anatomy, physiology, and pathology (taught by members of the hospital staff and a regular visiting M.D. from Michigan); the anthropology of religion (taught by a professor from Regis College in Denver); and spiritual anthropology (taught by Robert Sardello, a co-founder of the Dallas Institute of Humanities and Culture and author of a number of books on depth psychology and the soul).[12] Therese tied it all together with her own lectures and demonstrations on the principles of music-thanatology, which she continued to develop and deepen. Some of the students had difficulties trying to master so many disparate fields, however, and, in particular, seeing the relevance of medieval Latin death rituals to the work of easing the suffering of people dying today.

Part of the problem arose from my own work, which, insofar as it had to do with Cluny, had not progressed beyond the customaries themselves. As revealing as they are, they record the death ritual only in the manner of stage directions. That is, they say who did what and when, but do not give the full text of what was said or sung. To save space, the authors and scribes referred to the spoken and sung elements of all religious services at Cluny (like prayers and chants, all of which were standardized and well known) simply by their incipits, that is, the three or four words with which they began. Because of this, while the customaries make the structure of the ritual process very clear, they obscure most of what was specific to its meaning and spirituality. The students absorbed the anthropology of ritual pretty easily, especially since one of the other visiting professors, Alice Reich, a colleague of Therese's from her time at Regis University, was a cultural anthropologist. With her help, they could see how the death ritual at Cluny fit the model of a "rite of passage" to accompany a change in status. But they wanted more than that. They wanted to know what was actually said and sung at Cluny. They wanted lyrics as well as music. So I set about reconstructing the Cluniac death ritual in its entirety, filling in the texts of the various chants, prayers and other spoken elements from other sources. There are few existing manuscripts of the Cluniac liturgy from the eleventh and twelfth centuries, but the influence of the customaries was so great that I was able to find most everything in contemporary manuscripts for affiliated houses.[13]

In moving to the particulars of what was said and sung for the dying and the dead at Cluny, I was led back from the universally human aspects of the Cluniac death ritual to a deeper consideration of its peculiarly monastic and medieval features. As a historian and medievalist, this was an important breakthrough, and very much improved my own work. Trouble was, as we began to read and discuss the individual prayers, antiphons, and psalms in the context of the music-thanatology program, wide gaps began to appear between the sensibilities of the students and those of the monks of medieval Cluny. For all their beauty, the psalms and prayers of the Cluniac ritual can be unsettling to contemporaries. They speak of humility, love, and grace but also of vengeance, sin, punishment, and the assaults of the devil, and they do so in a way that many in the program found uncongenial. In one exercise, therefore, I suggested that the students write their own prayers, using the Cluniac ones simply as literary models, expressing their personal spirituality in the ancient cadences of the medieval Church. That worked to a degree, but seemed untrue to both the Cluniacs and the music-thanatologists in training.

In the end, I concentrated on putting the medieval sources in a larger context, arguing that the Cluniac death ritual was less a model of a blessed death in the modern world than a forerunner of the work that the students would do as music-thanatologists today. Thus, I began to emphasize the place of the Cluniac rituals within the long history of attitudes and responses to death and dying in Europe and European cultures, a history that had brought us to a place where the need for something like music-thanatology would be felt strongly enough for someone to invent it. By historicizing the religious values of the Cluniac materials, though, I ended up suggesting that the students should feel free to mold their understanding and practice of music-thanatology to their own and their patients' needs. Therese was sensitive to these issues, but her conception of music-thanatology was so strongly rooted in her Roman Catholic faith and her training in medieval music that it could not be fully captured or expressed in purely secular, or even non-Christian, terms.

Another problem connected with my particular contribution to music-thanatology was the way in which the fruits of my research could be misunderstood by people with no firsthand experience of the field. Therese's work, which garnered a lot of media attention, perhaps inevitably attracted imitators, who sometimes garbled the connection between medieval Cluny and music-thanatology. A 2003 article in *The New York Times*, for example, on a program founded by Edie Elkin called "Bedside Harp," which was then being instituted at the Robert Wood Johnson University Hospital in Hamilton, New Jersey, casually (indeed, almost brutally) noted that "In the 13th century, Cluny monks in France used the harp to help people die."[14] In 2006, a similar article on a couple of graduates of the "International Harp Therapy Program" developed by Christina Tourin claimed that "During the Middle Ages at the monastery of Cluny in France, harpists played to the dying to ease their journey to the next world."[15] There is no evidence of the use of harps in the death ritual at medieval Cluny and nothing I had ever written or taught suggested otherwise. But once any connection was made between the contemporary use of harps to comfort the dying and medieval Cluny, there seems to have been a tendency to make that connection closer than it actually was.

Happily, there has been no recent evidence of this kind of confusion. Around the same time as the article about the two graduates of her program appeared, Ms. Tourin sought me out and we talked the matter through. Her website currently makes no mention of Cluny, and her program seems to have expanded well beyond care for the dying to encompass the general use of harps in therapeutic situations of all kinds.[16] This shift has itself rendered less tempting the types of confusions noted above. Other programs have also moved away from the exclusive focus on end-of-life care that makes music-thanatology unique, while coverage in the press has focused on graduates of the Missoula program, who are careful to make the relationship between the medieval past and the modern present clear. Thus, it is now more common simply to read about "the monks of Cluny, France, who regularly included rituals of song in their care for the dying" or that music-thanatology's "roots extend at least back to the monastic medicine of Benedictine monks in eleventh-century Cluny, France."[17] Such claims establish a historical pedigree for the profession and, while not very revealing of medieval realities, are at least correct.

The near death and rebirth of music-thanatology

At times, the School of Music-Thanatology in Missoula felt like a cross between an experimental graduate program and a charismatic religious community. I should not have been surprised, since Therese once told me that she had seriously considered founding a religious order rather than a secular profession. Her ultimate choice to pursue music-thanatology as a "palliative medical modality," however, begged the question of why music-thanatology should be anchored in the medieval Christian past at all.[18] Non-Christian students, who did not share the understandings of incarnation and redemption familiar to Christians, wondered how Christ-centered traditions could (and even whether they should) be the basis of a practice meant to serve people of all faiths, or none at all. If the thing that made music-thanatology a palliative medical modality was its therapeutic application of sound to comfort the dying, why could it not be conceived of in other than Christian terms? I wondered these things too.

This problem was complicated by the very thing that made music-thanatology different from any other medical modality: the expectation that all practitioners would be contemplatives, actively engaged in an ongoing process of spiritual development. Therese refers to this ongoing process as *metanoia*, from the Greek word for "repentance" or "change of heart," and regards it as an essential feature of music-thanatology. Through *metanoia*, music-thanatologists develop, as Therese has put it, "the capacities to make themselves and a certain level of interiority available to others. They serve. There is no public display of self. There is transparency." They also labor to "ensoul the world (and the world of medicine) through purified heart forces. ... "[19] These are stirring goals, but subtle and obviously hard to measure. By making the transform-ation of the self through *metanoia* a requirement of the program, Therese was raising the bar extremely high for those who wanted to go out into the world as music-thanatologists. And, in the hierarchy of the school, Therese was the only one who could really assess a student's level of transparency, or spiritual transformation.

As academic dean, Therese oversaw every aspect of the curriculum of the school. As CEO of the Chalice of Repose Project, she directed every step in the development of the field. She did not want music-thanatology to be confused with music therapy. She worried that it would lose its integrity if its practitioners lost their highly focused sense of what made their profession distinctive.[20] And only those students who fully measured up to her rigorous standards achieved certification. Some dropped out during the initial two-year program, some failed or did not complete their comprehensive exams, and some never finished the required academic paper. The highly intensive nature of the program, which brought together motivated and idealistic groups of adults for two years of shared work, created tight bonds among most of the students. These bonds were strained when one or more of them did not measure up (whether musically, academically, or otherwise) to the demands of the training.

As pressing and thorny as such issues were, they did not lead to the collapse of the project in Missoula. The controversy which led to the near death of the program revolved more around the future of the profession than its past. While a fraction of the 15 members of the first class to graduate from the school in 1994 found positions at institutions elsewhere, most stayed on to become either resident faculty at the School of Music-Thanatology, or members of the staff and administration of the school, or the Chalice of Repose Project. The rest became practicing music-thanatologists at St. Patrick Hospital or Missoula Hospice. The situation was not much different for the next couple of classes, but it became harder and harder to stay on in Missoula. There were no more faculty and staff positions and the area was already well served by music-thanatology. The profession, and the pool of trained and certified music-thanatologists, had grown enough by the time the class of 2000 was finishing up that the need for established paid professional positions outside Missoula was becoming critical.

Given its nature, it is no wonder that music-thanatology found its first home at Missoula's St. Patrick hospital, a Catholic institution originally established in 1873 by pioneer nuns of the order of the Sisters of Providence. Nor is it surprising that the first medical institutions outside of Missoula to consider hiring music-thanatologists as full-time staff would be other Catholic hospitals, like Sacred Heart Medical Center in Eugene, Oregon, founded by another nineteenth-century order, the Sisters of St. Joseph of Peace, and Providence St. Vincent Hospital in Portland, Oregon. However, both Sacred Heart and Providence St. Vincent wanted to house music-thanatology in their departments of pastoral care. Therese resisted that idea, in part because it undercut music-thanatology's status as a medical modality.

Just as this controversy was brewing, tension emerged over the issue of re-certification. Therese and the resident faculty (two graduates of the class of 1994, and one each from the classes of 1996 and 1998) wanted all certified music-thanatologists to apply to them for regular refresher courses and re-certification. However, a number of graduates of the program, especially those who had been working on their own for some time, felt that re-certification should be overseen by all the professionals in the field, organized into an association. Furthermore, many supported those who wanted to do the work they had trained for, even if they had never been certified. The community split, with Therese and the resident faculty in Missoula on one side and most everyone else on the other. Providence St. Vincent eventually hired two certified music-thanatologists, one from the class of 1994 and one from the class of 1996, but by that time, the damage had been done and the school was shutting down.

The closing of the school in 2002 and the fracturing of the music-thanatology community was a painful process for all involved. Of the 63 total graduates, less than half had achieved certification, and not all had found work in the field, let alone full-time professional positions. Without a school to train and certify more practitioners or an organization to oversee continued professional development and re-certification, there was a real possibility that the practice of music-thanatology would wither away. But that has not happened. Since relocating the Chalice of Repose Project to Mount Angel, Oregon, Therese has begun a new training program using a distance-learning model.[21] While that is not likely to provide enough new music-thanatologists to keep the profession growing, it will assure that her core conceptions of the field, its nature, and its purposes remain influential.

At the same time, most of the graduates of the School of Music-Thanatology in Missoula have found employment in some measure as music-thanatologists. They have also organized a professional group, the Music-Thanatology Association International (MTAI), and started a new training program through Lane Community College in Eugene, Oregon, from which the first class of eight students graduated in 2009.[22] The MTAI is very clear in acknowledging Therese's role in creating their profession and training most of them, and recent media coverage has made a point of this, no doubt at the urging of her former students.[23] Yet, there has been no official reconciliation. This may be because the MTAI sees itself as "a certifying body for the field of music-thanatology ... responsible for the maintenance of professional standards for the field as well as for the provision of a process for qualified individuals to demonstrate proficiency in those standards."[24] Or perhaps it is because they have recently certified a number of practitioners who went through the Missoula program but did not achieve certification from Therese, whose CORP website asserts: "The Chalice of Repose Project is the only organization able to verify the music-thanatology education of our own past or present associates."[25] From the point of view of an outsider, though, the fact that both CORP and the MTAI are alive and well is a sign that the profession has survived its first great crisis and that the prognosis for its future is bright.

The past and the present of music-thanatology

The MTAI lists 39 separate competencies required for certification in music-thanatology, under the categories personal, musical, medical, clinical, thanatological, and professional. The medieval death rituals at Cluny appear in the description of only one of those, the last of five thanatological competencies, as follows:

> Demonstration of a basic understanding of how the history of death and dying in Western Latin Christendom from antiquity to the present affects the current predominant attitude toward death in western [sic] culture. This includes specifically an historical and anthropological understanding of the medieval Cluniac customaries and the contemporary hospice movement.[26]

It is gratifying to see that my work has a place in the current understanding of the field by those most active in it, and also to see that they have incorporated it into their professional training in more or less the way I had come to teach it over the course of my time in Missoula. But I am struck by the contrast between the small part Cluniac death rituals play in music-thanatology and the relatively large amount of attention given to them in media accounts. It suggests the attractiveness of grounding responses to contemporary dilemmas in knowledge about the past. To say that the practice of music-thanotology has roots in the middle ages explains its distinctive use of modal music, but it also gives it a kind of counterweight, of tradition and lost wisdom, against the negative aspects of dying in a modern medical setting.

It remains to be seen if music-thanatology will achieve the status of a palliative medical modality in quite the sense that Therese hopes. Most music-thanatologists working in hospitals are housed in pastoral rather than palliative care departments and in Catholic institutions, whose faith traditions have the same roots as music-thanatology itself. The use of the medieval past may, thus, have restricted the ability of music-thanatology to spread to hospitals in general, at least so far. But it is hard to imagine a different outcome given the peculiar origins of the field in the life and learning of Therese Schroeder-Sheker. Music-thanatology has made a real impact on end-of-life care, bringing beauty and spirituality to life in music played for the dying. There are now two separate pathways into the profession, the Chalice of Repose Project and the Music-Thanatology Association International, and the field is growing. Music-thanatology's relationship with the medieval past may have complicated Therese's quest to re-infuse death with meaning and grace, but it is hard to imagine how, without it, this pioneering approach to care for the dying would exist at all.

Notes

1 F.S. Paxton, *Christianizing Death: The Creation of a Ritual Process in Early Medieval Europe*, Ithaca, NY: Cornell University Press, 1990.

2 P. Ariès, *Western Attitudes Toward Death: From the Middle Ages to the Present*, trans. P. M. Ranum, Baltimore, MD: Johns Hopkins University Press, 1974, pp. 102–03.

3 F.S. Paxton, "*Signa mortifera*: Death and Prognostication in Early Medieval Monastic Medicine," *Bulletin of the History of Medicine* 67, 1993, 631–50; F.S. Paxton, "The Early Growth of the Medieval Economy of Salvation in Latin Christianity," in *Death in Jewish Life: Burial and Mourning Customs in Medieval Ashkenaz and later Communities*, ed. S. Reif, A. Lehnhardt and A. Bar-Levav, Turnhout: Brepols, forthcoming.

4 For the practice of music-thanatology as described in the following paragraphs, see T. Schroeder-Sheker, *Transitus: A Blessed Death in the Modern World*, Missoula, MT: St. Dunstan's Press, 2001, pp. 15–21.

5 Schroeder-Sheker, *Transitus*, p. 41.

6 D. Knowles, *The Monastic Constitutions of Lanfranc*, London: Nelson, 1951; rev. ed. C.N.L. Brooke, Oxford: Clarendon Press, 2002.

7 F.S. Paxton, *A Medieval Latin Death Ritual: The Monastic Customaries of Bernard and Ulrich of Cluny*, Studies in Music-Thanatology 1, Missoula: St. Dunstan's Press, 1993.

8 A. van Gennep, *The Rites of Passage*, trans. M. B. Vizedom and G. L. Caffee, Chicago: University of Chicago Press, 1960.

9 This paper was also later published, in booklet form, for use in the curriculum of the School of Music-Thanatology: F.S. Paxton, *Liturgy and Anthropology: A Monastic Death Ritual of the Eleventh Century*, Studies in Music-Thanatology 2, Missoula: St. Dunstan's Press, 1993.

10 G. Murphy, *Early Irish Lyrics: Eighth to Twelfth Century*, Oxford: Clarendon Press, 1959; repr. Dublin: Four Courts Press, 1998, pp. 52–53.

11 Schroeder-Sheker, *Transitus*, pp. 35–36.
12 E.g. R. Sardello, *Facing the World With Soul: The Reimagination of Modern Life*, New York: HarperCollins, 1994; R. Sardello, *Love and the Soul: Creating a Future for the Earth*, New York: HarperCollins, 1995.
13 The results will appear as F.S. Paxton, *The Death Ritual at Cluny in the Central Middle Ages*, Turnhout: Brepols, forthcoming.
14 M. Kochman, "Well Being: Call it the Singing Cure," *The New York Times*, 2 March 2003. Online. Available HTTP: <www.nytimes.com/2003/03/02/nyregion/well-being-call-it-the-singing-cure.html> (accessed 10 December 2010).
15 R. Melander, "A Gentle Cradle of Sound," *The Lutheran*, April 2006. Online. Available HTTP: <www.thelutheran.org/article/article.cfm?article_id=5812&key=33779342> (accessed 10 December 2010).
16 C. Tourin, *The International Harp Therapy Program*. Online. Available HTTP: <www.harprealm.com> (accessed 10 December 2010).
17 I. Verzemnieks, "Music in the Time of Dying," *The Sunday Oregonian*, 14 January 2007. Online. Available HTTP: <www.sacredflight.org/articles/Oregonian01142007.pdf> (accessed 10 December 2010); J. B. Frazier, "Trained Harpists Practice 'Prescriptive Music'," Associated Press Wire Story, 24 July 2009. Online. Available HTTP: <www.msnbc.msn.com/id/32127877/ns/health-more_health_news/> (accessed 10 December 2010).
18 Schroeder-Sheker, *Transitus*, p. 79.
19 Schroeder-Sheker, *Transitus*, pp. 70–71.
20 Schroeder-Sheker, *Transitus*, pp. 64–70.
21 The Educational Programs of the Chalice of Repose Project are described online. Available HTTP: <http://chaliceofrepose.org/ed-overview/> (accessed 10 December 2010). They include a "Master's Degree Program in Music-Thanatology" in collaboration with the Catholic University of America in Washington, D.C. scheduled to begin in 2009, but the most recent mention of Therese or music-thanatology on Catholic University's website is A. Cassidy, "Playing Music to the Dying," Summer 2005. Online. Available HTTP: <http://publicaffairs.cua.edu/cuamag/sum05/discourse.htm> (accessed 10 December 2010).
22 I. Verzemnieks, "Music-Thanatologists Provide Comfort during Life's Final Journey," *The Oregonian*, 25 July 2009. Online. Available HTTP: <www.oregonlive.com/living/index.ssf/2009/07/musicthanatologists_provide_co.html> (accessed 10 December 2010). Also see the website of the Music-Thanatology Association International. Online. Available HTTP: <www.mtai.org/index.php> (accessed 10 December 2010), and the description of the new Music-Thanatology Training Program. Online. Available HTTP: <http://lanecc.edu/ce/music/index.htm> (accessed 10 December 2010).
23 See, e.g., Frazier, "Trained Harpists," and Verzemnieks, "Music-Thanatologists."
24 MTAI, "Certification." Online. Available HTTP: <www.mtai.org/index.php/certification> (accessed 10 December 2010).
25 "History at a Glance: Thirty-Six Years and Vibrant (1973–2009)." Online. Available HTTP: <http://chaliceofrepose.org/36-year-history> (accessed 10 December 2010).
26 MTAI, "Certification." Online. Available HTTP: <www.mtai.org/index.php/certification#thanatological> (accessed 10 December 2010).

Suggestions for further reading

Medieval practices

Ariès, P., *The Hour of Our Death*, trans. H. Weaver, New York: Vintage, 1981.
——, *Western Attitudes Toward Death: From the Middle Ages to the Present*, trans. P. M. Ranum, Baltimore, MD: Johns Hopkins University Press, 1974.
Paxton, F. S., *Christianizing Death: The Creation of a Ritual Process in Early Medieval Europe*, Ithaca, NY: Cornell University Press, 1990.

——, "Curing Bodies – Curing Souls: Hrabanus Maurus, Medical Education, and the Clergy in Ninth-Century Francia," *Journal of the History of Medicine and Allied Sciences* 50, 1995, 230–52.

——, *The Death Ritual at Cluny in the Central Middle Ages*, Turnhout: Brepols, forthcoming.

Contemporary approaches

"Hospice." Online. Available HTTP: <http://en.wikipedia.org/wiki/Hospice> (accessed 8 December 2010).

"Hospice: The Hospice Concept." Online. Available HTTP: <http://www.hospicenet.org/html/concept.html> (accessed 8 December 2010).

Music-Thanatology Association International website. Online. Available HTTP: <http://www.mtai.org/index.php> (accessed 10 December 2010).

Schroeder-Sheker, T., "Chalice of Repose Project: The Voice of Music-Thanatology." Online. Available HTTP: <http://chaliceofrepose.org/> (accessed 8 December 2010).

——, *Transitus: A Blessed Death in the Modern World*, Missoula, MT: St. Dunstan's Press, 2001.

4

MARRIAGE

Medieval couples and the uses of tradition

Ruth Mazo Karras

Imagine a situation in which two people live together in a joint household over a period of years, are widely acknowledged as a couple and may even refer to each other as spouses, and have children together, yet they are unable to get formally married even if they wish to. Since the law does not recognize the union as a marriage, the partners do not have the same rights as spouses; for instance, they have no right upon death or the dissolution of the union to any property they may have shared, and their children may be legally related to only one of the parents. This describes same-sex unions in most of the contemporary United States, where only a handful of states allow same-sex couples to marry or register civil unions, while the majority of states have laws that explicitly prohibit marriage between two people of the same sex. It also describes clerical unions in the middle ages. Legally invalid as marriages after the Second Lateran Council of 1139, these unions were nonetheless common throughout the middle ages. In the late middle ages, clergy living with partners were so common in some regions as to be unremarkable. The women were most often called concubines, but they could also be called hearthmates (*focariae*) or, by opponents of the practice, priests' whores. Other types of unmarried couples, whether in the middle ages or today, might run into some of the same legal problems, but same-sex couples today and clerical couples in the middle ages represent two sizeable groups who were structurally excluded from marriage.

Clerical marriage was objurgated by church reformers in the eleventh century and by traditionalists reacting to a new wave of reformers in the sixteenth century, in both cases using many of the same terms used by opponents of same-sex marriage today. Clerical marriage, critics said, went against God's will, as expressed in scripture or otherwise. It brought filthy practices into something that should be pure. The celibacy of Jesus was held up as a model just as the heterosexuality of Adam and Eve is today. Medieval and Reformation-era writers in favor of clerical marriage also made some of the same arguments as those made today by the marriage equality movement: that it promotes stable relationships rather than promiscuity, and that it is a matter of basic fairness.

In discussing the medieval and early modern debates about clerical marriage, I draw on material written over a fairly long chronological span. The debates in the eleventh century and in the sixteenth century were different in many ways, notably in the divergent ways people thought about church authority and about church control of property in the two periods. Nevertheless, the debates in the eleventh century shared a number of arguments with those in the sixteenth, and can be seen as part of the same historical trajectory. My purpose here is not to elucidate particular texts in their entirety and in their specific historical contexts, but rather to make a broad comparison over a fairly long period of development. Indeed, in the broadest terms the issues discussed here go back to late antiquity and the ancient world, when discussions about sexual activity and continence, for both clergy and laity, were central to early Christianity as well as to other religions. I begin here with the eleventh century because that is when discussion decisively shifted from the topic of continence in general onto the terrain of clerical marriage in particular, with a strong emphasis on the difference between clergy and laity.

The analogy between discussions of clerical marriage in the pre-modern period and those of same-sex marriage in the contemporary era is not exact. The former were concerned with the ways in which the clergy should set an example for the laity, an issue which does not arise in the contemporary discussions of marriage equality, though it can arise in discussions of gay and lesbian clergy. Further, the most important argument made by the pro-marriage side in the two contexts is quite different. The most important argument used in favor of clerical marriage both in the middle ages and during the Reformation was the lesser evil argument, namely that chastity was the ideal for everyone, but so few people were called to it that marriage was a necessary institution. This argument does not feature prominently in the same-sex marriage debate, in which both sides agree that marriage is a good thing. Nor do many people currently make the argument that the reason we should allow same-sex couples to marry is that they are not capable of living chastely. The contemporary marriage equality movement's most important argument is that marriage in the United States is a civil right and that to limit it to opposite-sex couples denies constitutional equality. For example, the Massachusetts Supreme Court held: "That exclusion is incompatible with the constitutional principles of respect for individual autonomy and equality under law."[1] This argument was not made in the middle ages, when marriage was a matter for the church rather than the state and when it was not self-evident that all men were created equal.

But other arguments made now were also made then. The fact that even some of the same points were made in very different contexts is interesting, not because it shows us that things have not changed but because it shows us that they have. The sense of déjà vu we get from the striking parallels in these two very different situations – namely arguments for clerical marriage and arguments for same-sex marriage – reminds us that the same supposedly immutable religious principles can be put to the service of very different goals in different historical circumstances. Even if the arguments do not change, the world in which they are made does. This is the lesson we can learn from studying the medieval experience of marriage: the idea of what constitutes marriage, including who may participate in it and who may not, is not an eternal tradition but has always changed with the society in which is it situated. The remainder of this essay examines some recurring themes in the marriage debate under four separate rubrics: appeals to scripture, notions of purity, conceptions of social order, and the social reality of toleration for non-sanctioned practices.

The appeal to scripture

The medieval debate, and at least one side of the modern one, are both informed by notions of "what God wants," as determined mainly through scripture. Most commonly invoked are examples from the Old Testament, along with the teachings of Jesus and of Paul from the New Testament.

The Old Testament includes married priests. But pro-celibacy medieval authors argued, on the basis of Luke 1:23, that the priest Zechariah did not cohabit with his wife while he served in the Temple. Since Christian priests serve every day, they are therefore required to abstain continuously from sexual relations, and thus may not marry.[2] They interpreted "those who have made themselves eunuchs for the sake of the kingdom of heaven" (Matthew 19:12) to mean those who deliberately reject sexual activity. They also cited numerous passages from the letters of Paul, who wrote that "it is good for a man not to touch a woman" (I Corinthians 7:1), told the unmarried and widowed that "it is good to abide even as I" (I Corinthians 7:8), and pointed out that "He that is without a wife, is solicitous for the things that belong to the Lord, how he may please God. But he that is with a wife, is solicitous for the things of the world, how he may please his wife." (I Corinthians 7:32–33).[3] The unmarried state of Jesus was also adduced. But pro-marriage authors also cited key Pauline passages from I Corinthians, such as "for fear of fornication, let every man have his own wife, and let every woman have her own husband" (7:2) and "if they do not contain themselves, let them marry. For it is better to marry than to be burnt" (7:9) along with "Marriage honourable in all" (Hebrews 13:4) and "It behoveth therefore a bishop to be ... the husband of one wife" (I Timothy 3:2).

It should be noted that none of these texts explicitly says that priests may not marry, nor that they may. Interpretation is required. The same is true of biblical justifications for the restriction of marriage to couples of opposite sexes, *pace* fundamentalists who believe that their reading of the Bible is clear and does not require exegesis. All the examples of marriage in the Bible are between a man and a woman, but it is never explicitly stated that that is what, *by definition*, marriage *is*. Even Mark 10:6–9, which argues that marriage between a man and a woman should be permanent, does not explicitly restrict marriage to this configuration. Furthermore, the familiar texts about men lying with men being an abomination (Leviticus 18:22 and 20:13) do not specifically mention marriage, although there is clearly room for an *a fortiori* argument there. The literature (both scholarly and pastoral) discussing the exegesis of these texts, along with similar passages from Romans and I Timothy, is vast, but rarely touches on marriage. At the same time, proponents of gay marriage also cite the Bible, notably David's love for Jonathan (II Samuel 1:26) and Ruth's for Naomi (Ruth 1:14), to show that the "Judeo-Christian tradition" sanctions same-sex love, although in these cases as well there is no specific reference to marriage.

Although determination of "what God wants" was important to both sides in the medieval and early modern debates, it is far more central to the anti side in the contemporary debate than it is to the pro. Despite an attempt to frame the argument in terms of social good (the preservation of an important institution, the welfare of children) – indeed, campaigns against same-sex marriage often try to make a completely secular case in order to avoid the "separation of church and state" criticism – the rhetoric of the opposite-sex-only position depends heavily on scripture.[4] The marriage equality movement, on the other hand, tends to argue either that scripture is irrelevant because of the separation of church and state, or that it needs to be understood in its historical context rather than as immutable. The way in which modern heterosexual marriage is already quite different from biblical marriage is a frequent butt of satire, although such satires tend to dismiss Christian beliefs about the supersession of the Old Testament by the New.[5]

Purity

The reason why Old Testament priests, and by extension Christian priests, were to abstain from sexual relations had to do with ritual purity. The idea that the priest should be in a pure state when he touches the body of God, coupled with the idea that the female body is essentially impure, underlay the celibacy argument, at least from the eleventh century when the importance of Eucharistic theology came together with the reform movement's effort to undergird the church's power by sharply distinguishing the clergy from the laity. This, of course, is quite different from anything in the contemporary gay marriage debate. However, the visceral revulsion for women, at least those who were sexually active, that was expressed in the clerical marriage debate has its points of resemblance to the revulsion for homosexual activity that finds its way into the gay marriage debate. A variety of authors and church councils beginning in 386 referred to sexual intercourse on the part of a priest, even with his wife, as pollution or contamination.

Peter Damian is the most famous and influential exponent of this revulsion. Writing to Pope Nicholas II in 1059, he said that priests with wives "make themselves one flesh with a whore." Addressing the priests, he said: "At the imposition of your hand the holy spirit descends, and with it you touch the genitals of whores."[6] In a 1064 letter to Bishop Cunibertus of Turin he described priests' wives in these terms:

> Charmers of clerics, appetizers of the devil, expulsion from paradise, venom of minds, sword of souls, poison of drinkers, toxin of banqueters, matter of sin, occasion of ruin ... harem of the ancient enemy, hoopoes, screech-owls, owls, wolves, leeches ... whores, prostitutes, lovers, wallows of greasy pigs, dens of unclean spirits, nymphs, sirens, witches, Dianas ... through you the devil is fed

> on such delicate banquets, he is fattened on the exuberance of your lust ...
> vessels of the anger and furor of the Lord, stored for the day of vengeance
> ... impious tigers, whose bloodstained mouths cannot refrain from human
> blood ... harpies, who fly around and seize the lord's sacrifices and cruelly devour
> those who are offered to the Lord ... lionesses who like monsters make careless
> men perish in the bloody embraces of the harpies ... sirens and Charybdis, who
> while you bring forth the sweet song of deception, contrive of the ravenous sea
> an inescapable shipwreck ... mad vipers, who because of the impatience of the
> burning lust of your lovers mutilate Christ, who is the head of the clergy.[7]

Damian was far from the only medieval writer to describe the effect of a woman's body on a priest as polluting.[8]

Now, Peter Damian was a much better stylist than the author(s) whose prose appears on godhatesfags.com, one of the web sites of the Westboro Baptist Church; but the ideas that sodomites are

> wicked and sinners before the Lord ... violent and doom nations ... abominable
> to God ... worthy of death for their vile, depraved, unnatural sex practices ...
> called dogs because they are filthy, impudent and libidinous ... produce by
> their very presence in society a kind of mass intoxication from their wine made
> from grapes of gall from the vine of Sodom and the fields of Gomorrah which
> poisons society's mores with the poison of dragons and the cruel venom of asps. ...[9]

are not far from how Damian thought that heterosexual relations pollute the holy body of Christ. The more polite form of this argument, which is much more widespread, is that "same sex relationships are immoral" or homosexuality is a "sexual perversion," as found for example in testimony before the Vermont legislature when it was considering same-sex marriage legislation.[10] In general, contemporary public discourse is much less virulent than Peter Damian's eleventh-century diatribes.

Social order

The argument that "People of the same sex shouldn't be allowed to marry because I personally find gay sex repulsive," although it may be in many people's minds, is not generally made publicly by those who want to appear to be mainstream political players. A mainstream liberal like Howard Dean can articulate the genteel version ("it makes me uncomfortable") and still, like President Barack Obama, claim to support civil unions on equal rights grounds.[11] Nor, as mentioned above, do those opposed to same-sex marriage rely on scripture as a rhetorical strategy when dealing with an audience broader than just the evangelical community. Rather, along with an appeal to tradition, they make an argument on the basis of social order, namely: to allow people of the same sex to marry would threaten the institution of marriage because the very term would become meaningless, and would give social sanction to something that is not acceptable. As Glenn Stanton of Focus on the Family says:

"The terms 'husband' and 'wife' would become merely words with no meaning. 'Mother' and 'father' would become only words. Parenthood would consist of any number of emotionally attached people who care for kids. Gender would become nothing."[12] Same-sex marriage, in the words of the draftsman of the Defense of Marriage Act, would provide "official affirmation, celebration, subsidization and solemnization of behavior that is harmful to the people who engage in it and to society."[13] It would erode respect for marriage generally, thus causing more marriages to break up and more people to have children out of wedlock:

> If marriage becomes just one form of commitment in a spectrum of sexual relationships rather than a preferred monogamous relationship for the sake of children, the line separating sexual relations within and outside of marriage becomes blurred, and so does the public policy argument against out-of-wedlock births or in favor of abstinence.[14]

Without looking too deeply at the logic of this argument, let us merely note that a similar argument became prominent at the time of the Reformation, when defenders of the status quo insisted that allowing priests to marry would erode the institution of marriage. In fact, said the Bishop of Merseburg in 1523: "it is better that a priest through weakness sins with a poor whore than that he takes a wife, against his vow and against the custom of the church."[15] Thomas More, writing in 1532, thought that priestly marriage was worse than "double or treble whoredom," and reformers in 1541 accused Bishop Stokesley of London of having said that it was better for a priest to have a hundred whores than a wife.[16] In his response to Luther in 1521, Jerome Emser wrote that allowing priests to marry would allow everyone else to slip out of their obligations as well. If priests should be allowed to marry because of human frailty, then should not wives be allowed to cheat on their husbands, and young men to steal money from their fathers to give to whores?[17]

The counter-argument to this point was nearly identical in the twenty-first and the sixteenth, if not the eleventh, century. If the goal is to have an ordered society and less promiscuity, then surely permitting more rather than less marriage is the better option.

A married reformed priest, argued William Tyndale in 1530, did not threaten "men's wives, daughters, and servants."[18] He would live a respectable life with his own wife and children. Similarly, the conservative columnist David Brooks argued in 2003 that committed, exclusive relationships (i.e. marriage) are the basis of society, and that society's interest is best served by encouraging all people, including gay ones, to enter into such relationships, thus building a culture of fidelity rather than one of contingency: "We shouldn't just allow gay marriage. We should insist on gay marriage. We should regard it as scandalous that two people could claim to love each other and not want to sanctify their love with marriage and fidelity."[19] The contemporary journalist Jonathan Rauch makes a similar argument: if gay people cannot marry, this normalizes the unmarried state and allows straight couples to choose not to marry, which he thinks is a bad thing. Further, marriage is a stabilizing influence on promiscuous gay men.[20] Johann Eberlin, a Franciscan follower of Luther, wrote in

1522 with a similar idea: "If I am not permitted to have a wife, then I am forced to lead publicly a disgraceful life, which damages my soul and honor and leads other people to damnation."[21] Clerical marriage advocates and same-sex marriage advocates are making essentially the same point: that such couples should be allowed, perhaps even required, to have a normal domestic life like everyone else. Allowing them to do so is a matter of basic fairness; requiring them to is a matter of morality and social order. However, arguments of this sort have rarely been used in debates over state legislation; in that arena, the pro-marriage equality side has traditionally preferred the language of rights to the language of morality.[22]

Opponents of gay marriage have sometimes deemphasized the moral angle and relied on the language of rights, as in Maine, where in 2009 the group Stand for Marriage Maine invoked the individual rights of those who disagree with same-sex marriage.[23] But they have generally favored moral arguments, including values associated with some of the three goods of marriage delineated by Augustine of Hippo early in the fifth century. The idea that a stable and committed relationship is better than a promiscuous one speaks to the value of fidelity (*fides*), Augustine's first good. The sacramental nature of marriage (Augustine's second good) is not one of the main points at issue in the same-sex marriage debate today, in large part because the public debate focuses on civil rather than religious marriage. But Augustine's third good of marriage, that is offspring (*proles*), is definitely at issue. Same-sex marriage opponents argue that the purpose of marriage is the begetting of children, and that homosexual couples cannot do this. As former Senator Rick Santorum said: "Marriage is not about affirming somebody's love for somebody else. It's about uniting together to be open to children."[24] Opponents cannot, however, push this point too hard, because it risks invalidating the marriages of opposite-sex couples who cannot or choose not to have children, or the authenticity of the parental bond between opposite-sex couples and their adoptive children.

It is the *defense* of same-sex marriage on the grounds of the interests of children that most clearly resembles the pre-modern defense of clerical marriage. There are an estimated 160,000-plus same-sex coupled households in the US, and possibly as many as two million; it has been estimated that these households might involve as many as three million children.[25] Many same-sex marriage advocates argue that the welfare of these children would be best served by permitting those who are parenting them to establish legally recognized family units.[26] Likewise, argued the English reformer George Joye in 1541, the clergy do have children, and if clerical marriage is not permitted then the families with their "natural dear children" would be "drawn asunder, as it were with wild horses."[27]

Toleration in practice

The question of the position of the children of both types of unions (clerical and same-sex) reminds us that the question was – and is – not just one of theology and social theory. It was and is also a question of practical law and of practical attitudes. Polls show that a majority of Americans today oppose same-sex marriage, but there is a sizeable minority who support it; if civil unions are an option, then a majority support legal recognition.[28] If there had been such a thing as public opinion polling in the Middle Ages, the result would likely have been much the same for clerical marriage. Certainly the evidence of practice from medieval documents points to an institution that was, like same-sex marriage in the early twenty-first-century US, simultaneously tolerated and not tolerated.

Papal records from the later middle ages contain tens of thousands of petitions from the sons of priests seeking dispensations from illegitimacy so they too could enter the clergy (and some too from daughters who wished to become nuns), and there must have been many, many more couples who did not have sons who wanted to become clerics.[29] The records of any medieval ecclesiastical jurisdiction will show a large number of priests being fined for sexual activity. It is not always possible to tell whether these are casual or long-term liaisons; it is also not always possible to tell whether the prosecutions are the result of a zealous official or of community opinion. The records I am currently working with, from late fifteenth-century Paris, do give us some idea. When priests appear in court fined for keeping concubines, they must have come to the attention of the authorities in some way, yet many of these cases involve couples who are accused of having been together for years. Perhaps the authorities only recently found out about the offense, but many other people would have known, and clearly did not care enough to inform on the couple. As long as a couple lived quietly together and did not disturb their neighbors, many people were not bothered by it. Others, of course, were. And no doubt it was easier in a city like Paris than in a village to live one's life without arousing the neighbors' concern. But the point is that we can no more identify *the* medieval attitude toward clerical marriage than we can identify *the* contemporary attitude toward same-sex marriage.

A given individual's opinion of clerical marriage during the middle ages probably depended a great deal on that individual's relationship with the local priest and his partner, if he had one, just as people's attitudes toward homosexuality today may depend a great deal on whether they have any friends or family members whom they know to be gay. Indeed, the behavior of actual people in the real world informs one of the key arguments in both instances, a sort of amalgam of the lesser evil argument used in the pre-modern era and the equality argument used today. This argument says that the behavior of the group whose marriage is under discussion is better than that of couples who are allowed to marry, and that they therefore deserve to be allowed to marry. George Joye wrote, in 1541:

> Both great men, mean, and low of every sort many [*sic*] keep whores besides their own wives, contrary to their own open vows and promises. ... Is it sin for a poor priest to keep him only to his own lawful wife and no sin at all to the lay married man besides his wife to keep whores?[30]

Joye was making essentially the same argument as someone who says it is not fair that heterosexuals who barely know each other can get married, or marry multiple times without having their fitness for marriage questioned, while a committed gay couple cannot marry at all.

Learning from the medieval debate

The ways Christians understand their society and interpret scripture change over time. The majority of Christians in the world today belong to denominations that allow clerical marriage. Even in those that do not, opinion is changing. Polls indicate that a majority of US Catholics (in one survey, 63 percent) do not believe that a celibate clergy is necessary.[31] The Catholic Church allows married men to become priests in some of the eastern Catholic rites or if they have converted to Catholicism after marriage. Married Anglican priests who convert to Catholicism, such as those converting as a result of Pope Benedict XVI's 2009 invitation, can remain priests, although they are not eligible to be bishops. Clerical celibacy today is a discipline, not a doctrine. To the extent that the "Judeo-Christian tradition" is taken as a standard for judging contemporary claims to marriage equality, that tradition has indeed changed over time.

A prohibition on the marriage of same-sex couples is as bound to particular historical circumstances – and as mutable – as the prohibition on clerical marriage in the middle ages. History does not teach us what marriage should be, but it does teach us that marriage changes and develops depending on the needs of the society in which it exists. The argument from tradition has been powerful in the history of clerical marriage, in which both sides have claimed authority from the Bible and the early church, and it is powerful today in the debate over marriage equality, but it is ultimately misleading, because traditions do change and are reinterpreted by each generation.

This knowledge will not change the minds of some religious believers. Preventing priests from marrying was wrong, they will say, and was based on a misinterpretation of scripture. It is good that most Christian denominations have returned to the true way on that point, they might continue, but preventing same-sex couples from marrying is entirely different, because it is based on a correct interpretation of scripture. For those who believe they know what scripture means, and that there is only one correct interpretation which is consistent across all societies, history has no relevance. For others, however, knowing that laws and ideas about marriage change over historical time can reinforce their willingness to institute the most just and equitable marriage practices possible.

Notes

1 Goodridge v. Massachusetts Department of Public Health, 440 Mass. 309 (2003), 313.
2 Peter Damian, *Letter* 112, in *Die Briefe des Petrus Damiani*, ed. K. Reindel, 4 vols, Vol. 3, Munich: Monumenta Germaniae Historica, 1983, p. 270. These same scriptural arguments turn up in the Catholic Reformation: see e.g. Salzburg Provincial Synod, 15–28 May 1537, in *Acta Reformationis Catholicae Ecclesiam Germaniae Concernentia Saeculi XVI*, ed. G.Pfeilschifter, Vol. 2, Regensburg: Verlag Friedrich Pustet, 1960, p. 425.

3 All biblical passages (English translation) are from the Douay-Rheims Bible. This is the modern English translation closest to the Latin "Vulgate" version that predominated in medieval Europe.

4 A great many examples of this are aggregated online. Available HTTP: <www.whatisprop8. com/religious-viewpoints.html> (accessed 6 December 2010).

5 Examples online. Available HTTP: <http://irregulartimes.com/index.php/archives/ 2009/09/09/the-traditional-equation-marriage-1-man-1-woman-1-woman/> (accessed 6 December 2010); and <www.godlessgeeks.com/LINKS/BiblicalMarriage.htm> (accessed 6 December 2010).

6 Damian, *Letter* 61, ed. Reindel, Vol. 2, pp. 214–16.

7 Damian, *Letter* 112, ed. Reindel, Vol. 3, pp. 278–79. See M. McLaughlin, "The Bishop as Bridegroom: Marital Imagery and Clerical Celibacy in the Eleventh and Early Twelfth Centuries," in *Medieval Purity and Piety: Essays on Medieval Clerical Celibacy and Religious Reform*, ed. M. Frassetto, New York: Routledge, 1998, pp. 223–24; D. Elliott, *Fallen Bodies: Pollution, Sexuality, and Demonology in the Middle Ages*, Philadelphia: University of Pennsylvania Press, 1998, p. 101.

8 See, e.g., Humbert of Silva Candida, "Responsio sive contradictio adversus Nicetai pectorai libellum" 21 and 26, in *Acta et scripta quae de controversiis ecclesiae Graecae et Latinae saeculo undecimo composita extant*, ed. C. Will, Lippe: G. Elmert, 1861, pp. 137, 147.

9 These phrases, with biblical citations, can be found online. Available HTTP: <www. Godhatesfags.com> (accessed 6 December 2010) and – without biblical citations – at sites critical of Westboro Baptist such as Crank.Dot.Net. Online. Available HTTP: <www.crank.net/hate.html> (accessed 6 December 2010).

10 K. Hull, *Same-Sex Marriage: The Cultural Politics of Love and Law*, Cambridge: Cambridge University Press, 2006, p. 183.

11 K. Burge, "SJC: Gay Marriage Legal in Mass.," *The Boston Globe*, 18 November 2003. Online. Available HTTP: <www.boston.com/news/local/massachusetts/articles/2003/ 11/18/sjc_gay_marriage_legal_in_mass/> (accessed 6 December 2010).

12 G.T. Stanton, "Is Marriage in Jeopardy?" pp. 3–4. Online. Available HTTP: <www. johnankerberg.com/Articles/_PDFArchives/social-issues/2SI0804F.pdf> (accessed 6 December 2010).

13 R.H. Knight, "Talking Points on Marriage: Giving 'Gay' Relationships Marital Status Will Destroy Marriage." Online. Available HTTP: <www.orthodoxytoday.org/articles2/ KnightMarriage.php> (accessed 6 December 2010).

14 M. Spalding, "A Defining Moment: Marriage, the Courts and the Constitution." Online. Available HTTP: <www.heritage.org/research/reports/2004/05/a-defining-moment-marriage-the-courts-and-the-constitution> (accessed 6 December 2010).

15 *Handlung des Bischofs von Merseburg mit den zwei Pfarren von Schönbach und Buch* (1523), repr. in *Flugschriften aus den ersten Jahren der Reformation*, ed. O. Clemen, 4 vols, Leipzig: Verlag von R. Haupt, 1907, Vol. 1, p. 87.

16 T. More, *The Co[n]futacyon of Tyndales answere made by syr Thomas More knyght lorde chau[n]cellour of Englonde*, London: William Rastell, 1532, p. 254; J. Sawtry [G. Joye], *Thedefence of the Mariage of Priestes: Agenst Steuen Gardiner bishop of Wynchester, Wylliam Repse bishop of Norwiche, and agenst all the bishops and preistes of that false popissh secte, with a confutacion of their vnaduysed vowes vnadvysedly diffined: whereby they haue so wykedly separated them whom God cowpled in lawfull marriage*, Antwerp: Jan Troost, 1541, p. 5.

17 H. Emser, *Wider das vnchristenliche buch Martini Luters Augustiners, an den twetschen adel*, in *Luther und Emser: ihre Streitschriften aus dem Jahre 1521*, ed. E. L. Enders, Neudrucke deutscher Literaturwerke des XVI. und XVII. Jahrhunderts 83, Halle an der Saale: M. Niemeyer, 1890, p. 85.

18 W. Tyndale, *An Answer to Sir Thomas More's Dialogue*, ed. H. Walter, Cambridge: Cambridge University Press, 1850, p. 164.

19 D. Brooks, "The Power of Marriage," *The New York Times*, 22 November 2003. Online. Available HTTP: <www.nytimes.com/2003/11/22/opinion/22BROO.html> (accessed 7 December 2010).
20 J. Rauch, *Gay Marriage: Why It Is Good for Gays, Good for Straights, and Good For America*, New York: Holt, 2004, pp. 7, 78.
21 J. Eberlin von Günzberg, *Syben frumm aber trostloss pfaffen flagen ire not einer dem anderen und ist niemant der sye troste Gott erbarme sich ire*, trans. W. E. Phipps, *Clerical Celibacy: The Heritage*, New York: Continuum, 2004, p. 152.
22 Hull, *Same-Sex Marriage*, p. 153.
23 "The Threat to Marriage." Online. Available HTTP: <www.standformarriagemaine.com/?page_id=119 > (accessed 8 December 2010).
24 Rauch, *Gay Marriage*, p. 106.
25 Rauch, *Gay Marriage*, p. 74; T. Simmons and M. O'Connell, "Married-Couple and Unmarried-Partner Households: 2000," US Census Bureau, February 2003, pp. 9–11. Online. Available HTTP: <www.census.gov/prod/2003pubs/censr-5.pdf> (accessed 8 December 2010).
26 S. Goldsmith, "Let My Two Moms Marry! On Stonewall Anniversary, Kids of Gay Parents Join Same-Sex Marriage Fight," *The New York Daily News*, 27 June 2009. Online. Available HTTP: <www.nydailynews.com/ny_local/2009/06/27/2009-06-27_let_my_two_moms_marry_on_stonewall_anniversary_kids_of_gay_parents_join_samesex_.html> (accessed 8 December 2010); S. Wildman, "Children Speak for Same-Sex Marriage," *The New York Times*, 20 January 2010. Online. Available HTTP: <www.nytimes.com/2010/01/21/fashion/21kids.html> (accessed 8 December 2010).
27 Sawtry, *The defence of the Mariage of Priestes*, p. 5.
28 The similar results of multiple polls are summarized online. Available HTTP: <www.pollingreport.com/civil.htm> (accessed 8 December 2010).
29 L. Schmugge, *Kinder, Kirche, Karrieren: päpstliche Dispense von der unehelichen Geburt im Spätmittelalter*, Zürich: Artemis & Winkler, 1995, p. 183.
30 Sawtry, *The defence of the Mariage of Priestes*, pp. 29–30.
31 D. Smiley, R. Samuels, and L. Yanez, "Poll: Most Miami-Dade Catholics Oppose Celibacy Vow," *The Miami Herald*, 11 May 2009. Online. Available HTTP: <www.palmbeachpost.com/news/content/state/epaper/2009/05/11/0511cutiepoll.html?cxtype=rss&cxsvc=7&cxcat=0> (accessed 8 December 2010); "Poll: US Catholics Would Support Changes." Online. Available HTTP: <www.cnn.com/2005/US/04/03/pope.poll/index.html> (accessed 8 December 2010).

Suggestions for further reading

Medieval practices

Armstrong-Partida, M. "Priestly Marriage: The Tradition of Clerical Concubinage in the Spanish Church," *Viator* 40, 2009, 221–53.
Boswell, J., *Christianity, Social Tolerance, and Homosexuality: Gay People in Western Europe from the Beginning of the Christian Era to the Fourteenth Century*, Chicago: University of Chicago Press, 1980.
Brooten, B., *Love Between Women: Early Christian Responses to Female Homoeroticism*, Chicago: University of Chicago Press, 1998.
Brown, P., *The Body and Society: Men, Women, and Sexual Renunciation in Early Christianity*, New York: Columbia University Press, 1988.
Brundage, J. A., *Law, Sex, and Christian Society in Medieval Europe*, Chicago: University of Chicago Press, 1987.
——, "Sexuality, Marriage, and the Reform of Christian Society in the Thought of Gregory VII," *Studi Gregoriani* 15, 1991, 68–73.

Frassetto, M. (ed.) *Medieval Purity and Piety: Essays on Medieval Clerical Celibacy and Religious Reform*, New York: Routledge, 1998.

Lea, H.C., *A History of Sacerdotal Celibacy in the Christian Church*, Boston: Houghton Mifflin and Company, 1867 (with numerous later editions and reprints).

Modern debates

Chauncey, G., *Why Marriage? The History Shaping Today's Debate over Gay Equality*, New York: Basic Books, 2004.

Donadio, R., "Vatican Keeps Celibacy in Rules on Anglicans," *The New York Times,* 9 November 2009 Online. Available HTTP: <http://www.nytimes.com/2009/11/10/world/europe/10vatican.html?_r=1&scp=5&sq=pope%20welcomes%20anglicans&st=cse> (accessed 8 December 2010).

Good Hope Metropolitan Community Church, "David Loved Jonathan More than Women" Online. Available HTTP: <http://www.goodhopemcc.org/spirituality/would-jesus-discriminate/david-loved-jonathan-more-than-women-ii-samuel-126.html> (accessed 8 December 2010).

Hull, K., *Same-Sex Marriage: The Cultural Politics of Love and Law*, Cambridge: Cambridge University Press, 2006.

Myers, D.G., and L.D. Scanzoni, *What God Has Joined Together: The Christian Case for Gay Marriage*, New York: HarperCollins, 2006.

Rauch, J., *Gay Marriage: Why It Is Good for Gays, Good for Straights, and Good For America*, New York: Holt, 2004.

"Ruth Loved Naomi as Adam Loved Eve." Online. Available HTTP: <http://www.wouldjesusdiscriminate.org/biblical_evidence/ruth_naomi.html> (accessed 8 December 2010).

Stand for Marriage Maine, "The Threat to Marriage." Online. Available HTTP: <http://www.standformarriagemaine.com/?page_id=119> (accessed 8 December 2010).

5

WOMEN

The Da Vinci Code and the fabrication of tradition

Felice Lifshitz

In Stieg Larsson's best-selling novel, *The Girl with the Dragon Tattoo*, each section opens with a chilling statistic: "Forty-six percent of the women in Sweden have been subjected to violence by a man," we read, "Ninety-two percent of women in Sweden who have been subjected to sexual assault have not reported the most recent violent incident to the police."[1] Sexual violence and physical abuse are in fact just two of many injustices that specifically disfavor women, injustices that at the same time – while coming in many different forms and degrees of severity – plague our whole society and cannot be reduced purely to "women's issues." In the economic sphere, women – mothers, daughters, sisters, partners – continue to face the glass ceiling at the highest levels of the corporate world and receive chronically low wages in "pink collar" ghettos. These forms of unequal access to resources could be multiplied across virtually every arena of contemporary life, making it difficult for women to achieve their full earnings potential over the course of a lifetime. The consequences often include economic dependency for much of the woman's life and grinding poverty in old age, affecting in turn the whole fabric of family and community. Larsson's response to these injustices is a powerfully feminist novel, whose tattooed female heroine overcomes the threat of potential victimization to neutralize three evil, exploitative, wealthy and respected men, while rescuing the male protagonist in the nick of time from near-certain death. Because I do not wish to spoil the surprises of this suspenseful thriller for those who have not read it, I will not reveal the details here; suffice it to say that in doing so she employs a combination of physical strength, financial savvy, linguistic skill, and technological prowess. The "pierced and tattooed punk prodigy Lisbeth Salander" is Larsson's effective answer to the paralyzing myth that women are naturally passive or perpetually victimized. His heroine belies his own alarming statistics, providing an exemplary role model who can inspire other women to refuse abject victimhood.

As a feminist and a medieval historian, I adopt a strategy similar to Larsson's in attempting to improve the situation for women in the present: to emphasize the degree to which women are *not* necessarily victimized today, and – more importantly here – were not necessarily victimized in the past. Despite conventional wisdom, the problems that undoubtedly exist today are not survivals from a near-universal pattern of the subjection of women inherited from traditional or pre-modern societies. The struggle to solve those problems now cannot be articulated as a fight for "modernity" and against the heritage of the "dark age" past – one that was rarely as bad as it is imagined to be. It is, certainly, vital to demythologize the medieval past in this respect. One famous emblem of that supposedly oppressive past, the "chastity belt," is actually a mythical object. No such contraption existed by which medieval husbands, enjoying plenitudinous spousal powers, could guarantee their wives' sexual fidelity. But aside from dispensing with myths such as chastity belts, we need to reconsider knee-jerk interpretations of practices normally seen as part of the matrix of a purportedly age-old patriarchal oppression of women. For instance – a fact worth bearing in mind in addressing the role of Muslim women today – veils are not necessarily marks of inferiority but can be empowering signs of dignified status, as they indeed were for Christian nuns and abbesses, many of whom commanded great wealth, respect, and power (including political authority) in medieval Europe. Equally, it is not necessarily unfair for sons to have inherited more real property upon the death of their parents than did daughters, as was stipulated in a large range of pre-modern legal texts from many parts of the world, given that the latter would already have received a portion of parental wealth (in cash and movables) as dowries at marriage. Even polygamy and concubinage, commonly decried as sexist methods of oppressing women, were routes of advancement for women of low social status, and primarily disadvantaged low-status men who could not find wives, given the monopolization of women by high-status men.

These considerations should diminish the extent to which women *as a group* can be seen essentially as a category of oppressed persons over all time. Such knowledge – like the character of Lisbeth Salander – de-naturalizes the image of women as weak and powerless. "Biology is destiny" anti-feminism assumes a universal subjection of woman to man that is either "natural" or "divinely ordained" or both, a subjection that cannot be altered by human legislation or social revolution. But the moment one accepts that patriarchal subjection has never really been universally true, that many women over many centuries have effectively taken control of their own destinies, then the heart is ripped out of nostalgic anti-feminist arguments about traditional society and the "good old days." The recognition that eternal patriarchal domination is a myth has another salutary consequence: When men recognize that they, as a group, have no "natural" or divinely ordained right to control women, they do not feel "queer" or "inadequate" when they realize that they, as individuals, do not in fact have such power. They will not, in consequence, feel tempted to seize their "unjustly usurped" power through engaging in the kinds of violence against women highlighted in *The Girl with the Dragon Tattoo*.

Yet not every reader will interpret the significance of Larsson's novel as I have. Different readers and listeners can activate radically different meanings from a single "text," including meanings diametrically opposed to the intentions of the author, speaker, or writer. This principle operates even within the context of this essay. Some readers might wrongly conclude from the many points of overlap that my orientation matches that of the "Independent Women's Forum" (IWF). The IWF, as I have done, emphasizes the ways in which women are *not* victims; indeed, they go so far as to claim that contemporary US culture promotes female supremacy. They accept that women face challenges and victimization outside the US, and decry genital mutilation, human trafficking, forced marriages, and other similar practices. But their principal intent, far removed from my own, is to counteract the supposedly topsy-turvy world of the contemporary US: to educate young women to embrace what are called "traditional marriages" in which they can feel "protected," to devote themselves to child-rearing before having a thought of a career (because "having it all" is a myth), and to stop worrying about rape, wage discrimination, gender bias, and domestic violence, none of which – in their view – represents a serious problem in the female-supreme culture of the US.[2]

It is precisely the audience question – the possibilities for multiple audience (mis)-interpretation – that prompted me to write this essay, in the body of which I will explore Dan Brown's stunningly popular novel *The Da Vinci Code*. The book topped the best-seller lists in multiple languages, far surpassing the already considerable success of Larsson's *Girl with the Dragon Tattoo*. One stark difference helping to account for the exceptional popularity of Brown's book, beyond that of Larsson's, lies in the divergent characters of their female protagonists. The brave and brilliant Lisbeth Salander, the girl with the dragon tattoo, is the very antithesis of the heroines of *The Da Vinci Code*, namely Sophie Neveu – who requires constant explanations of all developments from male characters – and her distant ancestor, Mary Magdalen. Sophie, and even more so Mary, are pale shadows of the robust Lisbeth Salander; yet they sparked feminist fervor in many a reader. How and why that should be, what it might mean, and why it might matter, are the questions at the heart of this essay.

Dan Brown faces Mary Magdalene

"Jesus was the original feminist," one of *The Da Vinci Code*'s characters, Sir Leigh Teabing, opines.[3] Reviewers also essentially perceived the work as feminist, treating the book as an inspiration to women and as a potential danger to the hierarchical Catholic Church, although some stopped short of attaching the precise term to the book. The review by Patrick Anderson, originally published in *The Washington Post*, which did use the "F" word, was typical of audience response to the book, and deserves extensive quotation:

> The novel alternates between conventional chase scenes and the scholarly digressions that provide its special charm. ... Are you aware that the Catholic Church has for centuries repressed both women and the feminine side of early Christianity? During the Inquisition, for example, "Those deemed 'witches' by the Church included all female scholars, priestesses, gypsies, mystics, nature lovers, herb gatherers, and any women 'suspiciously attuned to the natural

world'. ... During three hundred years of witch hunts, the Church burned at the stake an astounding *five million* women." In a great many ways, the novel has a feminist slant, as when Langdon tells Sophie: "The Priory believes that Constantine and his male successors successfully converted the world from matriarchal paganism to patriarchal Christianity by waging a campaign of propaganda that demonized the sacred feminine, obliterating the goddess from modern religion forever." ... Read the book and be enlightened.[4]

I must leave aside the many false assertions of the book that are reflected in this particular review, beyond noting that the 2006 film version directed by Ron Howard wisely backed away from the hyperbolic absurdity of the five million murdered witches to a more reasonable number of 50,000.[5] My concern is not the misinformation in the book; rather, it is the reception of the book, and the chord it struck with critics and audiences alike. I acted as a local expert on the book in the Miami area at the height of the phenomenon, and gave numerous lectures and media interviews on the subject in a variety of venues (religious and secular, public and private) over the course of 2003 and 2004. Again and again, women enthusiastically expressed to me their reactions to the book, explaining how it had simultaneously enraged and uplifted them. Yet my contention is and has always been that *The Da Vinci Code* is more anti-feminist than feminist. At most it engages in a conflicted, muted, ambivalent form of feminism. Dan Brown's approach is in fact diametrically opposed to my own. His unsubtle conspiracy theory version of history refers to a quick and completely successful repressive movement accompanying the "conversion" of the fourth-century Roman emperor, Constantine. According to Brown, the "Vatican" immediately succeeds in suppressing the sacred feminine, with no resistance or hold outs except for a few knights (males all) who are "questing for the grail." Their quest entails speaking in a code "as a way to protect themselves from a church that had subjugated women, banished the Goddess, burned nonbelievers and forbidden the pagan reverence for the sacred feminine."[6] In this scenario, women are pushover patsies and passive victims who never even attempted to counter the new repressive regime, let alone succeeded in doing so. A charitable, nuanced view of the international success of *The Da Vinci Code* would probably explain that it satisfied many widespread feminist desires, but did so without fundamentally threatening some key masculinist conventions.

In the following pages, I will analyze what I call the "theology" of the novel, an admittedly incoherent, inconsistent set of ideas. My use of this term is not meant to accord it any level of serious intellectual or spiritual status. "Theology" remains the best word to describe Brown's treatment of Mary Magdalen, the royal queen who – according to his novel – bore Jesus's baby, and whose mortal remains have ever since been preserved, and protected from the evil members of Opus Dei, by the members of the Priory of Sion. Yet this Mary is simultaneously a goddess in her own right, a goddess furthermore who ought to be worshipped by men through *Hieros Gamos* (Holy Marriage), that is, the act of having sex with women. Chapter 60 is the main locus for Brown's theology, including the line: "The Priory of Sion, to this day, still worships Mary Magdalen as the Goddess, the Holy Grail, the Rose and the Divine Mother."[7] If one takes all the elements of Brown's theology seriously, he appears to set up the cult of Mary Magdalen as a competitor to the cult of Jesus Christ. Even more oddly, he implies that Jesus was not divine until the external intervention of Constantine declared him to be so (Chapter 55), but that Mary Magdalen was a legitimate goddess as well as descendant of a royal line.

Yet Brown's superficial inflation of the status of "the sacred feminine" in general, and of a female figure, Mary Magdalen, in particular, has surprisingly little impact on the message of the novel as a whole. Throughout *The Da Vinci Code*, the male is the ideal and only subject in Brown's theology, while women are no more than instruments or tools through which men reach the divine. Brown's concern is "that spark of divinity that man can only achieve through union with the sacred feminine."[8] This perspective does little more than invert the classic "Eve as man's downfall/Woman as temptation away from God" vision of gender relations; it does not recognize women as persons in their own right. Although he explains at length what a man must do in order to tread the pathway toward God (namely, have sex with a woman, decidedly *not* with another man), the author never even broaches the subject of how a woman might reach the divine. Moreover, the sacred feminine that men so desperately require is itself passive to the point of often being outright, lifelessly, inert. The apparently random women with whom male members of the Priory copulate in the *Hieros Gamos* rite have no active roles or any subjectivity in the story, any more than does Jesus's own version of the sacred feminine, Mary Magdalen. Brown's royal-blooded Magdalen, pregnant with Christ's daughter Sara, is secreted out of Palestine to Gaul, where she gives birth. The remainder of her life, at least as Brown describes it, includes nothing that could be classified as activity, which perfectly foreshadows her experience in death: two thousand years of being schlepped around in a sarcophagus by generations of Priory members. Her contribution to Brown's version of sacred history begins and ends with her ability to serve as a fertile vessel ("chalice") for Jesus's semen, a twist on the traditional view of the Holy Grail as a vessel for Jesus's blood (Chapter 60).

Brown's view of Mary Magdalen as little more than a baby machine is contradicted by both medieval sources and modern scholarship. He ignored a plethora of material that he could have used to create a portrait of a complex, active Mary. It is not that this material was necessarily historically reliable; in fact, very little is known about the New Testament figure of Mary Magdalen. Nevertheless, multiple works restoring Mary Magdalen to her "rightful" place as a central figure in early Christian history had fuelled the questing hopes of Christian women even already before the appearance of *The Da Vinci Code*. As the *Wikipedia* article on Mary explains (on a page whose neutrality is understandably disputed, but in an internet source which speaks to popular intellectual production), she was "one of the most important women in the movement of Jesus throughout his ministry," a woman who in the "late 20th and early 21st century" has regained her proper status "as a patron of women's preaching and ministry."[9] A 2003 article in *Time Magazine* could already place the newly published *The Da Vinci Code* into a larger "wave of literature, both academic and popular" on the Magdalen as "a rich and honored patron of Jesus, an Apostle in her own right, the mother of the Messiah's child and even his prophetic successor." This "wave of literature," including a number of best-sellers besides *The Da Vinci Code* itself, had "gained Magdalene a new following among Catholics who see in her a potent female role model and a possible argument against the all-male priesthood."[10] That Mary was the mother of the Messiah's child was obviously the take of Dan Brown, who drew on none of the other more active − if equally ahistorical − role possibilities for his portrait of the Magdalen.

Brown also failed to draw on the enormous body of (equally fantastical) medieval literature concerning Mary Magdalen, one of the most enthusiastically venerated saints of the entire period. Perhaps the single greatest distortion in the entire novel is the claim that "the Church outlawed speaking of the shunned Mary Magdalen."[11] To the contrary, there were many famous and completely orthodox (albeit currently discredited) narratives recalling Mary's life. The texts were used for many purposes, including for official liturgical celebration as part of a thriving pilgrimage cult with various centers − above all the Burgundian abbey of Vézelay, a UNESCO World Heritage site.[12] These narratives depart far more from patriarchal concepts of gender roles than does anything in *The Da Vinci Code*. The cult centers of the saint were located primarily in what is now France, because the Magdalen was believed to have immigrated to the area after the death of Jesus. Medieval biographies described her life in western Europe as the story of a preacher, teacher, missionary, and miracle worker, quite a far remove from Dan Brown's passive figure. She was certainly believed to have had a special relationship with Jesus, but not that of wife and mother to his child.

Here are some extensive selections from a popular biography of Mary that circulated widely in Latin Europe from the ninth or tenth century. The text exists in hundreds of medieval manuscript copies, in dozens of early modern and modern editions and, since 1989, in a cheap and easily available paperback English translation.

> When he [Jesus Christ] was led away in chains, all of his disciples fled, abandoning him. But loyalty did not forsake Mary Magdalene. The skin of her flesh adhered to the bones of the Saviour, for when Judas betrayed him, Peter denied him, and the ten apostles fled from him, there still was found in Mary Magdalene the courage of the Redeemer ... [Encountering the risen Jesus], bowing her head, numbly worshipping him, the disciple greeted her master, saying "Rabboni" (that is, "Master"). ... At last the Saviour was convinced that the love he had before taken such pleasure in had never ceased to burn in the breast of his first servant and special friend. ... Just as before he had made her the evangelist of his resurrection, so now he made her the apostle of his ascension to the apostles − a worthy recompense of grace and glory, the first and greatest honor, and a reward commensurate with all her services. ... Mary, seeing herself elevated by the Son of God, her Lord and Saviour, to such a high position of honor and grace ... as being among all women (except for the Virgin Mother of God) the most tenderly loved, the most cherished and the

dearest, could not do otherwise than exercise the apostolate with which she had been honored. ... The lover ceaselessly thought of her beloved, and in her meditation she burned with the fire of love, the inextinguishable fire in which she was daily consumed in the holocaust of insatiable desire for her Redeemer. ... From time to time she left the joys of contemplation and preached to the unbelievers or confirmed the believers in the faith, pouring into their souls the sweetness of her spirit and the honey of her words. ... Just as she had been chosen to be the apostle of Christ's resurrection and the prophet of his ascension, so also she became an evangelist for believers throughout the world. ... Mary performed miracles with inexpressible ease to establish the truth of her words. ... Never, or rarely, was anyone found who departed from her preaching unbelieving or without weeping.[13]

The story of Mary in this biography is just as fictional as Brown's picture in terms of "historical truth." But that is not the point. The point is that this text was orthodox, mainstream, and sanctioned by every level of the hierarchical church. It carried not the slightest taint of heterodoxy. One does not need to turn to the suppressed gospels of the Gnostics and questionable apocryphal acts, as does Brown, to find medieval people commemorating Mary Magdalen. There is simply no warrant for the assertion that her memory was suppressed by the church after Constantine. If anything, it was amplified, including in ways that were well intentioned in their original context.

For instance, Pope Gregory I "the Great" (590–603) preached and wrote repeatedly on the topic of Mary Magdalen, whose central place in Christian thought was secured by the fact that her encounters with the risen Christ (as narrated in several biblical passages) served as the required gospel readings accompanying the celebrations of the mass on several key days during the Easter season. In one of his gospel homilies, a sermon that immediately became very popular and influential as a model for future preachers, Gregory conflated a number of different female New Testament figures with that of Mary Magdalen. The woman actually named as the Magdalen in the Gospels first appears, along with "the 12" (male disciples) and several other women, among Jesus's constant followers; of Mary it is said that Jesus had driven seven demons from her at an earlier date (Luke 8). As befits one of his key followers, her presence is noted among the group of women who observed the crucifixion (Matthew 27) and went to Jesus's tomb to anoint his body, only to find it empty (Matthew 28). Mary Magdalen's biblical star turn comes during her extended one-on-one encounter with the risen Christ, described in John 20 and lovingly embroidered in the medieval biography quoted above; this passage (the famous *Noli me tangere* episode, in which the resurrected Jesus enjoins Mary not to touch him) formed the basis of Gregory's sermon for the Thursday after Easter, 591. There he identified her not only with the sister of Martha and Lazarus (John 11–12 and Luke 10) but also with the notorious former sinner who anointed Jesus's feet in the house of a Pharisee (Luke 7). This woman's unspecified sin is traditionally considered to have been prostitution; Gregory describes it as "bodily impurity."[14]

According to Dan Brown, the long-standing identification of Mary Magdalen with a whore, however penitent, was part of a "smear campaign" designed to "defame" Jesus's royal widow.[15] Brown displays here a profound misunderstanding of medieval spirituality. That the Magdalen had risen above a sinful past to become so special to Jesus rendered her that much more heroic and inspirational to other sinful humans; she also functioned as incontrovertible proof of the infinitely forgiving nature of Jesus. As Gregory wrote: "she had abandoned her wicked ways, and she washed away the stains of heart and body with her tears ... and she found such a position of grace with him that it was she who brought the message to his apostles. ... What ought we to see in this, my friends, except the boundless mercy of our Creator. ... Perhaps someone ... has lost the purity of his body: let him look on Mary, who purged away the love of her body by the fire of divine love. See how almighty God puts before our eyes at every turn those whom we ought to imitate."[16] Far from defamed and despised, Mary Magdalen functioned for centuries on end as an inspirational role model for Christian women and men alike.

Far more could be said about how the figure of Mary Magdalen was conceptualized during the European middle ages, all of which would give the lie to Dan Brown's presentation of her in *The Da Vinci Code*. I will limit myself to one final point, to address a question that may well have arisen in the minds of many readers. The Easter Thursday reading from the Gospel of John, including the "Do not touch me" (*Noli me tangere*) injunction from Jesus to Mary, might seem to imply that Jesus considered women to be in some way polluted or "untouchable." The fact that this biblical passage was highlighted in Christian liturgy would then seem to support Brown's arguments concerning the repression of women by the medieval Christian church. It is therefore worth noting that Gregory the Great, in the sermon discussed above, insisted that this was *not* "because the Lord refused the touch of women after his resurrection."[17] The pope went on to provide a plausible alternative explanation for Jesus's reticence, one that took all focus away from female sexuality or "impurity," an approach consistent with some of his other writings on women and ritual purity. For instance, in his correspondence with Augustine of Canterbury, whom he had sent to England to convert the population to Roman Christianity, Gregory argued against ideas of ritual impurity and pollution through sex, menstruation, and childbirth. He insisted, for instance, that a menstruating woman should not be forbidden to take communion or enter a church, for Jesus touched and healed a woman suffering from an excessive flux of blood – an event described in Matthew 9, Mark 5, and Luke 8. He went on to counter a whole range of prohibitions born of pollution anxiety, for instance inviting men who had had sex with their wives or experienced nocturnal emissions to take communion, make confession, and even celebrate the mass.

Rethinking religious tradition

Mary Magdalen is not the only female figure to have played a major role in European Christianity since its inception, including in ways completely authorized by "the church." The most obvious way, astonishingly unmentioned by Brown, is through veneration of Mary mother of Jesus, whose cult necessarily included celebration of the feminine as a procreative force. The physical reality of the Virgin Mary's corporeal motherhood was underlined by the celebration of the festival of her Purification on February 2, a festival well established by the latter part of the eighth century. Along with the Virgin's own Nativity (September 8), her Assumption (August 15) and the Annunciation (March 25), the Purification formed the quartet of major early medieval Marian feasts. Later centuries saw the expansion of this series. Mary, Mother of God, Empress of Heaven, Queen of the Angels, in some texts the co-redeemer and co-savior with her Son, was even considered capable, at the last judgment, of saving souls condemned by Jesus. It is true that some feminist scholars see the effects of the cult of the Virgin as more negative than positive for women, primarily because of her exceptionality. But that is beside the point. The enormous and officially promoted popularity of Mary mother of Jesus constituted a feminine aspect of Christian worship.

Once we begin to scratch the surface of our current knowledge about the status of women in the eyes of medieval male churchmen, it becomes clear that Dan Brown's blockbuster novel spreads a disturbingly false image. Under the guise of revealing "truths" about the sacred feminine that had supposedly been repressed for centuries by woman-hating medieval men, Brown effectively buried even deeper information, long known to specialists, about the importance of female figures in medieval Christianity. Much of this information is far more feminist than Brown's claim that Mary Magdalen was a woman of royal Jewish ancestry who became pregnant by Jesus Christ, and more conducive to the establishment of leadership and liturgical roles for Christian (including Catholic) women. For instance, one scholar has argued that the "inclusive Monotheism" of medieval Christianity combined belief in a supreme God with belief in a series of lesser deities, goddesses all, such as Reason, Charity, Love, Nature, Justice, Philosophy, Theology, Poverty, Right, Fortune, and the like. The sacred feminine was simply not suppressed in medieval Europe.

The normal reading of *The Da Vinci Code* as feminist derives, for many general readers, from their erroneous assumption that pre-modern Europe was characterized by an unremittingly repressive, male-dominated hierarchy. A novel built around the tale of how, in the supposed dark ages of the medieval world, the cult of Mary Magdalen was fostered within the institutional fabric of the church and helped medieval women justify their activities as preachers would seem – to such readers – like pure fantasy. It seems more reasonable for this audience to imagine that only a tiny handful of courageous priory members bucked the anti-feminist system of medieval Europe, a handful of exceptions proving the rule through their extraordinary courage and tenacity. But this is wrong, and the historian in me is outraged, not least because of our responsibility to provide justice to the dead. At the end of the day, I am persuaded by Edith Wyschogrod, who writes of our ethical responsibility as historians to give voices to those who now cannot speak for themselves, of an ethic that requires us to speak about the past based on our "eros for the dead," and our yearning for justice for them.[18] The departed who deserve justice include people like Gregory the Great and Mary Magdalen's anonymous medieval biographer.

Moreover, *The Da Vinci Code* provides no useful basis on which to foster gender equality and improve the position of women in the future, whereas the historical middle ages do. The reality of the middle ages already confounds any ahistorical view of the past as a stage for the eternal oppression of women. There is no need for fictional tales by modern novelists to provide positive pro-feminist imagery; it already existed in medieval texts and practices, frequently supported by institutional structures fostered by men. We should draw on this real past to make future progress, not flee history in the paranoid conviction that it has nothing to offer. A better understanding of medieval traditions concerning Mary Magdalen would make a world of difference.

Everywhere venerated, including by high-ranking male officials of the hierarchical church, as a special advocate for other sinners before the judgment seat of her beloved Jesus, Mary Magdalen even became a special patron of later medieval mendicant orders of friars like the Franciscans and the Dominicans. These were men who passionately identified themselves with the female figure of the penitent Mary. Imagine if this had been known to Meryl Streep, whose chosen theme for the commencement address she delivered at Barnard College in 2010 was "empathy." Now in the twenty-first century, for the very first time ever, Streep argued, heterosexual men are willing and able to identify with female characters. She lauded the development as positive, a sign that men are finally willing to recognize the fullness of humanity in women, surely a prerequisite for any truly egalitarian society. For her, the modern change is novel, revolutionary, an extraordinary breakthrough against millennia of cultural baggage.[19] This positive development should surely be fostered, but it can be done more effectively if the historical track record is better known. There is already a solid Western tradition of men identifying with female figures. In contrast, the "sudden breakthrough" perspective leaves such practices vulnerable, open to charges of being an unnatural, postmodern perversion, soon to vanish, like all unworthy ephemera, the next time a solid wind of "tradition" hits the United States.

Notes

1 S. Larsson, *The Girl with the Dragon Tattoo*, New York: Alfred A. Knopf, 2008, pp. 127, 445.
2 International Women's Forum. Online. Available HTTP: < www.iwf.org> (accessed 21 January 2011).
3 D. Brown, *The Da Vinci Code. A Novel*, New York: Doubleday, 2003, p. 248.
4 P. Anderson, "Holy Paper Chase! *The Da Vinci Code* by Dan Brown," *Washington Post*, 7 April 2003, p. C02. Online. Available HTTP: <www.washingtonpost.com/ac2/wp-dyn?pagename=article&node=&contentId=A43823-2003Apr6> (accessed 30 January 2011).
5 For a substantial series of corrections, see S. Newman, *The Real History Behind the Da Vinci Code*, New York: Berkeley Books, 2005.
6 Brown, *Da Vinci Code*, p. 239.
7 Brown, *Da Vinci Code*, p. 255.
8 Brown, *Da Vinci Code*, p. 310.
9 "Mary Magdalene," *Wikipedia*. Online. Available HTTP: <http://en.wikipedia.org/wiki/Mary_Magdalene > (accessed 21 January 2011).
10 D. Van Biema, "Mary Magdalene, Saint or Sinner? A New Wave of Literature is Cleaning Up her Reputation. How a Woman of Substance was 'Harlotized'," *Time Magazine*, 11 August 2003. Online. Available HTTP: <www.time.com/time/magazine/article/0,9171,1101030811-472868,00.html > (accessed 30 January 2011).

11 Brown, *Da Vinci Code*, p. 261.
12 For Vézelay, see World Heritage Convention, "Vézélay, Church and Hill." Online. Available HTTP: <http://whc.unesco.org/en/list/84> (accessed 21 January 2011).
13 *The Life of Saint Mary Magdalene and of her Sister Saint Martha,* trans. D.A. Mycoff, Kalamazoo, MI: Cistercian Publications, 1989, pp. 39–100.
14 Gregory the Great, *Homily* 25, in *Forty Gospel Homilies,* trans. D. Hurst, Kalamazoo, MI: Cistercian Publications, 1990, repr., Piscataway, NJ: Gorgias Press, 2009, p. 198.
15 Brown, *Da Vinci Code*, p. 244.
16 Gregory the Great, *Homily* 25, in *Forty Gospel Homilies,* pp. 198–99.
17 Gregory the Great, *Homily* 25, in *Forty Gospel Homilies,* p. 193.
18 E. Wyschogrod, *An Ethics of Remembering: History, Heterology, and the Nameless Others,* Chicago: University of Chicago Press, 1998.
19 "Commencement 2010: Keynote Address from Academy Award-Winning Actress Meryl Streep." Online. Available HTTP: <www.barnard.columbia.edu/commencement/rem_streep.html > (accessed 21 January 2011).

Suggestions for further reading

Medieval sources in English translation

Gregory the Great, *Forty Gospel Homilies,* trans. D. Hurst, Kalamazoo, MI: Cistercian Publications, 1990; repr., Piscataway, NJ: Gorgias Press, 2009.
The Life of Saint Mary Magdalene and of her Sister Saint Martha, trans. D.A. Mycoff, Kalamazoo, MI: Cistercian Publications, 1989.

Medieval women and gender

Classen, A., *The Medieval Chastity Belt: A Myth-Making Process,* New York: Palgrave MacMillan, 2007.
Clayton, M., *The Cult of the Virgin in Anglo-Saxon England,* Cambridge: Cambridge University Press, 2003.
Jansen, K.L., *The Making of the Magdalen: Preaching and Popular Devotion in the Later Middle Ages,* Princeton, NJ: Princeton University Press, 2000.
Meens, R., "Ritual Purity and the Influence of Gregory the Great in the Early Middle Ages," in *Unity and Diversity in the Church,* ed. R.N. Swanson, Oxford: Blackwell, 1996, pp. 31–43.
Newman, B., *God and the Goddesses: Vision, Poetry and Belief in the Middle Ages* Philadelphia: University of Pennsylvania Press, 2003.
Rubin, M., *Mother of God: A History of the Virgin Mary,* New Haven, CT: Yale University Press, 2009.
Stafford, P.A., "Powerful Women in the Early Middle Ages: Queens and Abbesses," in *The Medieval World,* ed. P. Linehan and J.L. Nelson, London: Routledge, 2001, pp. 398–415.
Warner, M., *Alone of All her Sex: The Myth and the Cult of the Virgin Mary,* New York: Simon and Schuster, 1976.

6

HOMOSEXUALITY

Augustine and the Christian closet

Mathew Kuefler

In November 2006, Ted Haggard resigned both as pastor of the New Life Church he had founded in conservative Colorado Springs and as leader of the US-based National Association of Evangelicals when it was revealed that he had been paying a gay prostitute, Mike Jones, for sex and drugs. Jones cited Haggard's hypocrisy (condemning homosexuality in public while engaging in gay sex in private), along-side the negative impact that Haggard's public pronouncements were having on gay issues, as the factors that motivated him to come forward. As genuinely shocked as Haggard's congregation and other evangelical leaders seem to have been, this sex scandal was only one in a series of similar incidents among conservative Christians in the US and elsewhere. The *Los Angeles Times* in September 2004 accused Paul Crouch, founder and president of the Trinity Broadcasting Network, the largest Christian television network in the US, of having paid a former male employee of the network almost a half million dollars to keep him from revealing a coerced sexual encounter. Similar examples date back to the earliest years of the movement. In 1916 John Balcom Shaw, Presbyterian pastor, college president, and one of the editors of *The Fundamentals* (the series of publications that lent its name to what became Christian fundamentalism) was disgraced by accusations that he had attempted the seduction of several young men at YMCAs and elsewhere around the country. Similar struggles and contradictions between belief and behavior can also be seen in the recent international crisis facing the Catholic clergy that resulted, for example, in the 1995 resignation of the Archbishop of Vienna, Hans Hermann Gröer, after allegations that he had coerced young men into sex. Charges of what is usually described as "pedophilia" against Catholic clergy in the US are not uncommon. According to one American report, four out of five victims of such illicit advances are male, most often boys in their teens.[1]

It is easy to be critical of such hypocrisy, since these individuals clearly do not live up to the sexual standards they impose on others. At the same time, it should also be clear that they have very likely wrestled mightily within themselves in trying to reconcile what they consider to be the demands of their faith with their personal feelings. It is vital to understand how persons like these can get caught up in the sort of shame and self-hatred that I call the Christian closet. The Christian closet is not a new phenomenon. Indeed, one sad tale of sexual desire and guilt that comes from the distant past may help illuminate the scandals that have become such a regular feature of the contemporary Christian landscape. My case study is especially significant, because it involves perhaps the most influential Christian theologian in the early medieval era: Saint Augustine of Hippo, a bishop of late fourth- and early fifth-century Roman North Africa.

Augustine described his struggles with his sexual desires candidly and in great detail in his *Confessions*, but he also helped cement into place the code of shame around sexual behavior that still regulates modern closeted Christians, and especially those who struggle with sexual desires for others of their own sex. Augustine's open mix of shame, grief, and regret speaks loudly even today, although if it has never been fully heard, since Augustine's revelations are shocking even for scholars. Insofar as Augustine's theology has been and continues to be foundational for many Christian thinkers, it should not be surprising that Christian leaders still occasionally recapitulate certain aspects of his discourse. However, because his own sexuality has been incompletely understood, the contemporary Christian debate on sexuality has not absorbed the full meaning of Augustine's insights on the power of sexual desire. Augustine's own pitiful story reminds us of the necessity of combining religious conviction with lived experience, and of the dangers of setting a sexual ideal that is impractical to follow.

Augustine's sexual trajectory

As my analysis of his *Confessions* demonstrates, sexual desire played a central role in Augustine's life. He referred to himself prior to his conversion to Catholic Christianity as a "slave to lust" (*libidinis seruus*). He represented his conversion as a commitment to "Continence" (*Continentia*), the female personification of sexual renunciation. Nevertheless, he experienced an ongoing struggle with his sexual passions even long after his conversion:

> But even now live in my memory … the images of such things that habit has fixed there, and while certainly they lack strength in attacking me when I am awake, in my dreams they result not only in pleasure but also in consent and what is very much like the deed. And so strong is the illusion of the image in my mind, in my body, that while I am sleeping these false visions persuade in ways that, when I am awake, true ones cannot.[2]

Augustine's struggle with sexual desire was no "private" matter. He understood his personal journey from lust to continence as representative of the universal human condition. Furthermore, he interpreted sexual passion as the primary site of human sin. For Augustine, sex provided the means for the congenital transfer of original sin (a concept he himself developed) from the first human parents, Adam and Eve, to the rest of the human race, and served as the greatest reminder of ongoing human sinfulness and frailty. It was to be avoided entirely, if possible, or otherwise limited to procreative sex within marriage. These ideas about sex influenced all generations of Christians that came after Augustine, down to the present day. Yet historians have not been sufficiently attentive to the likelihood that Augustine's own sexual past included homoerotic sexual expression (some scholars even expressly deny it), or to how his guilt about that past shaped his ideas about sex.[3]

Let us hear Augustine speak for himself about his sexuality. He described his young adulthood thus:

> What was it that pleased me, if not to love and to be loved? But the limit was not kept by one mind to another, that is to say, to the shining boundary of friendship, but exuded a fog of murky lust of the flesh and a pubescent outpouring and clouded over and eclipsed my heart, so that it could not discern the calm of love from the gloom of lust.

A bit further on, Augustine repeated the sentiment: "Thus I polluted the stream of friendship with the filthiness of desire and I clouded its clearness with infernal lust."[4] Traditional scholarship infers that Augustine was referring to his concubine, a woman he met in his youth when he lived in Carthage, but whose name is not even known to us. This interpretation is flawed, on a number of grounds.

To begin, Augustine's language of pollution and sinfulness seems too extravagant to refer to a concubine. In the passages which undoubtedly refer to his concubine, Augustine wrote soberly:

> In those years I had a woman, acknowledged not in that sort of union that is called legitimate, except that my wandering ardor, lacking in prudence, had hunted her down – but one, nonetheless, and I remained faithful to her bed.

He mentioned a concubine only once more, when he dismissed her so as to contract a formal marriage:

> She with whom I used to sleep was pulled from my side as an impediment to marital union; my heart, within which she held tightly, was torn and wounded, and bled. And she returned to Africa, vowing to me that she would refuse any other man and leaving behind with me my son by her.

Despite their bond, Augustine took another mistress after she left, even while he made plans to marry formally.[5]

Scholars have assumed that the woman Augustine dismissed and who returned to Africa is the same one as the one with whom he lived in his youth in Carthage, but we have so little information about the relationship that even that is not certain. More importantly, Augustine did not necessarily establish a relationship of *ongoing* co-habitation with a particular woman. Alypius, a man with whom Augustine was living in Milan, resented Augustine's approaching marriage (which never did take place) because it would have introduced a woman into their household.[6] Indeed, Augustine's reference to his concubine being "pulled from [his] side" may refer to a purely legal procedure rather than to any change in physical living arrangements. Roman law did not permit formal marriage (called *conubium*) between persons of widely differing social classes, but permitted a lesser form of marriage (called *contubernium*). Nonetheless, a man could not participate in the two forms of marriage at the same time. If this woman was Augustine's legal concubine, then a formal repudiation was required before he was legally free to contract a new marriage, even if they were not living together at the time, and that seems to be what he suggested in referring to this relationship as an "obstacle to marital union."[7]

Perhaps most importantly, it would have been extremely unusual for Augustine to refer to his relationship with his concubine as a "friendship" (*amicitia*), since that bond was considered in traditional classical culture only to be possible between men. While Christian ideas about spiritual equality between the sexes were making friendships between men and women possible in a new way at the beginning of the middle ages, such relationships still mostly happened within a context of mentorship rather than of mutuality. In any case, Augustine himself does not seem to have participated in such friendships with women. If there was any woman with whom Augustine shared an intimate bond, it was his mother, who followed him from North Africa to Milan and then to Rome, and remained with him until her death. Yet Augustine spoke approvingly of his mother's absolute submission to his father, as a slave to her master, in terms that belie any view of equality between men and women on his part.[8] Instead, Augustine's views on friendship seem to have conformed to the classical model. For instance, he implied that women were useful to men only for sex, and that only men could provide emotional and intellectual companionship to other men, asking in an apparently offhand manner: "How much more closely in cohabitation and conversation are two [male] friends together than a man and a woman?"[9] Elsewhere, he suggested that any discussion of love, even within a Christian context, should begin with the love between (also presumably male) friends.[10]

We must be careful to avoid being trapped by any notion of sexual identity which might force us to imagine that Augustine enjoyed sexual relations *either* with women *or* with men, but could not have done both. Many ancient Roman men were what we would consider to be bisexual today. Indeed, it would have been unexpected for someone in that day to have thought of sexual desire as something directed exclusively either at women or at other men. So Augustine's sexual involvement with women, and the mention of a son named Adeodatus, would not have precluded sexual involvement with men. Likewise, the modern fundamentalist Christian leaders involved in the scandals noted above were all married men.

A central feature of Augustine's experience of relationships was with other men. These connections included his deep admiration for learned men, as described in his *Confessions*, such as the Manichaean preacher whose arrival in Carthage he so greatly anticipated and who so disappointed him, and Ambrose, the bishop of Milan who brought him to Catholic Christianity. Then there was Alypius, with whom he lived in Milan and with whom he shared a growing attraction to Catholic Christianity. Both eventually became bishops in North Africa. Alypius was clearly an important fixture in Augustine's life, as the latter remembered it. For instance, Alypius was with him at the very moment that Augustine later believed was the turning point of his life: his conversion in the garden of the house that he and Alypius shared in Milan. Augustine called Alypius "extremely chaste" and his lifestyle one "of the utmost self-control" and contrasted Alypius with himself, still "bound by the disease of the flesh." He also called Alypius "the brother of my heart." After his conversion and election as bishop, Augustine continued to experience intense, close male friendships, as evidenced by the sometimes florid language he and his friends used in their letters to each other. Augustine called Nebridius, another north African living in Milan, his "sweetheart" (*dulcis*), and hoped after Nebridius' death that the latter would not forget him on earth while enjoying the pleasures of heaven.[11] Severus of Milevus, with whom Augustine also lived for a time in Thagaste, wrote to Augustine as his "sweetest brother" (*frater dulcissime*) and expressed the metaphorical desire to "suckle from the abundance of [his] teats" (*ubera*) in learning from him.[12]

What seems to us to be sexual language may not have been. This intimate language of friendship was commonly used in antiquity and the middle ages to describe intellectual or emotional as well as sexual companionship. At the same time, a contemporary of Augustine named Valerian of Cimelium specifically pointed out how the language of friendship between men could be used to disguise sexual relationships.[13] It is not always easy to distinguish those same-sex attachments in which the feeling is physical from those in which it is otherwise inspired, let alone from ones in which the sentiments are mixed or disguised (or sublimated, as we would say today). In Augustine's case, however, the attempt must be made, for the homoerotic aspect of Augustine's experience is key to understanding his interior struggles and how they shaped his extremely influential ideas about sexuality.

The friendship soured by lust

Let us return then to the youthful Augustine, to see what light he himself might shed on his feelings. After his studies in Carthage he returned home to Thagaste, also in North Africa. He wrote:

> In those years, in that time when I first began to teach in the city where I was born, I was paired with a friend, dear beyond measure through the companionship of our studies, the same age as me and flowering, as I was, in the bloom of adolescence.

Augustine described this connection as a sweeter joy than any other, even though he had already lived with his concubine. Augustine converted his friend to his Manichaean beliefs, and said of him, whom he also did not name, that "this man erred with me in his soul, and my soul was not able to be without him."[14]

Augustine used classical literary models to describe this friendship. Referring to the first *Ode* of the ancient Latin poet, Horace, he exclaimed:

> He said it well who said that his friend was half of his soul. For in my mind my soul and his soul had been one soul in two bodies, and my life was therefore frightful to me because I did not want to live with half a soul, and yet I also feared somehow to die lest he whom I had loved so much should be utterly dead.[15]

Latin literature provided abundant portrayals of deep male friendships, including in the works of extremely well known writers who were doubtless familiar to Augustine: the love between Nisus and Euryalus in the ninth book of Vergil's *Aeneid,* the love between Corydon and Alexis in the second book of Vergil's *Eclogues,* and the love expressed for Paullus in the fourth *Ode* of the poet Horace. Historical examples of intimate and even sexual male friendships were likely also known to Augustine, foremost among them the love between the Greek conqueror Alexander the Great and Hephaistion, or that of the Roman emperor Hadrian for the young man Antinoüs, whom Hadrian had deified after his death, and whose shrine at Carthage might still have been open in Augustine's youth.[16] Augustine explicitly compared his love for his own unnamed friend to that between the Greek heroes Orestes and Pylades, although he admitted that it did not equal theirs.[17]

The fact that Augustine and his friend were practicing Manichaeans is yet another reason to consider that their relationship might have been sexual. Many accusations of sexual immorality were made against this group, including the charge (leveled in Augustine's own day) that its "unchaste perversity, in the name of religion, commits crimes that are unknown and shameful even in brothels."[18] Certainly we must take such charges, made by those hostile to the group, with a grain of salt. Nevertheless, the sect's abhorrence for the material world (one of its chief beliefs) may well have led it to encourage non-procreative forms of sexuality. Augustine himself admitted that in marital relationships among Manichaeans "children are born against one's will."[19] Later in life he repeated the same comment, and accused his former coreligionists in somewhat vague language of a fondness for what seems to be fellatio.[20]

But the relationship between Augustine and his unnamed friend was cut short, for the friend fell ill and died, despite Augustine's constant ministrations. Augustine interpreted his friend's death as God's vengeance. He wrote in his *Confessions* (addressing himself directly to God):

> Behold, you were right there, at the heels of your fugitives, at the same time the God of vengeance and the fountain of mercy. ... Behold, you took this man away from his life, when scarcely a year in our friendship had passed, sweet to me above all sweetnesses of that life of mine.

His anguished outpourings show that Augustine was devastated and tormented by his loss:

With what sorrow was my heart cast in shadow, and however much I looked there was only death. My homeland was torture to me and my parents' home an exceeding unhappiness, and whatever I had shared with him had become without him an inhuman torment. I longed to see him everywhere, but he was not there, and I hated all things because he was not there nor could they say to me "Look, he is coming!" as when he was alive but absent.

Returning to the theme, he wrote:

> Oh, what madness that does not know how to love a human being as a human being! Oh, what idiocy that allows a human being to be more than a human being! That is what I was. And so I raged, I sighed, I wept, I was distraught, but there was neither rest nor help. I bore my soul, torn and bloodied and too weak for me to carry, yet I did not find anywhere that I might set it down. ... I hated all things, even the daylight and whatever was not what he was.

At one point, Augustine broke off his narrative to ask: "How can sweet fruit be picked from the bitterness of life, its groaning and weeping and sighing and lamenting?"[21]

The detail with which Augustine laid out his anguish is poignant even today. These passages concerning the loss of his youthful male friend are much more painful to read than is his description of his repudiation of his concubine, and obviously concerned a far more meaningful relationship. Even his grief at his mother's death, which he also recounted in the *Confessions*, does not seem so agonizing. A quarter of a century later, remembering and writing about this man's death reopened the wound in Augustine, and he wrote: "Look at my heart, my God, look within it: see what I remember, you who are my hope and who cleanses me from the dirtiness of such affections." The strength of feeling evoked at his friend's death seems even to have pulled Augustine into doubting God, and may have been at least partially responsible for generating in him a lifelong philosophical and theological preoccupation with the problem of the existence of evil.[22]

Augustinian theology and the Christian closet

When the older Augustine looked back to the time of his relationship with his deceased friend, he wrote with a profound sense of personal sin and guilt concerning the "abyss of corruption" he discerned within his earlier self, who had once acquiesced to "sins that are against nature."[23] What is more, he explicitly *countered* three arguments that might have justified such sins:

> Isn't it so that it is never wrong at any time or any place to love God ... and to love one's neighbor as one's self? And yet, sins that are against nature ought everywhere and always to be detested and punished, just as happened to the Sodomites. If all peoples did so, they would be held liable by divine law to the

same guilt of sin, for it is not thus done that human beings should be used in such a way. That relationship that we owe to God is violated, in fact, when that same nature of which he is the author is polluted by the perversity of lust. Against human custom, however, are also sins that ought to be avoided because they oppose tradition, so that the convention of a city or people, established by custom or law, should not be violated by the desire of any citizen or foreigner. It is shameful that any part should not fit with the large whole. Still, when God commands anything whatsoever against custom or convention, even if it had never been done there, it should be done, and if not done, it should be begun, and if not established, it should be established. ... But what sins are against you [Augustine asked God], who will not be corrupted? And what misdeeds can be against you, whom it is not possible to do harm? But at the same time you punish what these men do, because when they sin against you, they act indecently against their own souls, and their wickedness deceives them into either corrupting or perverting their nature, as you have made and ordained it, either by making immoderate use of the things that have been permitted or by becoming inflamed in their use of those things not permitted, which is against nature.[24]

Augustine here voiced arguments that will be familiar to anyone who follows the debate around the conservative Christian stance on homosexuality: that it can never be wrong to love, that human customs differ about sex, and that God is unaffected by (or perhaps not overly interested in) human sexual behavior. It seems he had once subscribed to these notions himself. But when he wrote these words, he dismissed them as invalid.

Augustine reveals to us how a new pattern for thinking about same-sex intimacy was becoming dominant through the spread of Christianity: to see it as sin. He was certainly not the only Christian to reject the classical tradition of intimate male friendship and the possibility of sexual intimacy between men.[25] Although he was not alone in his developing views, Augustine holds a special place in the history of the Christian closet. For one thing, he (like modern Christian evangelists and Catholic bishops) proudly asserted his countercultural role. It did not matter that many others might have believed homosexual acts to be sanctioned by law or popular opinion; he certainly did not consider such acts to be morally neutral, in keeping with his under-standing of the Christian tradition and the natural law. And then there is the element of tragedy: Augustine's condemnation fell upon himself as well as upon others.

There was a deeply personal aspect to Augustine's role in the creation of a new sexual orthodoxy that rejected homoeroticism. The biblical text most frequently used in this developing discourse was Paul's *Letter to the Romans*, which described one instance of sex between males as the result of idolatrous religion:

Although they claimed to be wise, they became fools and exchanged the glory of the immortal God for images made to look like mortal man and birds and animals and reptiles. Therefore God gave them over in the sinful desires of their hearts to sexual impurity for the degrading of their bodies with one another. They exchanged the truth of God for a lie, and worshiped and served created things rather than the Creator—who is forever praised. Amen. Because of this, God gave them over to shameful lusts. Even their women exchanged natural relations for unnatural ones. In the same way the men also abandoned natural relations with women and were inflamed with lust for one another. Men committed indecent acts with other men, and received in themselves the due penalty for their perversion.[26]

Paul was likely referring to the cult of a fertility goddess whose eunuch priests were widely known to have engaged in receptive homosexual practices. Augustine knew the cult too, for he admitted (with regret) having once attended some of its festivities even as he spoke out against them in his *City of God*.[27] Yet Augustine applied the Pauline text to all sexual relations between men, not simply those associated with the pagan fertility cult. This is clear from his verbal allusions to *Romans* in the passage from his *Confessions* quoted above, in which he denounced "sins against nature" and men "becoming inflamed."

The passage from *Romans* played a crucial role in Augustine's own sexual trajectory. He discussed the Pauline text thus in his *Confessions*:

> And thus I read there that even the unalterable glory of your incorruption [was changed] into idols and various representations, into the likenesses of images of corruptible human beings and winged beasts and four-legged animals and serpents. ... I was admonished to return to myself.

Augustine had abandoned the Catholic beliefs of his mother for the "irrational ideas" of the Manichaeans and, as a result, God allowed him to abandon right sexuality (marriage and procreation) for wrong sexuality (concubinage and a perverted friendship). Yet Augustine returned to himself, and converted to Catholic Christianity, after a dramatic moment in the garden with Alypius during which he heard a mystical voice telling him to "take and read." It was Paul's *Letter to the Romans* that he had at hand. This moment in the garden, and the death of his friend, are among the handful of places in the *Confessions* where Augustine recorded that he wept.[28]

After Augustine's conversion to Catholicism he abandoned his plans for marriage. For Augustine, turning to God meant projecting the entirety of his desire onto God. He would not even embrace the personified *Continentia*, who waited in her "chaste dignity" for him, but fell instead at the feet of God, towards whom he directed some of his most erotic utterances: "you glistened, you shined, and chased away my blindness; you glowed with flame, I drew breath and now I pant after you; I tasted and now I hunger and thirst; you touched me, and I was inflamed." The love he bore God was "an embrace that was not ended with its satisfaction." Augustine called God his true "bridegroom," while recognizing that he had been unfaithful to his rightful husband: "I did not love you and prostituted myself against you. ... for the friendship of this world is prostitution against you."[29]

The redirection of his love toward God was not without its costs. Augustine could not help but have regrets about what he had sacrificed. In the *City of God*, later in life, once again reflecting on the legend of Sodom, he wrote:

> It is fitting that those who were freed by angels were forbidden to look back, so that we might understand that he who is reborn through grace should not return in his mind to his former life, from which he was taken away, if he would escape the final judgment.[30]

Yet, throughout his life, Augustine was repeatedly tempted to look back. Sexual urges continued to trouble his thoughts. He experienced a desperate need to record his shameful past, and he produced a stream of anxious writings on the indelible power of lust. All of this lends personal poignancy to Augustine's theological notion that the presence of sin in the world, after the fall of Adam and Eve, meant that the human will was insufficient to control human bodies and their desires. It also reminds us how tortured some can be when the dictates of their religion conflict with their hidden desires.

Augustine was surely looking back yet again when, near the end of the *City of God*, he discussed some ornamental features of the human body: "the nipples on a man's chest, or the beard on his face, the latter of which is not for any protection but is a virile decoration." Then, with an almost audible sigh, Augustine expressed his pious hope: "a time is coming when we shall enjoy one another for our beauty alone and without lust."[31] But that time was not yet at hand. In the present life, Augustine faced the dilemma of conflicting human desires:

> If, therefore, everything appeals to [a human being] at the same time, don't those different desires tear at the human heart, when it is considered what we might embrace that is best of all? ... They contend with each other until he has chosen.[32]

Like the modern-day Christian leaders caught in webs of sexual scandal and deceit, Augustine felt obliged to choose between his own pleasure and his desire for salvation. Unlike them, he seems to have managed to preserve a life of outward chastity even if he occasionally indulged his secret, shameful desires in his mind. Meanwhile, what he could not permit himself to experience, he reviled in others. That is perhaps most clearly seen in Augustine's arguments against Jovinian, who refused to accept sexual expression as less virtuous and less Christian than sexual renunciation. It is still seen among those contemporary Christian leaders who revile homosexuality in public but seek homosexual companionship in secret. The tragic irony is that these leaders hold fast to a harsh standard of sexual conduct carved out by someone much like themselves, who struggled to suppress the sexual desires he believed separated him from God's love. Augustine chose to reject a part of himself, and it made him a rigid doctrinarian. His example serves as a lesson to all of us, believers or not, to sympathize with our fellow human beings in their struggles and to show them that there are many ways to love.

Notes

1 K. Terry, *et al.*, *The Nature and Scope of the Problem of Sexual Abuse of Minors by Catholic Priests and Deacons in the United States (The John Jay Report)*, Washington, DC: US Conference of Catholic Bishops, 2004. Online. Available HTTP: <www.bishop-accountability.org/reports/2004_02_27_JohnJay/index.html#exec > (accessed 16 January 2011).

2 Augustine, *Confessionum libri XIII*, ed. L. Verheijen, Corpus Christianorum Series Latina, 27, Turnhout: Brepols, 1981 (hereafter *Conf.*), 6.15.25, 8.11.27, and 10.30.41. Many English translations are available, including by R.S. Pine-Coffin, H. Chadwick, and M. Boulding. All the translations in this essay, from the *Confessions* and from other works, are mine unless otherwise noted.

3 For instance, A.G. Soble, "Correcting Some Misconceptions about St. Augustine's Sex Life," *Journal of the History of Sexuality* 11, 2002, 545–69.

4 *Conf.* 2.2.2 and 3.1.1.

5 *Conf.* 4.2.2 and 6.15.25.

6 *Conf.* 6.12.21.

7 *Codex Theodosianus* 4.6.3 and *Novella Valentiniani* 35.1, in *The Theodosian Code and Novels*, trans. C. Pharr, Princeton, NJ: Princeton University Press, 1952.

8 *Conf.* 9.9.19.

9 Augustine, *De Genesi ad litteram* 9.5, ed. J. Zycha, Corpus Scriptorum Ecclesiasticorum Latinorum, 28, Prague: Austrian Academy of Sciences, 1894, p. 273. The work is available in English translation as Augustine, *On Genesis*, trans. R.J. Teske, Washington, DC: Catholic University of American Press, 1991.

10 Augustine, *De Doctrina Christiana*, 1.20, ed. R.P.H. Green, Oxford: Clarendon Press, 1995. The work is available in English translation as Augustine, *On Christian Doctrine*, trans. D.W. Robertson, New York: Macmillan, 1958.

11 *Conf.* 8.8, 6.12.21, 9.4.7, 8.6, and 9.3.

12 *Epistle* 109, in *Sancti Aurelii Augustini Epistulae*, ed. K.D. Daur, Corpus Christianorum Series Latina, 31B, Turnhout: Brepols, 2009, p. 85.

13 M. Kuefler, *The Manly Eunuch: Masculinity, Gender Ambiguity, and Christian Ideology in Late Antiquity*, Chicago: University of Chicago Press, 2001, pp. 197–200.

14 *Conf.* 4.4.7.

15 *Conf.* 4.4.7.

16 R. Lambert, *Beloved and God: The Story of Hadrian and Antinoüs*, New York: Viking, 1984, p. 185.

17 *Conf.* 4.6.11.

18 *Novella Valentiniani* 18.1, in *The Theodosian Code and Novels*, trans. Pharr, p. 531.

19 *Conf.* 4.2.2.

20 Augustine, *Contra Faustum Manichaeum*, 22.30, ed. J. Zycha, Corpus Scriptorum Ecclesiasticorum Latinorum, 25:1, Prague: Austrian Academy of Sciences, 1891. The work is available in English translation as Augustine, *Contra Faustum (Answer to Faustus, A Manichean)*, trans. R.J. Teske, Hyde-Park, NY: New City Press, 2007.

21 *Conf.* 4.4.7, 4.4.9, 4.7.12, and 4.5.10.

22 *Conf.* 9.12.29–30, 4.6.11, and 4.4.9.

23 *Conf.* 5.10.18, 9.1.1, and 3.8.15.

24 *Conf.* 3.8.15–16.

25 Kuefler, *The Manly Eunuch*, pp. 166–70.

26 Romans 1:22–27 (New International Version).

27 Augustine, *De civitate Dei libri XXII*, 2.4 and 7.26–27, eds B. Dombert and A. Kalb, Corpus Christianorum Series Latina, 47–48, Turnhout: Brepols, 1955. The work is available in English translation as Augustine, *The City of God Against the Pagans*, trans. R.W. Dyson, Cambridge: Cambridge University Press, 1998.

28 *Conf.* 7.9.15, 7.10.16, 8.12.29, and 9.12.

29 *Conf.* 8.11.27, 10.27.38, 10.6.8, 4.15.27, and 1.13.21.

30 Augustine, *De civitate Dei*, 16.30, eds Dombert and Kalb, Vol. 48, p. 535.

31 Augustine, *De civitate Dei*, 22.24, eds Dombert and Kalb, Vol. 48, pp. 850–51.
32 *Conf.* 8.10.24.

Suggestions for further reading

Ancient and medieval approaches

Boswell, J., *Christianity, Social Tolerance, and Homosexuality: Gay People in Western Europe from the Beginning of the Christian Era to the Fourteenth Century*, Chicago: University of Chicago Press, 1980.

Brown, P., *The Body and Society: Men, Women, and Sexual Renunciation in Early Christianity*, New York: Columbia University Press, 1988.

Clark, E.A., "Friendship Between the Sexes: Classical Theory and Christian Practice," in E.A. Clark, *Jerome, Chrysostom, and Friends: Essays and Translations*, New York: Mellen Press, 1979, pp. 35–106.

Hunter, D., "Resistance to the Virginal Ideal in Late-Fourth-Century Rome: The Case of Jovinian," *Theological Studies* 48, 1987, 45–64.

Kuefler, M., *The Manly Eunuch: Masculinity, Gender Ambiguity, and Christian Ideology in Late Antiquity*, Chicago: University of Chicago Press, 2001.

——, "The Marriage Revolution in Late Antiquity: The Theodosian Code and Later Roman Marriage Law," *Journal of Family History* 32, 2007, 343–70.

Pagels, E., *Adam, Eve, and the Serpent*, New York: Vintage, 1988.

Williams, C., *Roman Homosexuality: Ideologies of Masculinity in Classical Antiquity*, Oxford: Oxford University Press, 1999.

Augustine

Brown, P., *Augustine and Sexuality*, Berkeley: Center for Hermeneutical Studies in Hellenistic and Modern Culture, 1983.

——, *Augustine of Hippo: A Biography*, Berkeley: University of California Press, 1967.

Burrus, V., M.D. Jordan, and K. MacKendrick, *Seducing Augustine: Bodies, Desires, Confessions*, New York: Fordham University Press, 2010.

Jonte-Pace, D., "Augustine on the Couch: Psychohistorical (Mis)readings of the *Confessions*," *Religion* 23, 1993, 71–83.

Miles, M.R., "Sex and the City (of God): Is Sex Forfeited or Fulfilled in Augustine's Resurrection of the Body?" *Journal of the American Academy of Religion* 73, 2005, 307–27.

Power, K., "*Sed unam tamen*: Augustine and his Concubine," *Augustinian Studies* 23, 1992, 49–76.

Sawyer, E., "Celibate Pleasures: Masculinity, Desire, and Asceticism in Augustine," *Journal of the History of Sexuality* 6, 1995, 1–29.

Modern controversies

"Amid Allegations, Haggard Steps Aside," *Rocky Mountain News*, 2 November 2006. Online, Available HTTP: <http://www.scrippsnews.com/node/15833> (accessed 16 January 2011).

Corley, F., "Cardinal Hans Hermann Gröer: Disgraced Archbishop of Vienna," *The Independent*, 27 March 2003. Online. Available HTTP: <http://www.independent.co.uk/news/obituaries/cardinal-hans-hermann-groer-592499.html> (accessed 15 December 2010).

"List of Christian Evangelist Scandals." Online. Available HTTP: <http://en.wikipedia.org/wiki/List_of_Christian_evangelist_scandals > (accessed 15 December 2010).

Lobdell, W., "Ex-Worker Accusing TBN Pastor Says He Had Sex to Keep His Job," *Los Angeles Times*, 22 September 2004. Online. Available HTTP: <http://articles.latimes.com/2004/sep/22/local/me-tbn22> (accessed 15 December 2010).

Lofton, K., "Queering Fundamentalism: John Balcom Shaw and the Sexuality of a Protestant Orthodoxy," *Journal of the History of Sexuality* 17, 2008, 439–68.

Terry, K., *et al.*, *The Nature and Scope of the Problem of Sexual Abuse of Minors by Catholic Priests and Deacons in the United States (The John Jay Report)*, Washington, DC: US Conference of Catholic Bishops, 2004. Online. Available HTTP: <http://www.bishop-accountability.org/reports/2004_02_27_JohnJay/index.html#exec > (accessed 16 January 2011).

7

SEXUAL SCANDAL AND THE CLERGY

A medieval blueprint for disaster

Dyan Elliott

Once upon a time in the early fifth century there was a holy man named Sylvanus, the bishop of Nazareth. Sylvanus was a good bishop with a reputation for sanctity. So imagine the shock of a noble matron when she found Sylvanus under her bed, presumably planning to take her by force. The woman called out in alarm, and Sylvanus responded with a string of foul language loud enough to wake the neighborhood. When the outraged public drove Sylvanus from their midst, he was forced to seek refuge at the tomb of his friend, St. Jerome. The crowd was out for blood and armed assailants stepped forward. But Sylvanus overpowered each of them, turning the sword against its owner. Eventually the pontiff collapsed and died.

The story is apocryphal, invented in the fourteenth century to buttress the cult of Jerome. Yet this representation of a cleric's reprehensible behavior points to a timeless issue for the church: from at least the second century, the clergy attempted to distinguish themselves from the laity through their more rigorous sexual standards, culminating in the imposition of celibacy upon western European (Latin) clergy. They even appropriated Christ's rhetoric of the "angelic life:" Jesus declared that in the next life there would be no marriage, but people would live like angels (Matthew 22:30).[1] But clerics were not exempt from the laws of gravity, and, as the example of Sylvanus suggests, by raising themselves to such heights, they only had further to fall. The clergy's identification with celibacy predetermined that their most visible and notorious scandals would be sexual.

Christ prepared his followers for the possibility of public disgrace, commenting "it must needs be that scandals come" (Matthew 18:7). This seeming resignation was, however, balanced by grim warnings: "woe to that man by whom the scandal cometh" and "he that shall scandalize one of these little ones [children] that believe in me, it were better for him that a millstone should be hanged about his neck, and that he should be drowned in the depth of the sea" (Matthew 18:6). One possible interpretation of these remarks is that there might be some merit in concealing shameful behavior.

Fortunately, the resolution to the story of Sylvanus is that the bishop was innocent. The malefactor was not Sylvanus but a demon in the shape of Sylvanus attempting to destroy the bishop's good name. Nor was it Sylvanus who broke the prohibition against clergy shedding blood by slitting the throats of his parishioners; it was presumably Sylvanus' patron, Jerome, standing up for his friend. Sylvanus' demise was not a judgment from heaven after all; it was a direct response to his prayers that God receive his soul.[2]

If one were reading against the grain, the bizarre story of Sylvanus could serve as an exemplary tale revealing the degree of denial and falsification church authorities were prepared to undertake to suppress scandal. This essay considers some ways in which the church responded to scandal in the past, on both theoretical and practical levels, and how this history resonates with modern revelations concerning clerical sexual abuse. Numerous researchers with different backgrounds have identified the modern church's effort to conceal this criminal behavior as a systemic problem. Garry Wills refers to "structures of deceit;" Myra Hidalgo likens the church's secrecy to the configuration of an incestuous family; former federal investigator Leon Podles points to the correlation between the clerical gay subculture and the high proportion of male victims; and canonist Thomas Doyle denounces a two thousand year paper trail of abuse. Many studies have also attempted to link contemporary abuses with the compulsory celibacy of priests, resulting in both attacks on and impassioned defenses of this principle.

Despite the differences in perspectives and methodology, these critics share the underlying assumption that the bishops' attempts to conceal the criminal behavior of their subordinates resulted in a hideous distortion of the church's mission. It seems impossible to deny this allegation. What I challenge, however, is the tacit premise that the suppressions and denials endemic among the higher clergy (bishops and above) is a corruption of procedure or an abuse that has crept into church governance. I suggest that, in fact, this pattern of evasion has been shaped by centuries of discussion in canon (church) law and theology about how to contend with clerical criminality and scandal. Although my primary focus is the high middle ages (eleventh and later centuries), my investigation necessarily reaches back to the first century of Christianity for theological and canon law precedent. This long continuum of clerical culture is the key to understanding the crisis of the present day church.

The clerical school for scandal

The concept of scandal is all about being your brother's keeper. The word scandal is derived from a Greek verb that means "to cause another to stumble." A given act need not be sinful in and of itself in order to be scandalous: the salient attribute is its ability to occasion sin in another. St. Paul makes this distinction when queried about whether it is licit to eat food sacrificed to idols (I Corinthians 8:1–13). The consumption of such food is not sinful, Paul reasons, but the act can be misinterpreted and thus should not be encouraged. A person who eats the meat although aware that this can cause sin in another is a sinner. The important thirteenth-century theologian,

Thomas Aquinas differentiated between active scandal (when sinning or the appearance of sinning leads another to fall) and passive scandal (when an individual's words or deeds, however blameless, lead another to sin).[3]

To acknowledge the full force of scandal is to recognize that appearances matter – tremendously. The disciplinary guidelines for the medieval clergy reflect this awareness on many levels. In keeping with Old Testament strictures such as Leviticus 22:24 and Deuteronomy 23:1, there was, for example, a prohibition against ordaining a person who lacked a body part. What perhaps began as a kind of pollution taboo was eventually interpreted as instituted to avoid scandalizing the faithful. Thus in the high middle ages, pastoral theologians like John of Freiburg reasoned that someone lacking a visible body part should not be ordained. Even if only missing a piece of a finger, a man could not say mass because his deformity might repel parishioners.[4]

Most often, disciplinary sanctions were directed at voluntary behavior. In the third century, a number of clerics attracted to celibacy attempted to set up housekeeping with the growing numbers of women who chose to live as virgins consecrated to God. But church authorities were united in pronouncing the relations between priests and these virgins scandalous and worthy of suppression. The first evidence for such relations occurs in a letter of Cyprian, bishop of Carthage (d. 258), denouncing a deacon who lived with two consecrated virgins and shared their beds. The bishop insisted that the women submit to gynecological examinations to ensure their virginity was intact before their readmission to the church. But Cyprian acknowledged that such proofs only spoke to their physical condition, casting no light on the more crucial question of spiritual integrity.[5] In 325, the Council of Nicea outlawed relations between priests and their "surreptitious virgins" and drew up a list of unobjectionable housekeepers that included "a mother or sister or aunt, or ... any person who is above suspicion."[6]

The priests and the virgins were chastised openly. But it could have gone the other way. Although Christ had little use for hypocrites, his injunctions against scandal could be used to support a strategic hypocrisy. In the early church, a priest caught openly in a heinous sin, such as fornication with a spiritual daughter, was ineligible for the public penance that expiated mortal sin – he had to be deposed (lose his priestly office). Nor could any person who had ever done public penance be ordained.[7] Yet the severity of these penalties could forestall denunciations: a person who incriminated a cleric had to be ready to assume the heavy responsibility of destroying a man's career.

The church's fear of scandal could thus result in discretion detrimental to a priest's soul. But whatever offense was kept from public awareness did not undermine the efficacy of his ministry. True, in the fourth and fifth centuries, a group known as the Donatists maintained that any sacrament performed by a priest guilty of a mortal sin was invalid. This movement, however, was trounced by Augustine of Hippo (d. 430), who argued that the sacraments remained undefiled by a minister's personal demerits.[8] There are sound reasons why the Donatist position was pronounced heretical: consider the spiritual paranoia that would ensue if baptisms were invalidated by the secret sin of the officiating priest. Yet in condemning the Donatists, the church countenanced the possibility of the priest as secret sinner, moldering in his own private hell yet with his priestly power intact.

Beginning in the sixth century, a new path opened up for the private expiation of sins. The ancient practice of public penance gradually gave way to private confession by an individual to a priest, a tradition spreading from monastic communities in the British Isles to continental Europe. In a letter of 853, Hrabanus Maurus, archbishop of Mainz, a city in modern Germany, presents this form of confession as the preferred option for criminal priests: "it seems to me that those caught publicly in perjury, theft, fornication, or other crimes of this sort should, according to the canons, fall from their rank because this would create a scandal; those whose crimes are hidden can acknowledge [them] through secret confession ... with a priest present to assign penance; through fasts, vigils, alms and sacred prayers, these people might hope for pardon from God, with their rank preserved."[9] Clearly Rabanus believed that private confession could do double duty for a sin that was also a crime – at least for the clergy. In the ninth century, most clerics agreed with this view.

As the church became increasingly preoccupied with its corporate identity and jealous for its good name, it was anxious to dress this developing policy on scandal in as much authority as possible. Authority meant antiquity. So we also find a prescription for contending with a priest's secret sin in a canon (church law) attributed to the fourth-century Council of Gangra but really part of the ninth-century Pseudo-Isidorean Decretals, a set of forgeries upon which many far-reaching claims for clerical authority are ultimately based. This text deals harshly with a fornicating priest. It assigns the offender a series of tapering fasts that last 13 years and stipulates that all the while he wear sackcloth and implore God's mercy. During this marathon of penance, he "should not go out in public lest the flock of the faithful suffer scandal; nor ought the priest to repent publicly just like a layperson."[10] These canons were included in the *Decretum*, the authoritative collection of church law compiled by the twelfth-century jurist, Gratian.

In short, public penance was the province of the laity. For clergy, the dread of scandal, and the private remedy of confession, drew a curtain of silence over vice, especially sexual. The dangers of this expedience are symbolized in a late eleventh-century edifying tale (*exemplum*) recorded by Goscelin of St. Bertin. The story, ostensibly demonstrating the devil's attacks on the holy and God's mercy on the truly penitent, concerns a holy hermit named Alexander. A demon disguised as a monk kidnaps a princess and entrusts her to Alexander's care.[11] The hermit raises the child, only later to seduce and impregnate her. Alexander's demonic friend convinces him to murder the girl, arguing that a single murder is preferable to the scandal from the fall of someone reputed to be so holy. This demonic monk, "that excellent teacher of perdition," helps bury the girl.

This pastiche of lust, sin, and crime is finally put to rights: Alexander's hands become stuck in a tree for some 15 years, a miracle that facilitates his penance. He confesses his offense to a king who was passing through the forest on a hunt. Realizing that the murdered girl must be his daughter, the king exhumes the body and discovers it miraculously intact. The fallen hermit is released with a touch of the holy cadaver's uncorrupted finger and forgiven by the king. The two men then build a monastery in the girl's honor.

This story folds sin and crime into a unified offense expiated through private penance. The fact that the king happens to be the girl's father yet is unbothered by the revelation of Alexander's dark deed suggests that both justice and kinship yield before the "benefit of clergy" – a legal provision exempting clerics from secular courts that was bitterly contested by public authorities. Equally unsettling is the story's focus on Alexander to the detriment of the girl he seduces. This nameless woman is a mere instrument for the hermit's spiritual odyssey, providing opportunities for his temptation, sin, repentance, and absolution. She even has to die to fulfill this role. Yet her incorrupt body and its ability to generate a miracle point to a posthumous reward: her restored purity and perhaps sainthood.

Clerics seducing clerics

The experience of Goscelin's near-contemporary, Peter Damian, demonstrates how apprehension over scandal was also expressed on a corporate level, where any attempt to critique or reform the clergy's behavior was seen to constitute a worse scandal than the offenses critiqued. In 1049, Damian addressed a treatise, *The Book of Gomorrah* to Pope Leo IX, in which he attacked what he perceived as scandalous same-sex relations that he claimed were rife among clergy. According to Damian, the church punished anal intercourse (sodomy) by the clergy with deposition, but it ignored less grievous forms of intimacy like mutual masturbation. His treatise appeals for the broader sanctioning of such behavior, including penalties as harsh as deposition. Damian anticipated opposition, as is apparent in his Afterword: "He [who] accuses me of being an informer and delator [denouncer] of my brother's crime, let him be aware that I seek with all my being the favor of the Judge of conscience. ... Who am I, when I see this pestilential practice flourishing in the priesthood to be a murderer of another's soul, by daring to repress my criticism? ... I should become responsible for another's crime."[12] In short, by exposing such sins Damian was, in his own way, acting as his brother's keeper, while saving his own soul.

The political context for Damian's intervention was the eleventh-century reform of the church. During this period, the clergy separated itself once and for all from the laity, with clerical celibacy one of the most prominent dividing lines. The case against clerical marriage was made vigorously, sometimes involving physical violence against married priests and their families. And yet, this reforming climate was far from receptive to Damian's charges. With the exception of Damian, the reformers had one sexual misdemeanor on their minds: clerical marriage. Unlike same-sex relations, such marriages could pose material threats to the church's integrity. Clerical families divided the priest's loyalty to the church, which relations with another cleric might, arguably, consolidate. Furthermore, clerical marriage produced children who might claim their father's property – the church's property. Haunting some reformers, too, was that clerical offspring might constitute a potential priestly caste.

The kind of dangerous liaisons Damian was targeting could not compete with these concerns. The pope thanked him for his efforts, agreeing that sodomy should be punished by deposition, but leaving everything else much as it was.[13] Leo's successor, Alexander II, was apparently more sensitive to the treatise's potential for scandal. Damian complains to a friend that Alexander borrowed one of his works, allegedly to make a copy, but refused to return it.[14] In all likelihood the text was *The Book of Gomorrah*.

Some scholars are reluctant to take Damian's critique literally, suggesting, for instance, that his invocation of sodomy was a rhetorical device. But the fact that "the clerical vice" came to be a euphemism for homosexual relations suggests otherwise. Yet Damian remains a solitary whistle blower. Modern scholars have reviled *The Book of Gomorrah* as a homophobic performance, which it clearly is. Still, what is brave about the book is that it is an insider's view; Damian broke ranks with the clergy and cast a harsh light on their hypocrisy. What is cowardly, though, is also that it is an insider's view; Damian fails to break ranks with the clergy by prioritizing the safety of the laity. At no time does he show interest in the impact that predatory seducers, hiding behind a commitment to chastity, might have on their spiritual charges.

Damian did show concern about the exploitation of younger clerical subordinates, however, which he presented as pervasive among the clergy. Yet while there is much evidence (for instance, records of bastard children) for breaches of clerical celibacy with concubines, documentation of clerics preying upon minors is rare. Instead, we must rely on innuendo, as in an anecdote related by Walter Map (d. *c.* 1208–10). Walter describes how he once heard a Cistercian abbot recounting miracles performed by Bernard of Clairvaux, the order's superstar. Among them was a tale of a failed miracle. According to the abbot, a father besought Bernard to save his ailing son, but when Bernard arrived the boy was dead. Seemingly undaunted, Bernard prostrated himself upon the boy's body, prayed at length, and then got up. "But the boy," the abbot reported, "did not get up; he lay there dead." Upon hearing this story, Walter quipped: "[Bernard] was the most unlucky of monks … I have heard before now of a monk throwing himself upon a boy, but always, when the monk got up, the boy promptly got up too."[15] The abbot was understandably chagrined.

Walter's anecdote indicts Bernard, the Cistercians, and the regular clergy (clergy who belong to monastic orders) in one swoop. But it also tacitly suggests the ongoing abuse of children in monasteries, whether boys sent for schooling or those offered by parents as future monks. The dearth of explicit evidence for such abuse comes as no surprise. If the incident was kept private, a cleric could simply avail himself of sacramental confession, a practice which produced no written record. Furthermore, the concept of "reserved sin" that arose in the high middle ages obscures the documentary trail for such offenses. A "reserved sin" was one sufficiently serious to require the intervention of a higher authority, often the bishop. The gravest sins were reserved for the papal penitentiary, and presumably many clerical sexual irregularities found their way there. Still today, the Vatican papal penitentiary remains closed to public scrutiny.

One social environment where we can look for sexual exploitation of the young by clergy is the university. Attended by many students who were minors (under age 14), medieval universities were clerical institutions; both masters (professors) and students were clerics. Universities had their own courts and jails. Yet even these institutions, from which one might expect decent records, withhold on such matters as sexual abuse. A singular case in the Register of Merton College, Oxford, suggests why. On 21 July 1492 Richard Edmund, Bachelor of Arts and Fellow of the College, was accused of "sins against nature." The list of charges against him included:

(1) Incit[ing] and provok[ing] various and different youths to the sin against nature ... unto the greatest peril of your soul and the immense scandal of our college.

(2) Visit[ing] suspect spots within the university ... [where] you are particularly suspected of unchaste behavior in peril of your conscience and the greatest scandal to our house.

(3) Indulg[ing] in nocturnal prowling within the university to the scandal of the college and you plotted and incited others to do this with you.

(4) Often laying outside the college suspiciously unto the great scandal and infamy of the college.

Edmund was asked to write down the offenses of which he was guilty. He was, however, encouraged to take two or three days to deliberate, since admitting to the first article would result in automatic expulsion. Edmund claimed he did not want a deferment but still pondered the articles at length. Finally, in the presence of the warden and assorted masters, he wrote "Yes" beside the first, most grievous charge, and "No" beside the others. The warden sent the other masters out of the room and asked Edmund who introduced him to this sin. Edmund answered that it was someone dead but whom the warden had known well. The warden asked Edmund how often he had indulged in that "worst crime." "With greater frequency of late," Edmund replied.

The warden then called back the witnesses to report "secretly" on what he had learned. He wished to take counsel as to how to "preserve the honor of the said bachelor." Soon after the meeting, however, it came to the warden's attention that Edmund had "begun to excuse himself over the article concerning the sin against nature, claiming that the warden and the other witnesses had lied. He denied the crime entirely and all the other things that he had conceded earlier." Disturbed by the rumor, the warden gathered six senior masters to assist him, as required by statute, and summoned Edmund, who again denied the charge. Asked why he had written "Yes," Edmund claimed he had been informed that the warden already had enough witnesses for conviction. After much back and forth, with Edmund confessing then denying, one boy whom he had "induced to the said sin" agreed to testify. The masters thereupon unanimously agreed to expel Edmund: "we concede to you the favor of remaining until Christmas, for the honor of the college; but after that we expel you from our college on account of your demerits which were sufficiently proved by the college in our presence. And we declare you are expelled in perpetuity." Edmund then sought grace on his knees, again confessing to the first article and confirming his guilt. He also named four youths whom he had seduced.[16]

The process was scrupulous, deliberate and, perhaps most important from the college's perspective, discreet. Indeed, the college was so successful in suppressing the scandal that Edmund appears on the list of newly made doctors in the faculty of arts on 12 February 1483 – a mere month and a half after he left Merton.[17] We can assume that Edmund, armed with his doctorate, got a position at a college ignorant of his past – and that he went on to seduce other students.

Predatory pastors and their superiors

The mechanisms described above would not only deflect charges of clerical misconduct but shield defendants from most serious consequences. This reflexive self-protectiveness placed the laity at a disadvantage. Yet as Goscelin's tale of Alexander suggests, the false holy man who preyed upon female followers was ubiquitous in fact and fiction. The virginity of the anchoress Christina of Markyate (d. after 1155) was threatened by a series of clerics, high and low (her first assailant was a bishop).[18] But rebuffing a cleric could lead to other dangers. When a young woman repulsed the sexual overtures of Gervais of Tilbury (fl. c. 1176), she inadvertently revealed that her attachment to virginity was a product of her affiliation with the Cathar heresy. The rejected suitor made sure she was burned. Likewise, Robert Le Bougre (d. after 1239), the first papal inquisitor, attempted to seduce a matron under the cover of sacramental confession. When she resisted, he tried to have her condemned as a heretic.[19]

Peter Damian expressed fear that two clerical partners in sin might desecrate the sacrament by absolving one another.[20] He had not foreseen that confession would itself offer opportunities for clerics to seduce laypeople – the sin of solicitation, as it became known by the early modern period. The occasions for this clerical sin became more frequent as the laity gradually embraced private confession. In 1215, the Fourth Lateran Council in Rome declared it mandatory for every Christian to confess once a year during Easter week. Failure to comply resulted in excommunication. The council stressed (and arguably introduced) the celebrated seal of confession, threatening any loose-lipped priest with perpetual penance in a monastic prison.[21] The stability required by the new discipline heightened the potential for sexual abuse: a penitent had to confess to the same confessor, usually the parish priest, however ineffectual or reprehensible he might be.

The requirement for celibate clergy to listen to sins of sexually active laity was perhaps a bad idea. Not surprisingly, many pastoral authorities were sensitive to the hazards that confession might afford. Raymond of Peñafort (d. 1275) instructed priests to sit across from women confessants and never look them in the eye. Antoninus of Florence (d. 1459) required priests to confess women with witnesses present, to impose limits on the time spent with female confessants, and to make themselves unpleasant by "using harsh and rigid words." John Gerson (d. 1429), Chancellor of the University of Paris, advised that priests might avoid lascivious thoughts by lying cruciform on the floor when hearing an attractive woman's confession. Male religious (monastic) orders were often reluctant to assume pastoral care of religious women because of the potential for sexual temptation.

But what to do when these measures failed and the priest succumbed to temptation? The manner in which he was disciplined depended on who knew about his transgression. By the high middle ages, clerical culture had the benefit of centuries in which to weigh the advantages of secret sin with private atonement against public denunciation and punishment. This discussion was deepened by the casuistry and the interplay of question and answer associated with scholasticism, a form of academic discourse that emerged in the twelfth and thirteenth centuries. The scholastic approach to secret sin is exemplified by Henry of Ghent (d. 1293), a secular master at the University of Paris, one of the greatest scholars of his generation. According to Henry, the secret sin not only suspends the normative operation of church discipline, but potentially undermines the church's responsibility to the laity.

Henry uses the principle of fraternal correction, an obligation stressed in monastic rules, as a probe for exploring the secret sin. He presents the hypothetical case of a monk who secretly knows that a brother has committed a mortal sin. Would it be sinful for him to bypass a private warning and go straight to the offender's superior? Henry's answer is yes. Such a move would mean infamy for the cleric and scandal for the church. But what if the sinner is indifferent to the private warning and refuses to amend his behavior? Henry declares that private admonition would be most effective coming from the offender's superior, a stance that seems to argue for disclosure. He nevertheless cautions against the monk making incriminating revelations, lest the sinner deteriorate "on account of the greater shame, or greater fear of punishment." Indeed, if the would-be-corrector suspects that his warning might backfire, he should bypass fraternal correction altogether and hold his peace.[22]

Henry also entertains the possibility of enlisting help from others aware of the sin – the equivalent to the modern day intervention. If the monk still refuses to amend, Henry at first argues that the offense "ought to be revealed in public. For to do otherwise would be to neglect the health of one's neighbor." He supports this with an analogy from the Augustinian Rule (a code of conduct for hermits supposedly written by Augustine in the fifth century), which likens ignoring a sin to a physician remaining silent about a wound. Yet Henry ultimately rejects any rationale that would urge disclosure. He deems the comparison to the physician unsuitable because "a corporal wound does not bring disgrace as a spiritual wound does." Indeed, Henry portrays the person who is prepared to reveal another's sins not as a potential disciplinarian, but as a traitor. Here he quotes Augustine again: "if your brother were to sin among you, correct him among yourselves. … Why? Because he sinned among you. … Those sins perpetrated in the presence of all ought to be corrected in the presence of all. Those sins perpetrated in secret ought to be corrected in secret." Henry then relates how Augustine volunteers the example of Joseph who, upon realizing Mary was pregnant, did not take vengeance or accuse her. Instead he silently determined to send her back to her family "expecting it to be known to others what he knew."[23]

Henry was not entirely insensible to dangers in the course of inaction he recommends. He writes: "Certain hidden sins … incline to the detriment of the neighbor and the public good, [so] some say that if the delinquent is not corrected by [the prelate] privately, the sin ought to be revealed by his public denunciation." Nevertheless, Henry refutes this view. "But although [this solution is] technically licit, it is not the good of the delinquent which is principally sought, but the public; it does not comply with the precept of fraternal correction in which the good of the delinquent is principally sought."[24] The sinful cleric's benefit thus trumps public safety.

Henry thus creates a world where the sinful cleric's spiritual wellbeing and public good are in conflict – a clash always resolved in the cleric's favor. The similarity between this value system and the behavior of modern-day prelates becomes even more evident when Henry considers another question: What if an abbot learns through confession that a monk assigned to a parish corrupts his parishioners? Must the abbot recall him to the abbey? Henry's position remains unchanged: The confessor is powerless to act upon information received from confession alone. What the abbot hears in confession he hears as God. In his public role of abbot, however, his knowledge is limited to what he can know as a man.

The compartmentalization in this answer was unassailable: The abbot's two personae were theoretically separate and could not pool their information. Henry makes this concession, though. As the secretary of God, the confessor "in secret can have the intention of moving [the penitent] for his salvation and that of others, but in public he ought to have a reason and occasion for moving him without scandal and suspicion."[25] Henry also stipulates that the abbot should not hurry to move the offending cleric, lest he arouse suspicion. Nor was the abbot to warn members of the monastery, to which he sends the monk, of the man's past offenses.

Another question, which Henry considers independently from the secret sin, presents possible obstacles to the abbot's powers to move the monk. What if an abbot presented a monk to the bishop for the care of souls, who then instates the monk in a parish, as standard procedure would dictate? If the abbot recalled the monk to the cloister, should he obey? Or is he under obedience to the bishop who orders him to stay put? Henry answers that the monk must obey the one who has "control over care of souls," in other words, the bishop, though the abbot is doubtless better acquainted with the monk's personal habits.[26] One by one, Henry closes off possible remedies, rendering the field of abuse virtually a closed system in which the perpetrator remains in place.

Henry's code of ethics also made it extremely difficult for lay penitents sexually involved with their confessors to end the relationships. He questions whether a parish priest can absolve a female parishioner with whom he has sinned sexually, and if she is permitted to go to another priest for confession without her former lover's permission. The short answer to the first question is yes: The efficacy of the sacrament remains undiminished, whether or not the priest has reformed. As to the second question, Henry is more tentative: He argues that to seek another confessor contradicts the Fourth Lateran Council's injunction of confessional stability. Yet, he concedes, if the woman fears the priest will solicit sex from her again, she may ask his permission to go to another priest. If he refuses, she may act of her own will. The female penitent is, however, forbidden to reveal any details that might "result in infamy for her own priest."[27]

Needless to say, Henry offers no solution for the cleric who lacks a vocation for chastity. This is clear from Henry's merciless discussion of another hypothetical situation: A man who tries but fails to contain himself sexually and eventually enters a monastery in the hopes that monastic discipline will help. This monk promises himself that if he finds that way of life despicable, he will leave – which happens. Is he bound to return to the monastery, asks Henry? Yes, he concludes, because a vow cannot be conditional. The monk is as bound to monasticism as a husband to the wife he loathes.[28]

Henry's answers illuminate the role theology played in creating and sustaining a safe haven for clerical vice, one as sordid as it was secure, in which the priest and the layperson are perpetually locked in the roles of predator and victim. His perspective on the secret sin was representative of thirteenth-century theologians and their casuistry. One might conclude that this deference to the cleric burdened with a hidden sin struck a mighty blow in favor of the individual. Yet according to the church's corporate logic, each cleric was not just an individual, but a symbol for the entire church. As long as his sin was concealed, it remained the sole property of the clerical perpetrator. The church did its best to keep it that way. Any serious steps to punish the offender were only to be taken if non-clerics knew of the sin. When a cleric's infamy was revealed to the world, the shame belonged to the entire church. The church was prepared to go to great lengths to stave this off.

Past present

Medieval canon law and theology did not die with the dark ages. Gratian's *Decretum* and key supplemental texts continued to be authoritative until 1917, when a new compendium, the *Code of Canon Law*, was introduced. In the Code and a revised version of 1983, the concern over scandal continues to intrude on clerical discipline. Both modern texts maintain that a hidden offense should never be brought to light by public penance; penalties for infractions are lightened, even alleviated, if there is risk of scandal; and judges are encouraged to excuse first-time offenders.[29] Each version of the Code forbids superiors from utilizing knowledge gained through sacramental confession for decisions pertaining to administration or governance – thus eliminating Henry of Ghent's solution for the abbot who, as God's secretary, could look for an opportunity to move his sinful charge.[30]

Certain omissions in the 1983 Code are especially alarming; they provide even surer cover for delinquent clerics. Gone is the laity's obligation to denounce under pain of excommunication any danger to the faith or public good, including solicitation, in confession. No longer is the opportunity for private judicial correction limited to two occasions before the case goes to trial. Summary justice and extra-judicial remedies have disappeared, eroding the bishop's capacity to discipline sinful clerics.[31] The 1983 Code also seems more tolerant of sex crimes. While the 1917 Code declares that priests guilty of grave sexual offenses, such as the corruption of minors, "are suspended, declared infamous, and are deprived of any office, benefice, dignity, responsibility, if they have such, whatsoever, and in more serious cases they are to be deposed," the revised version is more equivocal: "the cleric is to be punished with just penalties, including dismissal from the clerical state if the case warrants."[32] The new directions regarding members of religious orders are murkier still. Although a member of a religious institution must be dismissed for committing murder, assisting in an abortion, or open concubinage, other sexual infractions, including sex with a minor, are negotiable if "the superior judges that dismissal is not entirely necessary and that the correction of the member and restitution of justice and reparation of scandal can be sufficiently assured in some other way."[33]

That the modern church has concealed so many reprehensible crimes for so long is a sad tribute to the ancient policies still underwriting canon law. No rank of church governance is immune from this rampant irresponsibility, as is painfully corroborated by the example of Pope Benedict XVI. In his earlier capacity as Archbishop of Munich and Friesing, Benedict seems to have been complicit in relocating a sex offender to another parish, where the priest went on to abuse other children. Equally disturbing are new revelations about Benedict's 20-year prefecture of the Congregation for the Doctrine of the Faith, the office presently responsible for handling the cases of sexually offending clerics. Far from living up to his reputation as reformer, Benedict, it now appears, did little more than obfuscate and foot-drag. To date, the Vatican has resisted adopting the zero-tolerance policy for abuse promulgated by the American bishops in 2002.

In their quest to explain the church hierarchy's indifference to the laity's suffering, a number of analysts have identified the phenomenon of clericalism: a corporate narcissism that spawns a reflexive sense of entitlement, which in turn justifies the suppression of horrendous scandals. Researchers have also drawn parallels between this behavior and that of multinational corporations such as Enron, whose executives suffer from similar delusions of grandeur and engage in analogous cover-ups. Although arguably the oldest multinational, the church is distinguished from these other corporate structures by at least one important factor: Its response to scandal is hallowed by an ideology others cannot claim. Even directors of the most craven of corporations recognize when they break the law; the church elite, in contrast, uphold a theology of clerical privilege and scandal that has evolved over millennia.

Perhaps a more germane analogy for the church's corporate persona is the military. From ancient times, clerics have referred to themselves as "soldiers of Christ." This self-identification is more than mere rhetoric. Monastic quarters seem to have been modeled upon military barracks. The church has its own law, courts, and discipline, offering striking parallels with military counterparts. The ritual of defrocking priests is probably indebted to military court martial. Most important, the military exists in a similar binary opposition with the civilian world as clergy with laity. Intrinsic to both elite corps is some condescension, even contempt, for the outside world. We need only compare General Stanley McChrystal's injudicious critique of the Obama administration with the modern church's tendency to protect clerics at the expense of laity.

How can change be effected in a culture as enclosed and self-protective as that of the church? A symbolic act such as the resignation of the current pope, however unlikely, would constitute an important assurance of the desire to change. Yet much more is required than symbolic pledges. I believe the only way to break through church elitism is by a massive "laicization" of its hierarchy. This can most effectively be achieved with the abolition of clerical celibacy: the discipline the eleventh-century reformers used to set the clergy above the laity and the deceptive screen behind which clerical predators operate. This solution is not nearly as radical as it sounds. In the early church it was assumed that even bishops would be married, while the Greek Orthodox church still has a married priesthood. In other words, such reform would hearken back to apostolic times rather than representing a revolutionary initiative like the ordination of women. Indeed, the Catholic Church has paved the way for a married clergy by accepting married priests who, opposed to the ordination of women, leave the Anglican/Episcopalian church. And a married clergy is a timely solution: At present, the pool of candidates for the priesthood in Europe and North America is drying up, primarily due to the lack of candidates willing to embrace clerical celibacy. A married clergy would draw from a larger, and hence healthier, pool of candidates. Priests who were parents might also develop a more protective attitude to minors. Finally, if clerical celibacy was no longer the hallmark of the priesthood, the church's fear of sexual scandal would be greatly diminished.

Is it worse to sin out in the open or in secret? The theologian Peter Abelard (d. 1142) raised this intriguing question in his pioneering scholastic work "Yes and No" (*Sic et Non*). He assembled an array of authorities, one set urging the sinfulness of publishing one's sins and the other condemning the hypocrisy of the concealed sin.[34] Abelard envisaged *Sic et Non* as an exercise book for students – it was their task to reconcile these conflicting sources, not his. As the lover of Heloise and a man twice condemned for heresy, Abelard knew a thing or two about scandal. Yet I doubt even this brilliant thinker could have answered so impossible a question. It is a scandal the modern church has the hubris to believe it can.

Notes

1 Biblical passages in English translation are from the Douay-Rheims Bible. This is the modern English translation closest to the Latin "Vulgate" version that predominated in medieval Europe.
2 Pseudo-Cyrillus, *De miraculis Hieronymi* 5, *Patrologia Latina* 22, cols 299–302.
3 Thomas Aquinas, *Summa Theologica* 2a 2ae 43 art.1, resp. AD 4, trans. T. Heath, London: Blackfriars, 1972, Vol. 35, p. 113.
4 John of Freiburg, *Summa confessorum* bk. 2, tit. 1, q. 6, Rome: s.n, 1518, fols 52v–53r.
5 Cyprian, Letter 4, *The Fathers of the Church: St. Cyprian, Letters 1–81*, trans. Sister Rose Bernard Donna, Washington, DC: Catholic University of America, 1964, pp. 10–14.
6 I Nicaea (325) 3, *Decrees of the Ecumenical Councils*, ed. N.P. Tanner, Washington, DC: Georgetown University Press, 1990, Vol. 1: *Nicaea I to Lateran V*, p. 7.
7 *Epistola decretalis papae Siricii* 14, cited in Gratian, *Decretum* Dist. 51 c. 5, *Corpus Iuris Canonici*, ed. A. Friedberg, Leipzig: Bernhard Tauchnitz, 1879, Vol. 1: *Decretum Magistri Gratiani*, cols 204–05.

8 See *The Letters of Petilian, the Donatist* 2.69, in *St. Augustine: The Writings Against the Manichaeans and Against the Donatists*, ed. P. Schaff, Nicene and Post-Nicene Fathers Series 1, Vol. 4, Edinburgh: T & T Clark, 1887; repr. Peabody, MA: Hendrickson Publishers, 2004, p. 547.

9 Gratian, *Decretum* Dist. 50, c. 34, col. 193.

10 Gratian, *Decretum* Dist. 82, c. 5, col. 292.

11 Goscelin, *Liber confortatorius*, trans. W.R. Barnes and R. Hayward, in *Writing the Wilton Women: Goscelin's Legend of Edith and "Liber confortatorius,"* ed. S. Hollis, *et al.*, Turnhout: Brepols, 2004, p. 190.

12 Peter Damian, Epistle 31, *Letters*, trans. O.J. Blum, Vol. 2, Washington, DC: Catholic University of America, 1990, pp. 7–10, 49, 50.

13 See Leo's letter, included as a preface: Damien, *Letters*, Vol. 1, pp. 4–5.

14 Damian, Epistle 156, *Letters*, Vol. 7, p. 80.

15 Walter Map, *De nugis curialium: Courtiers' Trifles*, dist. 1, c. 24, ed. and trans. M.R. James; rev. C.N.L. Brooke and R.A.B. Mynors, Oxford: Clarendon Press, 1983, pp. 80, 81.

16 *Registrum annalium Collegii Mertoniensis 1483–1521*, ed. H.E. Salter, Oxford: Oxford University Press, 1923, p. 62.

17 *Registrum*, p. 169.

18 *The Life of Christina of Markyate: A Twelfth-Century Recluse*, ed. and trans. C. H. Talbot, Oxford: Clarendon Press, 1987, pp. 42–43, 112–19.

19 Ralph of Coggeshall, *Chronicle*, in *Heresies of the High Middle Ages*, ed. and trans. W. Wakefield and A. Evans, New York: Columbia University Press, 1991, pp. 251–52; C.H. Haskins, "Robert le Bougre and the Beginnings of the Inquisition in Northern France," in *Studies in Mediaeval Culture*, Oxford: Clarendon Press, 1929, pp. 193–244.

20 Damian, Epistle 31, *Letters*, pp. 16–18.

21 IV Lateran 21, *Decrees of Ecumenical Councils*, Vol. 1, p. 245.

22 Henry of Ghent, *Quodlibet IX*, ed. R. Macken, in *Henrici de Gandavo opera omnia*, ed. G.A. Wilson, Leuven: Leuven University Press, 1979, Vol. 13, p. 318.

23 Henry of Ghent, *Quodlibet IX*, ed. R. Macken, pp. 314–15, 320.

24 Henry of Ghent, *Quodlibet IX*, ed. R. Macken, pp. 315, 316.

25 Henry, *Quodlibet VIII*, 29, in *Quodlibeta Magistri Goethals a Gandauo doctoris solemnis: Socii Sorbonici: et archidiaconi Tornacensis cum duplici tabella* (Paris: Vaenundantur ab Iodoco Badio Ascensio, 1518; reprt. Louvain: Bibliothèque S.J., 1961), Vol. 2, fol. 337r. (The *Quodlibet* of Henry of Ghent is currently being edited by Leuven University. This text has yet to be edited for the series.)

26 Henry, *Quodlibet IV*, 35, in *Quodlibeta Magistri Goethals*, Vol. 1, fol. 148v.

27 Henry, *Quodlibet IX*, ed. R. Macken, pp. 304–05.

28 Henry, *Quodlibet VIII*, 23, in *Quodlibeta Magistri*, Vol. 2, fols 333r-v.

29 *The 1917 or Pio-Benedictine Code of Canon Law* (hereafter *PB*), trans. E. Peters, San Francisco: Ignatius Press, 2001, 2288, 2290, 2312.2–3; *Code of Canon Law* (hereafter *CC*), trans. Canon Law Society of America, Washington, DC: 1983, 1340, 1344, 1352.

30 *PB* 890; *CC* 984.

31 See *PB* 904, 2368.2, 1935.2, 1949, 2183–85, 2186–88, 2191.1; cf. 2222.2, 2311.

32 *PB* 2359.2; *CC* 1935.2.

33 *CC* 695.1.

34 Abelard, *Sic et Non: A Critical Edition*, 149, ed. B.B. Boyer and R. McKeon, Chicago: University of Chicago Press, 1977, p. 509.

Suggestions for further reading

Medieval asceticism, confession, and penance

Elliott, D., "Women and Confession: From Empowerment to Pathology," in *Gendering the Master Narrative: Women and Power in the Middle Ages,* ed. M. Erler and M. Kowaleski, Ithaca, NY: Cornell University Press, 2003, pp. 31–51.

John Cassian, *Conferences*, trans. B. Ramsey, New York: Paulist Press, 1997.

John Chrysostom, "Instruction and Refutation Directed Against Those Men Cohabiting with Virgins," in E. Clark, *Jerome, Chrysostom, and Friends: Essays and Translations*, New York: Edwin Mellen, 1979, pp. 164–208.

Lea, H.C., *A History of Auricular Confession and Indulgences in the Latin Church*, 3 vols, Philadelphia: Lea Brothers, 1896.

McNeill, J. and Gamer, H. (eds) *Medieval Handbooks of Penance*, New York: Columbia University Press, 1990.

Medieval clerical culture and sexuality

Arnold, J., "The Labour of Continence: Masculinity and Clerical Virginity," in *Medieval Virginities*, ed. A. Bernau, R. Evans, and S. Salih, Toronto: University of Toronto Press, 2003, pp. 102–18.

Barstow, A.L., *Married Priests and Reforming Papacy: The Eleventh-Century Debates*, New York: Edwin Mellen, 1982.

Boswell, J., *Christianity, Social Tolerance, and Homosexuality: Gay People in Western Europe from the Beginning of the Christian Era to the Fourteenth Century*, Chicago: University of Chicago, 1980.

Elliott, D., *Fallen Bodies: Pollution, Sexuality, and Demonology in the Middle Ages*, Philadelphia: University of Pennsylvania, 1999.

Frassetto, M. (ed.) *Medieval Purity and Piety: Essays on Medieval Clerical Celibacy and Religious Reform*, New York: Garland, 1998.

Haliczer, S., *Sexuality in the Confessional: A Sacrament Profaned*, New York: Oxford University Press, 1996.

Karras, R.M., *From Boys to Men: Formations of Masculinity in Late Medieval Europe*, Philadelphia: University of Pennsylvania Press, 2003.

——, "Thomas Aquinas's Chastity Belt: Clerical Masculinity in Medieval Europe," in *Gender and Christianity in Medieval Europe: New Perspectives*, ed. L. Bitel and F. Lifshitz, Philadelphia: University of Pennsylvania, 2008, 52–67.

——, *Sexuality in Medieval Europe: Doing Unto Others*, New York: Routledge, 2005.

Lea, H.C., *A History of Sacerdotal Celibacy in the Christian Church*, 2 vols, New York: MacMillan, 1907.

Leyser, C., "Cities of the Plain: the Rhetoric of Sodomy in Peter Damian's *Book of Gomorrah*," *Romanic Review*, 86, 1995, 191–211.

Müller, W., "Pardons for Sexual Misconduct: Routine and Papal Intervention in the Later Middle Ages," in *The Roman Curia, the Apostolic Penitentiary, and the Partes in the Later Middle Ages*, ed. K. Salonen and C. Krötzl, Rome: Institutum Romanum Finlandiae, 2003, pp. 171–81.

Swanson, R.N., "Angels Incarnate: Clergy and Masculinity from Gregorian Reform to Reformation," in *Masculinity in Medieval Europe*, ed. D.M. Hadley, London: Longman, 1999, pp. 160–77.

Taglia, K., "'On Account of Scandal': Priests, Their Children, and the Ecclesiastical Demand for Celibacy," *Florilegium*, 14, 1995–96, 57–60.

Modern times

Berg, A. (director) "Deliver Us From Evil," 2006 documentary film.

Doyle, T., A.W. Sipe, and P.J. Wall *Sex, Priests, and Secret Codes: The Catholic Church's 2000-Year Paper Trail of Sexual Abuse*, Los Angeles: Volt Press, 2006.

Frawley-O'Dea, M.G., *Perversion of Power: Sexual Abuse in the Catholic Church*, Nashville, TN: Vanderbilt University Press, 2007.

Hidalgo, M.L., *Sexual Abuse and the Culture of Catholicism: How Priests and Nuns Become Perpetrators*, New York: Haworth Press, 2007.

Phipps, W.E., *Clerical Celibacy: The Heritage*, New York: Continuum, 2004.

Podles, L.J., *Sacrilege: Sexual Abuse in the Catholic Church*, Baltimore, MD: Crossland, 2008.

Wills, G., *Structures of Deceit: Papal Sin*, New York: Doubleday, 2001.

8

LABOR

Insights from a medieval monastery

Martha G. Newman

The great inhumanity of capitalism, the economist Paul Krugman has written, is that it treats labor as a commodity, to be calculated and analyzed as if it were analogous to a bushel of apples. "There would be no excuse for an economic system that treats people like objects," he continues, "except that, as Churchill said of democracy, capitalism is the worst system known except all those others that have been tried from time to time."[1] In modern economies, the value ascribed to work is linked to its cost as a commodity and the market value of its products. Yet we feel an unease with the idea of work solely as a commodity; work provides a sense of identity and meaning as well as a paycheck. "What do you want to *be* when you grow up?" we ask our children, associating their careers with their very existence. Both Studs Terkel's interviews from the early 1970s and recent studies in behavioral economics imply that the value and meaning we find in our labor need not have direct correlation with its financial reward.

Whereas we have a language easily at hand to describe workers as commodities, we struggle to find a vocabulary to express the human importance and meaning of our work. The quantitative character of modern economics and management dominates our understanding of work and the conditions of labor. Work tends to be valued according to its pay, despite the inequities of a free market that compensates speculation and entertainment over the production of goods and services, and despite the associated difficulty of evaluating non-paid work, whether volunteer activities or household labor and child-rearing. Campaigns for unionization, for improving the conditions of work, or for instituting a living wage still function within the assumptions of market capitalism; for the most part, they endeavor to modify or regulate the market, but not to undermine it. Even studies of job satisfaction retain the social scientific assumptions of economics and express the intangible in quantitative terms, often analyzing worker opinions so as to further increase productivity. The prevalence of this economic language obscures what are often felt but unarticulated ideas: that our work transforms our bodies, our minds, and our sense of who we are, and that people have the capacity to gain a sense of satisfaction from their labor that cannot be quantified.

The inhumanity of treating people as commodities was central to Karl Marx's nineteenth-century critique of capitalism. Yet Marx was better at identifying the ways in which capitalism alienated workers than he was in describing the ideal integration of a worker with his or her work. In the early twentieth century, Henry Ford's assembly line innovations and the growth of scientific management treated people not just as commodities but as machines: Charlie Chaplin's Little Tramp in the movie *Modern Times* (1936) satirized the dehumanizing characteristics of this assembly line labor. The current conditions of global capitalism have extended such management beyond the assembly line to blur distinctions between blue-collar and white-collar work; as Simon Head details in *The New Ruthless Economy*, call center workers are taped and timed and given scripts to manage their interchanges. Open offices, cubicles, and computer programs that record keystrokes have a similar effect on jobs in the information sector. Even highly paid professionals are not immune; American doctors complain that their schedules are increasingly managed by insurance companies ostensibly concerned about accountability and value. If Studs Terkel interviewed today's workers, could he still find people who articulate their pride and sense of value in their work?

In the contemporary global economy, the older association of work with identity also becomes more difficult. If people are now likely to change jobs numerous times over their lives, what have they grown up to *be*? Similarly, how should we think of the relationship of identity and work when people not only hold multiple jobs sequentially, but often must hold two jobs simultaneously in order to make ends meet? Sadly, one of the places that the association of work with identity is clearest is in the literature about unemployment; people have long noted the effect of lack of work on self-esteem. But can we only talk about the non-quantitative aspects of work when work itself is absent?

If it is difficult in modern societies to resist the quantitative language of productivity, the problem in medieval Europe appears in the inverse. The quantitative measurement of productivity was then in its infancy. In the twelfth and thirteenth centuries, European society gradually transformed from a subsistence economy into a commercial one and began to participate in a world trading system that stretched from the Mediterranean world to China. In this essay, I will explore ideas about work and its relation to human identity suggested in writings from milieux that participated in this changing medieval economy. I do not seek to address the origins of this new commercial economy, nor to examine the beginning of the modern language of economics; others have done that. Nor do I intend to hold medieval Europe up as some pre-capitalist utopia, immune from the inhumanities of the market; medieval society had its own inhumanities. Understanding medieval ideas about work cannot solve the inequities of modern capitalism. But comparing medieval discussions about the value of labor with modern assumptions about work can help us to understand our own attitudes better – and to see the implications of associating work with our identity and sense of self.

The study of work in the middle ages

The study of work in the middle ages has long been dominated by the influence of the German sociologist, Max Weber (d. 1920). Weber used the medieval period as a foil against which he traced the supposed influence of Protestantism on the development of capitalism in the early modern period. Even now, as in Weber's scholarship, the middle ages are still sometimes portrayed as a period that restricted innovation and economic development; according to this view, a suspicion of labor was inherited from the antique world and then augmented by a Christian interpretation of work as punishment for the fall of humankind as narrated in the biblical Book of Genesis. Yet historians of the medieval economy have largely overturned this stereotype by exploring the formation of a commercial economy in late medieval Europe, the development of banking and techniques of investment, and the conditions of work for men and women in craft and trade organizations.

The study of medieval ideas about work has lagged behind these economic histories. By the fourteenth century, we begin to have documents of practice produced by guilds and merchants; from these, medievalists can reconstruct social conditions for both men and women, especially in urban areas. In rare cases, we can even hear the ideas of the people who did the labor. Before the fourteenth century, in contrast, most documents describing work express the perspectives of churchmen and their often prescriptive comments to the laity. Still, scholars have critiqued Weber's portrayal of medieval society, arguing that, as early as the Carolingian period, churchmen began to stress the productivity of labor rather than its value as penance for sin; this intellectual change corresponded with increasing agriculture yields. Such ideas developed further in the twelfth and early thirteenth centuries as theologians began to consider how to compensate urban workers for their production, as merchants began to quantify time, and as technological innovations began to transform natural products.

The relationship between medieval attitudes toward labor and the actual conditions of work, though, remains debated. To illuminate their interaction, I shall look at some accounts of visions and other miracles that monks of the Cistercian order collected and recorded in the last decades of the twelfth century and the early years of the thirteenth, and juxtapose these narratives with Cistercian sermons and theological treatises. The miracle stories appear initially to have been part of the order's oral culture, in which the monks recounted exemplary tales of their illustrious brethren as part of a process of spiritual formation and a way of asserting the special holiness of their communities. Such stories are neither interviews nor ethnographies: Rather, like the Cistercian sermons and treatises, they are didactic documents, intended to present their audiences with a lesson. However, unlike the sermons and treatises, which were mostly composed by abbots, the stories provide a glimpse of Cistercian ideas about the physical labor the monks performed in and for their monastic communities.

There are a number of reasons to study the Cistercians' ideas about work. First, this monastic order developed at a moment in which commercial exchange began to dominate the medieval economy. The first Cistercian abbey of Cîteaux was founded in 1098, and by the time the monks from this community and its affiliated abbeys had formed an order and articulated their regulations, they found themselves positioned to take advantage of the growth in trade and commerce. Although they retained the basic economic assumptions of older forms of European monasticism, in which monks exchanged prayers for donations of property, they modified the means of exploiting this land, substituting their own labor and that of hired workers for the agricultural production of a subject peasantry that typically enjoyed at best limited freedoms. Furthermore, through the Cistercian emphasis on poverty and simplicity in ornamentation, and their communities' location on lands better suited for pasturage than the cultivation of grains, many of these monasteries produced goods such as wool, whose market value created revenues that the monks could then use for further economic development. The monks' skills also enabled technological innovation. These circumstances affected the monasteries' relationship to their land and to their patrons and inserted at least the wealthier Cistercian abbeys into the emerging commercial economy.

Second, Cistercian monasteries created texts written by people who actually did physical labor. This is unusual, not just for the middle ages, but even for more modern periods; more often than not, the people writing and theorizing about work are not laborers themselves. In the middle ages, the widespread concept of a tripartite division of society into "those who pray, those who fight, and those who labor" expressed a real distinction between literate clerics, warrior aristocrats, and the great majority of unlettered peasants and artisans who worked with their hands. One of the distinctive elements of the Cistercians' monastic observances was the requirement that the monks did manual labor. Rival monks often noted and criticized this practice, questioning why the Cistercians curtailed the time spent at prayer and in the performance of the mass in order to harvest grain and cut down trees.

There are important caveats, though, to understanding the Cistercian writings about work as produced by workers. Somewhat paradoxically, the Cistercians' insistence on dividing their days between labor and prayer, rather than defining their prayer as work, led to the creation of distinctions within their monasteries that were based on work. Although all the monks performed some labor, within a few decades of its foundation, the order had established a lay brotherhood composed primarily of illiterate men who spent more time at work and less time at prayer than the monks. These lay brothers, who were celibate and took vows, often ran the monasteries' granges, negotiated sales, and were perhaps responsible for many of the order's technological innovations. The monks who wrote about work were mostly men from elite backgrounds who had voluntarily chosen their ascetic life; their perspectives may well have differed from those of lay brothers whose work was less voluntary yet whose illiteracy meant they had no control over their appearance in written documentation. We should also bear in mind that the monastic houses we are considering were all male; unsurprisingly, the members of these single-sex communities tended not to notice work done by women, even while they sometimes described theoretical differences between male and female labor. Yet such limitations mean their writings express some of the social tensions encapsulated in ideas about the value of labor – a further reason to study the Cistercians. Overall, medieval Cistercian thought about work was noticeably different from our dominant quantitative modes of thought. But it hints at concepts that may help us today gain a clearer picture of the relationship between work and individual identity, our sense of who we are as human beings.

A Cistercian theology of work

Medieval thinkers inherited a triple legacy of ideas about work and its significance. As already mentioned, the first inheritance came from classical antiquity, an era whose authors, generally all members of the social elite, denigrated manual labor in favor of cultured leisure. Interwoven with those classical ideas was the second inheritance: The culture of the Germanic and Celtic peoples who prized both the fighting values of their warriors and the skills of their artisans, especially smiths. This reverence for smiths and artisans received biblical justification in the figure of Tubal-Cain who, according to Genesis, first instructed humans in metalworking (Genesis 4:22). The third inheritance was the ambivalent legacy of ancient and early medieval Christianity, in which the meaning of work was understood through the lens of the Christian interpretation of the Fall. On the one hand, labor resulted from God's cursing of Adam and Eve; women were doomed to the pains of childbirth and men were compelled to toil and sweat to bring from the ground the plants of the field (Genesis 3:16–19). On the other hand, human work could imitate God's work of creation; even before the Fall, God placed Adam in Eden "to till it and keep it" (Genesis 2:15). The New Testament expressed comparable ambivalence: Jesus asked his disciples to compare themselves to the birds of the air and the lilies of the field who neither work nor spin (Matthew 6:25–29 and Luke 12:27), while Paul, in his letters, described himself and the apostles as laborers who, "with toil and labor," work night and day so as not to burden others, because those who do not work should not eat (2 Thessalonians 3:8–10).

Some of the biblical ambiguity subsides with a careful examination of the Latin vocabulary of the Vulgate (the Latin translation of the Bible popular in the middle ages). Latin, like Greek and later European languages, had two distinct words for work. The Vulgate uses forms of *operari* to denote both God's creation and Adam's care for Eden; in contrast, Adam's toil after the expulsion from the Garden is described with forms of the verb *laborare.* The Psalms echo this vocabulary, often clustering together the words for toil, pain, and sweat (*labor, dolor, sudor*). Similarly, when Jesus in the New Testament speaks of working for the food that is eternal, and the disciples ask how to perform the works of God, the words for "work" are all variations of *operari*, whereas passages promising rest to those who work (I Corinthians 15:58, or Matthew 11:28) use variations of *labor. Laborare* thus has connotations of toil, pain, and effort, while *operari* has broader implications, suggesting action, deeds, and mental or spiritual as well as physical endeavor. We find echoes of this distinction in English. In this essay, I use "labor" and "work" interchangeably to describe both employment and those unpaid activities such as childrearing and housekeeping that are connected to maintaining human livelihood. But the English "labor" still retains implications of toil and pain as well as designating work in economic terms, while "work" extends beyond economic activities to invoke scientific and theological concepts of energy, force, and action.

The Latin vocabulary of Cistercian authors follows the usage in the Vulgate. In the writings of the Cistercian abbot, Bernard of Clairvaux, variations of *operari* commonly refer to the actions of God and the Holy Spirit or the effect of the virtues. *Labor*, however, often appears with *dolor*, which replicates the language of penitence and suffering in the Psalms. When Bernard employs both *laborare* and *operari*, he frequently distinguishes between earthly toil and the "good works" that encourage or reward such effort. Yet it is important to note that "labor" and related forms carry a considerable range of meanings in Cistercian literature. These terms can designate agricultural work, but they also describe the more general trials and struggles of life on earth, including those of Jesus, whose example the monks sought to imitate. Or they may refer to the effort put into ministry or preaching. The language portraying agricultural labor, whether plowing, hoeing, or pruning, is sometimes used metaphorically to express spiritual endeavors. Thus while the Cistercians stressed manual work as part of their monastic practices, their ideas and language about labor of this kind intertwined with discussions of other aspects of their religious life.

Cistercian monks never formulated a clear rationale for their emphasis on manual labor as part of their monastic life, but some writings indirectly reveal significant aspects of their thought. One of Bernard's earliest letters, for example, defending Cistercian customs to a relative who had left the Cistercians for the rival monastery of Cluny, puts into the mouth of the Cluniac prior the question, "How, truly, is it religion to dig the ground, to cut down trees, to haul manure?"[2] Bernard responds by associating such labor with a monk's other austere practices; with the exhaustion and hunger that comes from work, Bernard argues, his relative could have endured the simple food and scant bedding of Cistercian life. Bernard and other Cistercian abbots placed labor in a familiar dyad that contrasted activity and contemplation: periods of work prepared one for periods of contemplation, and the variation prevented a lack of fervor in either.[3] This position implies that manual labor has no intrinsic worth but is instead a new form of discipline making possible other, more familiar, forms of monastic asceticism.

Yet the inclusion of labor among Cistercian ascetic practices did not in fact mean it was understood to be without its own value. Studies of ideas about work often follow Weber in assuming that medieval Christians generally believed labor, a punishment for sin, to provide no positive benefit to the worker. Over the last decades, medievalists have realized that the extreme ascetic practices of some medieval holy men and women need not be seen as hatred or punishment of the body but rather as their exploration of the possibilities of human physicality; the discipline of asceticism can create the self rather than merely constraining it. The penitential character that medieval Christian thought attributed to labor can be understood in a similar fashion. Although Cistercian authors viewed the labor, sweat, and pain imposed upon Adam and Eve as a punishment and their own work as emulating that penalty, they placed these toils within a Christian theology of redemption; Christ's labor, sweat, and pain held out the possibility for human salvation. Penitential labor, then, disciplined the body, but through this discipline, Cistercians believed, work could produce a reformed human being.

Bernard of Clairvaux articulated these associated ideas in a sermon on the harvest. The sermon begins by stressing the penitential and ascetic quality of physical labor as a reminder to the audience of their exile and sins. During their lives, Bernard argues, his listeners would be afflicted with fasting, with vigils, with labor and arduous tasks, because these were actions of human penitence. Yet such physical acts were not only punishment; the work of the body shaped the work of the mind. Manual labor opened the mind so that it too could "toil in thought" and, through contemplation, suffer penance for human sinfulness.[4] For Bernard and other Cistercian abbots, such labor encompassed more than manual work: It included the toil and suffering of contrition in which a monk labored by meditating on the sacrifice of Jesus.[5]

Central to Bernard's understanding of this penitential labor was its voluntary character. In a sermon for Good Friday, Bernard divides people who "endured toil and pain" into three categories: Those who toil out of necessity, those who do so in order to satisfy their desires, and those who do so out of good will. Neither those who toil out of necessity nor those who toil to enjoy the products of their labor conform to "the image of the Son of God"; only those who choose a life of poverty and abandon all things to follow Christ can conform themselves to Jesus' labor and pain.[6] Bernard's praise of voluntary labor and critique of both necessary and productive work were closely allied with the Cistercians' ideas about conversion to monastic life. Cistercian monasteries refused to educate young children or accept them as monks offered by their parents; only adults were admitted to these communities. They viewed the decision to become a monk as the first step in learning to reform and discipline the will. Bernard was not alone among Cistercian writers in his scorn of necessary labor; the English abbot, Aelred of Rievalux, also distinguished the voluntary work of monks from the "curse" of the peasants.[7] Similarly, in much Cistercian thought, the voluntary character of monks' labor and pain separated their penitential actions from the labor not only of peasants but also of women who endured toil, sweat, and the pain of childbearing out of a necessity imposed by their social status and their sex.

Cistercian theological texts thus present the manual labor of the monks within a complex association of ideas and behaviors pertaining to penance. The monastic authors linked the effort of work with sweat and pain, and so with the punishment imposed on humans after the Fall; but at the same time, they valued such penitential behaviors as a way to reform human nature. For Cistercian theologians, it was important that these penitential acts were voluntary; unlike women who had to endure the pain of childbirth, or peasants who had to endure the effort and sweat of agricultural work, the monks chose a life of effort, sweat, and pain, and their voluntary behavior conformed, in their view, to the example of Christ's willing sacrifice. While the monks' work may have contributed to the economic well being of their communities, those Cistercians who wrote about it emphasized its contribution to the production of a reformed person. They valued labor not for the goods it produced but for its internal effect on the worker; like other penitential acts, it enabled the reform of the human self.

Cistercians at work: their stories

Sermons and treatises depict the theological ideas that Cistercian abbots associated with work and labor, but they are not the only texts in which the monks expressed their conceptions about work. Starting in the 1170s, the monks began to collect stories of visions and other miraculous experiences, some of which portrayed the monks at work. The collections were compiled at least a generation after the composition of most of the theological texts discussed above, and they appear to have recorded stories in oral circulation among Cistercian communities. In contrast to the theological texts, these stories do not combine the spiritual value of physical work with other forms of penitential labor but stress the importance of work in and of itself. Exactly how to understand this difference, however, is unclear. It might reflect the oft-noted observation that those who actually do physical work value it more highly than those who write about it; the narrators of the stories are monks who labored in the fields. Although still often expressing ideals, the particular characteristics of these stories and their variations show how these monks may have interpreted theological ideas and put them into practice. They also suggest that, over time, the monks broadened their understanding of the kinds of physical work that had spiritual value.

One oft-recounted story features the Virgin Mary visiting the Cistercian monastery of Clairvaux while the community worked to bring in the harvest. The tale occurs in three miracle collections, each containing a different version. The earliest two renderings appear in collections assembled in the 1170s. Offering dissimilar attitudes toward work, they suggest that these ideas were very much in flux. In one version, Mary's visitation takes place as the monks sweat and toil in the field. One monk, not working, watches three women walk among the laborers as if they were overseers, sent by their lord to inspect the harvest and guard against fraud. The monk challenges the women, only to learn that they are Mary, Elizabeth, and Mary Magdalene. According to the author of this version, the three women are indeed overseers intending to prevent fraudulent labor; they have come not because they suspect theft of the produce, but because they wish to inspect the monks working and to help guard these laborers against temptations [8] The story reinforces the penitential character of the Cistercians' work. Mary, as overseer, is less concerned about the crops than the monks' thoughts and intentions. Yet the tale also implies an unease with their manual labor. The author offers little explanation of why the labor has value other than mentioning that it was prescribed in the Benedictine Rule (the sixth-century code of monastic life that became normative in most medieval monasteries); and he hints that such work might contain spiritual dangers. His concern about hidden temptations suggests that some monks may have grumbled about their labor, perhaps especially when it was work their aristocratic culture deemed degrading. This is the only story about manual labor in this collection.

In a collection assembled by Herbert of Clairvaux also in the 1170s, the story of Mary's visitation appears alongside other tales about work. Rather than providing an implicit warning, this version instead confirms the holiness of the community and its labor. The monk who watches the arrival of Mary and her companions sees more than just the women: He can also discern how the monks' work shapes their interior disposition. "With great love in his soul," writes the author, "[the monk] began to consider the harvesters with both reflection and admiration, because clearly so many wise, noble, and elegant men, at that very moment, exposed themselves to labor and toil for the love of Christ. They undertook this labor in the boiling heat of the sun with such eagerness that it was as if they plucked the most sweet and fragrant apples in a garden of delights, or as if they feasted at a table full of the most elegant and delicious dishes."[9] Only then does the monk see the three women coming across the field; he watches them enter the cloister, spreading their grace among the monks and lay brothers. Mary's visitation, in this instance, offers a reward rather than spiritual protection. The story gives little sense that labor might provoke grumbling and discontent; rather, it celebrates the eager toil that the monks performed in love of Christ.

In both versions of the story, the visionary monk stands apart from those working, perhaps suggesting unease about reconciling visionary experience with practical labor. Yet a slightly later rendering of the tale in a collection by a German Cistercian, Engelhard of Langheim, portrays the visionary as himself working; he was the cellarer, the monastic official responsible for a monastery's economic welfare, and the one who often supervised the lay brothers.[10] In this case, the cellarer has his vision not during a day of hot and sweaty work but at its end, after he has paid the hired laborers, put the tools away, and entered the monastery. Not wanting to disturb his brothers who are already asleep in their dormitory, he rests in the cloister. There he sees Mary, holding a vase to her nose. As in the other accounts, the monk asks why women are in the monastery; Mary explains that she has spent the day visiting her monks in the field and collecting their sweat in her vase. "It has the most pleasant smell for me, and it is certainly worthy for my son and will return the highest reward," she tells the cellarer. But he is concerned about this reward. "How great is our labor for you which is not so much done out of voluntary devotion as out of the necessity of poverty?" he asks. Mary responds by quoting the Benedictine Rule: "Have you not heard that what is voluntary receives a penalty and duty earns the reward?" She further explains: "If duty receives the reward, what is voluntary now receives a part. But whether out of necessity or whether voluntary, what you do is mine. I claim all of your work for myself, and what I receive, I remunerate." Mary then disappears and the cellarer, "refreshed in hope, comforted in faith, and willing to work," falls asleep. When he recounts his vision to the rest of his community the next day, they are all aroused to work and begin to "toil and sweat" not in order to fill their baskets with grain but to allow Mary to fill her vase.

As in the other renditions of this vision, Engelhard's account considers the relationship between the monks' labor and their motivations. Especially noteworthy in Engelhard's telling of the story, however, is its reinterpretation of Bernard of

Clairvaux's ideas about voluntary and necessary labor. Whereas Bernard emphasized the value of voluntary labor as imitating the voluntary sacrifice of Christ, Engelhard reversed this position and stressed the value of work performed out of need even more than work chosen voluntarily. By attributing a line from the Benedictine Rule to Mary, he not only gave his position authority, but he also asked his monks to consider their relationship to the Rule and the various possible interpretations of "necessity" (*necessitas*) and "will" (*voluntas*). Engelhard's account also shows greater recognition than the other versions of the economic value of labor; the cellarer's story acknowledged the monastery's poverty, recognized the existence of hired laborers, and noted the need to care for the community's tools. Since the monks' work seemed to Engelhard's protagonist to be less voluntary than necessary, he was naturally concerned about its spiritual value. Mary's response affirms that she ultimately rewarded both forms of labor.

Engelhard's version of this story suggests a new Cistercian understanding of the value of labor that moves beyond voluntary asceticism. But his idea of work remains disconnected from the production of commodities; even though his protagonist was the cellarer, responsible for the monastery's economic welfare, the vision stresses the production of sweat as an offering to Mary and Jesus. The monks' work disciplined their bodies and shaped their thoughts. It is not clear if Engelhard's concept of work influenced his Cistercian contemporaries, yet it is akin to the ideas expressed by early thirteenth-century scholastics who began to find value in the involuntary labor of peasants.

Although Engelhard valued necessary as well as voluntary labor, his story still illustrates the perspective of the literate members of the monastery. It is more difficult to access the attitudes of the Cistercians' illiterate lay brothers toward their work. While regarded as full members of Cistercian communities, these brothers were clearly marked in the monastic customs as subordinate to the monks. Their labor – whether in agriculture, in artisanal crafts, or in trade – freed the monks for more extensive hours of prayer.

Starting around 1168, a series of lay brother revolts struck Cistercian monasteries. Stories about these uprisings, again written by monks, suggest that some abbots precipitated the problems by trying to instate customs that underscored the lay brothers' subordinate status. At the monastery of Schönau, for instance, a new abbot refused to continue his predecessor's custom of giving the lay brothers new shoes when he supplied shoes to the monks, while other lay brothers rebelled because their abbots refused them alcohol. Yet even if these revolts were triggered by the tightening of previously relaxed regulations, complaints about lack of shoes or alcohol may only have been the flashpoint for broader discontent; as the lay brothers at Schönau plotted to sneak into the monks' dormitory to slash the monks' new shoes, they complained that their "arduous and harsh work was intolerable."[11] They, of course, needed the shoes more than the monks.

The monks' stories about the lay brothers nonetheless sought to depict the spiritual value of the lay brothers' work. One story concerns a plowman who sees Jesus walking next to him, holding the whip and pole used to prod the oxen, while another describes a lay brother who succeeds in bringing ten buffalo across the Alps from Italy thanks to the efficacy of his prayers to St. Bernard of Clairvaux. The biography of the saintly lay brother Arnulf, from the abbey of Villers, furthers this message: the monk who wrote about Arnulf's life described him as using the agricultural implements associated with his work to develop a distinctive lay brother spirituality that emphasized his identification with the patience and obedience of Jesus on the cross.[12] What remains unclear in all these stories, though, is the extent to which they illumine lay brothers' own attitudes and experiences. Perhaps such tales, with their implied lessons about obedience and humility, only become popular in the last decades of the twelfth century as a way for the monks to try to quell lay brothers' discontent.

Conclusion

Medieval monasteries were economic units as well as places of prayer. Scholars have long recognized their importance in fostering technology and developing a productive economy. The Cistercians, especially, were early participants in Europe's new commercial economy, selling livestock and wool, and their monasteries became industrial workshops. They have sometimes been seen as enacting a Weberian Puritan paradox; their ascetic ideas encouraged the production of surpluses they then used for technological innovation and further economic development. Yet their ideas about work did not stress the importance of productivity, nor did they express the value of work in a quantitative fashion. Instead, medieval Cistercians understood the worth of manual labor within a Christian penitential framework, in which such work was both God's punishment for Adam and Eve's disobedience and an imitation of Christ's sacrifice. Yet such penance also reformed the human self by shaping both actions and inner intentions. At first these monks valued work primarily as an act of voluntary asceticism, but their stories and theological writings suggest that gradually they came to esteem necessary labor as well – a change that may reflect the monks' actual experience of economic conditions in their communities.

These medieval monastic writings remind us, then, that it is possible to separate the effort of working from the production of goods and services, and that this effort can itself have value in shaping who we are. Echoes of this concept of work still resonate in some modern critiques of capitalism. Pope John Paul II's encyclical *Laborem exercens* issued in 1981, for example, underscores how work creates the human subject and criticizes both capitalism and collectivist economic systems for losing sight of the value of the individual and his or her labor.[13] The pope's ideas, rooted in Catholic theology, reflect a long Catholic tradition of advocacy for workers' rights and a living wage – principles that have been incorporated into modern labor movements. Like Bernard of Clairvaux, John Paul II viewed the sweat and toil of human labor as part of the redemptive process by which a person conforms to the sacrifice of Christ. As with the Cistercians, the penitential character of human labor is not merely punishment for sin, but an opportunity to explore the potential in human existence.

It is hardly surprising that contemporary papal teachings about work draw on medieval monastic ideas about human labor. But can these monastic insights be transposed into a secular key? It seems that, as we search for ways to describe the value of labor outside of the quantified paradigms of production and consumption, we quickly slip into religious language. A series of modern heterodox economists borrow religious concepts without necessarily advocating a particular religion. Thus in the 1970s, E.F. Schumacher drew on Buddhist ideas to advocate work as a means of forming human character rather than of producing goods that satisfy human wants. More recently, Otto Scharmer has drawn on insights from mystical practice to explore the link between work and self-formation. Similarly, those who suggest that in local and artisanal work we can find an antidote to the alienating conditions of the modern workplace also tend to express the value of this work in language with religious underpinnings. For some reason, motorcycle repair seems especially to elicit such meditations, whether the consideration of a "metaphysics of value" in *Zen and the Art of Motorcycle Maintenance,* or the espousal of a virtue ethics in the more recent *Shop Class as Soulcraft.* Neither Robert Pirsig nor Matthew Crawford use the Cistercian language that describes labor as an imitation of Christ, but they still consider the ways that the contemplation and ascetic practice connected with work can help shape the self and form identity.

If understanding Cistercian ideas about work can help us see our modern forms of ascetic and contemplative practice, they also can help us observe the tensions in these modern meditations on labor and identity. Just as the Cistercian stories about work were written by those who had voluntarily chosen monastic life, so modern discussions of the contemplative and ascetic value of physical work tend to be written by those with means, the education, and the connections to choose a life of manual labor and to supplement it with second careers as authors. We do not know whether the lay brothers accepted the Cistercian monks' ideas about the value of their work or whether they saw the monks' stories as a disguise intended to cloak the lay brothers' exploitation. Similarly, it is not always evident today when language stressing the value of work serves to camouflage unfair conditions of labor, justifying exploitation by emphasizing the non-pecuniary benefits of work. Karl Marx, of course, saw this quite clearly. Describing religion as "the sigh of the oppressed creature, the heart of a heartless world, and the soul of soulless conditions," he recognized that religious ideas help soften hardship, but he also underlined that only with the abolition of such ideas could working people fully understand the actual conditions of their labor. Such debates still occur in modern labor history though with less attention to the explicit role of religion. For example, did adopting Japanese production practices in a General Motors auto plant in Freemont California provide a more satisfying (and more efficient) work environment, or did it just soften and disguise the differences in power between management and workers?

The medieval Cistercians developed their ideas about work on the cusp of an economic transformation, as Europe slowly shifted from subsistence agriculture to a commercial economy. Their ideas reflected traditional conceptions of the penitential qualities of work, but they modified these concepts to underline its positive value as well. They even began to suggest that such value could be found not only in the work of those who had the freedom to choose, but also in the work of those who had no choice. We seem today to be in the midst of another such transformation, in which the global spread of capital and information is altering the way we work. Many modern economists have noted the increased social cleavages caused by these changes: the division is no longer between professionals and blue collar workers, but rather between those people who can work within a specialized and localized environment – whether motorcycle repairmen or professionals with creative jobs – and those service workers and routine production workers who are at the mercy of an international market for labor. It is not surprising that recent considerations of the relation of work and identity call for work that is more local, more personal, and more autonomous, and posit the value of work as a kind of secular religion. But must this be a luxury only reserved for the few lucky enough to be able to choose the conditions under which they work? How do we create jobs for modern service workers and those doing routine production that recognize that workers are not only commodities and that their labor, too, shapes who they are? Medieval monastic concepts of labor cannot directly solve our contemporary problems, but they can help us explore the value of work outside of the production and consumption of commodities, and consider the ways that the effort of labor shapes both our bodies and our minds.

Notes

1 P. Krugman, *The Accidental Theorist and Other Dispatches from the Dismal Science*, New York: W.W. Norton, 1999, p. 1.
2 Bernard of Clairvaux, Letter 1.4, *Sancti Bernardi opera*, 8 vols, eds J. Leclercq, C.H. Talbot, and H.M. Rochais, Rome: Editiones Cistercienses, 1957–77, Vol. 7, p. 4.
3 Bernard of Clairvaux, *Sermones de diversis* 3.4, *Sancti Bernardi opera*, Vol. 6.1, p. 89; Gilbert of Hoyland, *Sermones in Canticum Salomonis* 23.3, *Patrologia Latina* (hereafter PL) 184, cols 120–21.
4 Bernard of Clairvaux, *Sermones de diversis* 37, *Sancti Bernardi opera*, Vol. 5, pp. 222–23.
5 See Guerric d'Igny, *De resurrectione Domini* 3.4, in *Sermons*, 2 volumes, *Sources Chrétiennes* (hereafter Vol. 202) 166, 202, ed. J. Morson and H. Costello, trans. into French by P. Deseille, Paris: Sources Chrétiennes, 1970–73, SC 202, p. 254; Isaac of Stella, *Sermo L in Naivitate Petri et Pauli*, PL 194, col. 1861.
6 Bernard of Clairvaux, *In feria IV hebdomadae sanctae, sermo de passione Domini* 12, *Sancti Bernardi opera*, Vol. 5, p. 65.
7 Aelred of Rievaulx, *Speculum caritatis* 2, in *Aelredi Rievallensis opera omnia I: Opera ascetica*, eds A. Hoste, C.H. Talbot, R.V. Plaetse, *Corpus Christianorum Continuatio Mediaevalis* (hereafter *CCCM*) 1, Turnholt: Brepols: 1971, p. 83.
8 *Collectaneum exemplorum et visionum Clarevallense e codice Trecensi 946*, ed. O. Legendre, *CCCM* 208, Turnhout: Brepols, 2005, pp. 289–90.
9 Herbert of Clairvaux, *De miraculis* 1.1, PL 185, col. 1273.
10 Munich, Bayerische Staatsbibliothek München, Ms. clm 13097 [Rat. civ. 97] fols 145v–146r.
11 Conrad of Eberbach, *Exordium magnum Cisterciense* 5.10. ed. B. Griesser, Rome: Editiones Cistercienses, 1961, pp. 292–98.
12 Goswin of Bossut, "The Life of Arnulf, Lay Brother of Villers," in *Send Me God: The lives of Ida the Compassionate of Nivelles, nun of la Ramée, Arnulf, lay brother of Villers, and Abundus, monk of Villers*, trans. M. Cawley, Turnhout: Brepols, 2003, pp. 129–51.

13 John Paul II, *Laborem exercens*. Online. Available HTTP: <www.vatican.va/holy_father/john_paul_ii/encyclicals/documents/hf_jp-ii_enc_14091981_laborem-exercens_en.html> (accessed 6 February 2011).

Suggestions for further reading

Cistercian spirituality and concepts of work

Bouchard, C.B., *Holy Entrepreneurs: Cistercians, Knights, and Economic Exchange in Twelfth-Century Burgundy*, Ithaca, NY: Cornell University Press, 1991.

Bynum, C.W., *Holy Feast and Holy Fast: The Religious Significance of Food to Medieval Women*, Berkeley, CA: University of California Press, 1987.

Holdsworth, C., "The Blessing of Work: The Cistercian View," in *Sanctity and Secularity*, ed. D. Baker, Oxford: Oxford University Press, 1973, pp. 59–76.

Newman, M.G., "Crucified by the Virtues: Laybrothers and Women in Thirteenth-Century Cistercian Saints' Lives," in *Gender and Difference in the Middle Ages*, ed. S. Farmer and C. Pasternack, Minneapolis: University of Minnesota Press, 2003, pp. 182–209.

Noell, B., "Expectation and Unrest among Cistercian Lay Brothers in the Twelfth and Thirteenth Centuries," *Journal of Medieval History* 32, 2006, 253–74.

Sullivan, L., "Workers, Policy-Makers, and Labor Ideals in Cistercian Legislation, 1134–1237," *Cîteaux: Commentarii Cistercienses* 40, 1989, 175–99.

The medieval economy and work

Abu-Lughod, J.L., *Before European Hegemony: The World System AD 1250–1350*, New York: Oxford University Press, 1991.

Bennett, J., *Ale, Beer, and Brewsters in England: Women's Work in a Changing World 1300–1600*, New York: Oxford University Press, 1996.

Epstein, S., *Wage Labor and Guilds in Medieval Europe*, Chapel Hill: University of North Carolina Press, 1991.

Farmer, S., *Surviving Poverty in Medieval Paris: Gender, Ideology and the Daily Lives of the Poor*, Ithaca, NY: Cornell University Press, 2002.

Freedman, P., *Images of the Medieval Peasant*, Stanford, CA: Stanford University Press, 1999.

Gimple, J., *The Medieval Machine: The Industrial Revolution of the Middle Ages*, Harmondsworth: Penguin, 1977.

Howell, M., *Women, Production, and Patriarchy in Late Medieval Cities*, Chicago: The University of Chicago Press, 1986.

Hunt, E., and J. Murray, *A History of Business in Medieval Europe 1200–1550*, Cambridge: Cambridge University Press, 1999.

LeGoff, J., *Time, Work and Culture in the Middle Ages*, trans. A. Goldhammer, Chicago: University of Chicago Press, 1980.

Little, L., *Religious Poverty and the Profit Economy in Medieval Europe*, Ithaca, NY: Cornell University Press, 1978.

Lopez, R.S., *The Commercial Revolution in the Middle Ages, 950–1350*, Cambridge: Cambridge University Press, 1976; repr. 1998.

Robertson, K., and M. Uebel (eds) *The Middle Ages at Work: Practicing Labor in Late Medieval England*, New York: Palgrave Macmillan, 2004.

Work in contemporary society

Crawford, M., *Shop Class as Soul Craft: An Inquiry into the Value of Work*, New York: Penguin, 2009.

Head, S., *The New Ruthless Economy: Work and Power in the Digital Age*, New York: Oxford University Press, 2003.

Krugman, P., *The Accidental Theorist and Other Dispatches from the Dismal Science*, New York: W.W. Norton, 1999.

Pirsig, R., *Zen and the Art of Motorcycle Maintenance: An Inquiry into Values*, New York: Morrow, 1974.

Reich, R., *The Work of Nations: Preparing Ourselves for Twenty-First Century Capitalism*, New York: Simon and Schuster, 1993.

Scharmer, C.O., *Theory U: Leading from the Future as It Emerges*, San Francisco: Berrett-Koehler Publishers, 2009.

Schumacher, E.F., "Buddhist Economics," in idem, *Small is Beautiful: Economics as if People Mattered*, New York: Harper and Row, 1973, repr. 1989.

Terkel, S., *Working: People Talk About What They Do All Day and How They Feel About What They Do*, New York: Pantheon Books, 1974.

This American Life, 26 March 2010, "403: NUMMI." Online. Available HTTP: <http://www.thisamericanlife.org/radio-archives/episode/403/nummi> (accessed 8 February 2011).

Warr, P., "Psychological Aspects of Employment and Unemployment," *Psychological Medicine* 12, 1982, 7–11.

9

DISABILITY?

Perspectives on bodily difference from the Middle East

Kristina Richardson

> The deaf person is he who does not pity someone painfully afflicted, and the mute person is he who does not open his mouth, though his body yearns to speak.
>
> Shihab al-Din al-Hijazi (d. 1471)

In the combat zones of Iraq, Palestine, Afghanistan, and Pakistan, the bodies of men, women, children, even fetuses have been physically transformed through the ravages of violence. Amputees, physically and psychologically wounded individuals, and people suffering from communicable diseases are numerous. The 2001 film *Kandahar,* by Iranian film director Mohsen Makhmalbaf, artfully conveyed the quiet dependence of male Afghan amputees on prosthetic limbs, depicting the extent to which colonial and postcolonial conflicts have distorted individual lives and bodies. In a scene set at a makeshift Red Cross desert camp, two female Russian aid workers notice that several Afghan men with amputed legs awaiting treatment have taken up their crutches and started walking away from camp. Calling out to them, the women ask where they are going but receive no answer. The director changes the camera angle so we can see what the men see: Prosthetic legs being airdropped by parachute to the camp. The men's faces register expectation, hope, relief, and determination: To acquire a long-awaited prosthesis.

In mainstream US media coverage of wars in the Middle East, the word "Afghanistan" – and more broadly, "the Muslim world" – has commonly appeared in close proximity to the word "medieval," almost invariably in ways that are hostile and disparaging, serving the interests of foreign military intervention. In this essay, I would like to turn the tables, asking what might be *gained* from re-envisioning the "Islamicate middle ages" in the specific field of "disability studies." I want to apply the fundamental question, "what is disability?" to a new geographical orbit encompassing the social, cultural, and political arenas in which Islam was a dominant factor in the medieval centuries, and in doing so, to raise new questions about "disability" itself as a means of capturing human realities. For this reason, the term will often appear in quotation marks. In the first part of this essay, in order to suggest the magnitude and urgency of the issue, I will examine the contemporary Middle East, where the lives of millions continue to be profoundly affected by bodily difference and cultural constructions of "disability" combine with the context of conflict to form a volatile cocktail, frequently endangering the lives and welfare of broader communities. In the second part, I will look at the socially constructed nature of "disability" and the distinct ways in which bodily difference was imagined in the medieval Islamicate world. Finally, we will see how attempts to remove bodily difference from medieval Cairo proved both impossible and undesirable. From this world, I will suggest, we can learn some valuable new perspectives for rethinking the issue in our own society.

Bodily difference, trauma, and suicide bombing

Afghanistan's "disability" crisis predates the coalition invasion that followed the attacks of 11 September 2001, but it has been greatly exacerbated by renewed warfare as well as the uneven access to quality health care. *New York Times* reporters have estimated that in 2008, 10 percent of Afghans were "disabled." The experience has been so totalizing that aid organizations and medical professionals report being overwhelmed by requests for medical assistance and advice. Dost Muhammad Khi-Ree, a semi-paralyzed Afghan emigrant to the United States, has returned to Afghanistan to advocate for victims there, visiting the ministries of health and of social affairs and disabilities, speaking out about making public buildings accessible, particularly health care facilities, and also making the case for introducing Afghan medical workers to American medical knowledge, which he credits for his adaptation to life with a physical disability.[1] Khi-Ree's advocacy efforts take on even greater urgency in light of recent findings by an Afghan pathologist in Kabul named Yusef Yadgari, who has examined the physical remains of hundreds of suicide bombers in Afghanistan. Yadgari has found that a majority – 60 percent – of all suicide attackers were "disabled" at the moment of attack. Some of these individuals were partially blind or leprous, some were cancer patients or amputees. Mental illness could not be evaluated through Dr. Yadgari's autopsy methods, but were such information known, the percentage of "disabled" suicide bombers would probably climb to nearly 80 percent.[2] Yadgari proposes a re-evaluation of approaches to reducing suicide attacks; greater effort should be made to eliminate poverty, to improve the lives of people with disabilities in the broadest sense, and to channel people's sense of empowerment through increased economic opportunity and access to knowledge. Ignorance and poverty constrain individual agency with devastating results. This model, which (as we will see) resonates closely with dominant medieval attitudes, consists mostly in broadening the possibilities for "disabled" lives, be they in terms of aesthetic appreciation or in terms of opportunity and social integration.

Anxieties about people with "disabilities" carrying out suicide attacks have also recently surfaced in Iraq. In mid-February 2008, the Iraqi government voted to enforce an obscure law introduced by Saddam Hussein to remove mentally "disabled" people and mendicants from urban streets. Such a move harks back to policies in thirteenth- to fifteenth-century Egypt of forcibly removing "blighted people" and beggars from Cairo streets, about which I will say more later.[3] Iraqi officials claimed that the susceptibility of mentally ill individuals, particularly disaffected youth, to the persuasive arguments of suicide bombing recruiters poses a real threat to efforts at stabilizing the nation. The example of a child with Down syndrome who detonated a bomb on election day in 2005 is often cited as an extreme example of how mentally "disabled" people and their family members must be protected from the allure of self-sacrifice or sacrifice of one's children.[4] Reports of "disabled" suicide attackers were so widespread that such ideas colored perceptions of suicide bombings. On 1 February 2008, two women strapped bombs to their bodies and detonated them in a crowded animal market in Baghdad, killing approximately 100 people. Reports immediately surfaced that both women had Down syndrome, adduced by examining their faces. Witnesses from US military officers and Iraqi civilians authoritatively corroborated this claim, which international media outlets faithfully reproduced. Only some weeks later were doubts cast on this depiction of the bombers, and the claim ultimately disproved. This incidence of media gullibility served as a cautionary tale about the unreliability of eyewitness accounts, about combat zones' emotionally charged atmospheres that obscure judgment, and about the imprecision of visual medical diagnoses made on severed body parts postmortem. Less acknowledged was that the willingness of military and political authorities to ascribe "disability" to suicide attackers indicated an anxiety founded on real circumstances: such people *could* physically engage in resistance efforts, terrorist acts, and crimes, they could mobilize their "unsightly" or "diseased" bodies in support of a cause, they could be historical actors and not just acted *upon* by medical professionals or charitable institutions. The media occurrence also upended the presumption of disability as a *consequence* of military engagement or a mark of patriotism, for here we saw disability preceding the sacrifice and being inconsequential to the efficacy of the terrorist act.

Marring the body has also been utilized as a means of escape from difficult conditions. In contemporary Afghanistan, photojournalist Stephanie Sinclair has documented Afghan women who have unintentionally survived self-immolation attempts and their communities' responses to such incidents.[5] Sinclair states that many of them had set themselves alight in direct protest of personal circumstances; she circumspectly does not raise the possibility that the women's burns resulted from intentional abuse from husbands or in-laws, though this possibility is strong. In this visually jarring collection of disfigured female bodies, the body functions as a site of protest against private discontents. If these women have indeed set their bodies on fire, then they have sent a resonant message to their own families and communities. Death or physical transformation, even if the latter is unintended, brings deliverance from unbearable situations.

Bodily difference in the contemporary Muslim world has often been the involuntary consequence, as well, of toxic environments. In 2009, rates of neural tube defects in newborns in Fallujah, Iraq, rose 15 times higher than rates just one year earlier.

Neural tube defects can cause infants to have larger than ordinary heads, cardiac and ocular deficiencies, and withered legs. Physicians suspect toxic materials used in battle since the arrival of US-led coalition forces in 2003 have contributed to this severe upturn in disability incidents.[6] The physical realities of those born in Iraq before the 2003 invasion have also changed; not all of this physical suffering is solely attributable to twenty-first-century warfare. Indeed, throughout the Middle East, sustained twentieth-century violence between Israeli and Palestinian fighters, Iraqi and Iranian fighters, US and Iraqi fighters, Taliban and Soviet fighters, and among fighters in the civil wars of Iran, Lebanon, and Iraq have made severe physical injury common in veteran and civilian lives.

Similarly, in the US and the United Kingdom, hundreds of thousands of wounded and "disabled" veterans have returned home, overwhelming the available health services for war veterans. For these men and women, too, medieval classifications of bodies may illuminate some blind spots in our contemporary notions of bodily difference. By consciously rethinking conceptions of wounded and otherwise marked bodies, we – as well as the medical, political, and religious authorities in the Middle East – can tailor new responses.

Imagining bodily difference: a medieval alternative

Modern classifications of the bodies of both human and non-human animals by their differences may feel natural to many of us. However, a brief look at the shifting terminology applied to bodily or psychological difference quickly reminds us of how these concepts are socially constructed, subject – and open – to change. In the southern African nation of Botswana, for instance, a woman who has undergone a hysterectomy or mastectomy is perceived as someone whose bodily integrity and gender are in question; the anthropologist Julie Livingston noted that one man divorced his wife after her hysterectomy because he "didn't want to be married to another man."[7] Our modes of classification often say more, then, about the classifiers than they do about the classified. In English, the development has moved from the outmoded "handicapped," "retarded," and "crippled" to the currently preferred terms "disabled," "physically or cognitively different," or "differently abled." These terms are intended to accord dignity and respect to whomever they are applied, but it is worth dwelling on the modern English term, "disability." The term implies a focus on the body's physical and cognitive limitations in comparison with a supposedly fully able body (disability scholars take issue with the notion that anyone is perfectly able-bodied, or whole, since we all operate within specific limitations). Even when function is restored to a "disabled" body – say through a prosthesis, an assistive device, a service animal, a cane, a crutch, or a wheelchair – a person is still not identified as able-bodied. Some scholars have linked this mode of classification with the rise of neoliberal capitalism, which values bodies for their productive labor (less in the case of women's reproductive labor), privileging the able-bodied as the ultimate citizen.[8]

In the Islamicate world, the dominant terminology has also undergone major transformations over the *longue durée*. The modern standard Arabic term *i'aqa* signifies what we English speakers understand as "disability"; it literally means hindrance or obstacle. The modern adoption of *i'aqa* to signify disability most likely stems from European and North American valuations of the able-bodied worker as the ideal participant in a functioning society, although one might well argue that the Iraqi government's decision to remove cognitively disabled people from public areas – troubling for many reasons – also stands as a tacit recognition that "disability" does not mean *inability*. But in the classical Arabic of the middle ages, the main term used to describe physical difference in human and non-human animals was *'aha*, meaning blight or damage. *'Aha* is not a word intrinsically linked to the human body – it could also be applied to crops, for instance – and does not connote physical *disability*, but rather suggests a mark that spoils the presumed wholeness, integrity, or aesthetics of something.

This terminology appears closely related to a set of attitudes radically different from those that dominate today. One finds in the Qur'an, a seventh-century document, a variety of verses about different types of what we would normally term "disability." Forty-eight verses are about blindness, seven about muteness, two about lameness, and two about leprosy.[9] Undeniably, people with these characteristics are not viewed as the same as their sighted, walking, healthy counterparts; in early Muslim religious/ legal writings, they are typically portrayed as downtrodden recipients of charity or medical intervention. "The blind and the seeing," God twice proclaims in the Qur'an, "are not alike."[10] Yet people with these physical conditions carry no adverse moral associations. The Qur'anic position on the moral state of such people is summarized in verse 48:17: "there is no blame on the blind, nor is there blame on the lame, nor is there blame on the sick." They are physically distinct, physically different, and difference is duly acknowledged as a condition of humanity. It is incumbent on every Muslim to respond ethically to human differences. For instance, certain accommodations are made for participation of physically different people in rituals, prayers, and other religious obligations, such as the waived obligation for those physically unfit to make a pilgrimage to Mecca. According to the influential Persian theologian al-Maturidi (d. 944), the presence of these people glorifies God's creation: if God can create single bodies that combine functioning and non-functioning parts or that combine physical beauty and ugliness without destroying the bodies, he must possess complex and truly awesome powers.

Physiognomy and physical markers of difference were in fact central to defining a person in the Islamic middle ages: that is, physical difference constituted a significant social category, along with such others as tribal affiliation, religion, and birthplace. Among these markers were nicknames. One of the most famous classical Arabic prose writers, Abu 'Uthman 'Amr al-Basri (d. 868/9), is chiefly remembered as "al-Jahiz": "the goggle-eyed man." Al-Jahiz's mid-ninth-century *Book of the Leprous, the Lame, the Blind, and the Cross-Eyed*, a lengthy work featuring hundreds of biographical anecdotes about people with physical impairments or intellectual differences, is worth visiting here. Among his subjects are governors, caliphs, farmers, female slaves, soldiers, mothers, and housewives who are variously depicted with humor, gravity, admiration, and contempt. In the introduction, al-Jahiz establishes that he "will mention what is said about people lacking beard hair and eyebrows, about people with warts, about hunchbacks and sufferers of many other illnesses, how body parts in these illnesses are described, and what emerges in poetry, anecdotes, parables, and traditions about them." His book contains a brief section on his fellow "goggle-eyed" people, and a short section of the text is even devoted to non-human animals with physical impairments like limping hyenas, wolves, lions, tigers, leopards, lynxes, cats, sparrows, starlings, gazelles, and even a dung beetle.[11] One striking feature of these biographical sketches is al-Jahiz's wide-ranging narrative voice. He makes no systematic attempt to portray his subjects in a particular light, resulting in a variety of stories, such as those featuring "disability" as retributive divine punishment (a man awakens semi-paralyzed the morning after killing his slave girl in a jealous rage), as no obstacle for superhuman warriors (a man loses his leg during battle, dips the stump in a pot of boiling oil to cauterize it, and continues fighting), as visual foil (an unattractive hunchbacked man wins the affections of a crowd of beautiful ladies), or perhaps as marker of sexual undesirability or low status (a woman with pocked skin repeatedly burns her co-wife with a hot rock so their husband will not prefer one over the other).

Perhaps to a twenty-first-century reader, anecdotes from al-Jahiz's book read as curiosities or the literary equivalents of freak shows. In its totality, however, *The Book of the Leprous* reveals a particular view of bodies that allows for bodily difference as a natural part of the social fabric.

Relocating "disability"

Environmental conditions in the later middle ages made illness and "disability" – including congenital birth defects, parasites, lice, leprosy, plague, and eye disease – prominent features in everyday life, easy to locate in the sources. Eye disease was strikingly widespread in Egypt. In March 1388, a contemporary chronicler recorded high winds blowing through the country, stirring up so much dirt and sand that women walking in the streets of Cairo were half-blinded. A century later, in 1481, an Italian Jewish traveler in Alexandria noted that in June, July, and August, a fierce wind "attacks people like the black plague, God forbid! Or makes them blind so that for five or six months they cannot see at all. Therefore it is that in Alexandria many people are found whose eyes are diseased."

From the mid-fourteenth century, epidemics spread quickly, frequently, devastatingly through the urban centers of the medieval Middle East. The disposal of masses of human remains proved difficult, a problem posing further threats to public health and sanitation. If a city's water supply became polluted, this rendered an entire urban population prone to contagion. Some of the images will resonate with modern TV viewers: in the medieval Islamicate world, as in Europe, plague victims sometimes suffered from swelling of the glands in the necks, armpits, and groins but were most readily identified by the characteristic pustules that erupted and could permanently mar their skin or disfigure their bodies. Plague affliction was so ubiquitous and recognizable in the fourteenth century that al-Safadi (d. 1363) wrote an epigram about two lovers, one of whom had contracted the plague:

Plague boils broke out on the leg of my beloved,
But far be it for adversity to overshadow his grace.
So I said to [the critics], "There is nothing new in this, for have you ever seen
The dawn unaccompanied by the bright gleam of morning?"[12]

Just as dawn and morning are inseparable parts of the day, the beauty of the beloved
is inseparable from grace and thus impervious to blights.

Not everyone was so philosophical in the face of a public health crisis. The first
of several attempts to remove "blighted" human beings from the urban landscape of
Egypt occurred under the Mamluk Sultan al-Zahir Baybars I. In 1265–66, Baybars
assembled disabled people in a central market and ordered their transfer to
al-Fayyum, a Christian oasis settlement southwest of Cairo with many monasteries,
where he had established a separate living area for them. It is possible that the sultans
imagined these isolated Christian communities would show compassion to the ill and
"blighted," as monks had reputations for taking in travelers, wanderers, and the poor.
Yet although in this new place their basic needs were provided, many of the disabled
people returned to Cairo shortly after this forced migration. On 31 August 1330,
Sultan al-Nasir Muhammad decreed that all amputees and lepers living in Cairo and
Old Cairo must move to an unspecified location in al-Fayyum, but he appears to
have met with no greater long-term success. Similarly, in mid-September 1392,
Sultan al-Zahir Barquq ordered lepers and amputees to leave Cairo and its surrounding
areas. According to the fourteenth-century Egyptian historian, Ibn al-Furat, the
amputees soon returned to the city.

Political efforts to isolate and remove bodily difference from Cairo's landscape,
then, repeatedly failed. Part of the reason lies in the deeply ingrained cultural and
religious attitudes to which I have already drawn attention. Muslim theologians and
philosophers envisaged bodily difference as a natural facet of human variety, desired
by an omniscient, omnipotent God. This was the context that allowed the Cairene
writer, Shihab al-Din al-Hijazi (d. 1471) to formulate ideas that appear, quite
remarkably, to anticipate modern theories of bodily difference. Effectively, he
removed blight as a condition rooted in bodies, by locating it instead in behavioral
patterns and expectations in *society*. In al-Hijazi's view: "the deaf person is he who
does not pity someone painfully afflicted, and the mute person is he who does not
open his mouth, though his body yearns to speak." People who lack empathy for
their fellow human beings ignore, as though they cannot hear, the needs of their
fellow humans. Similarly, those who cannot speak up in defense of another human
being are blighted.

Al-Hijazi wrote these words when he was only 24 years old, ten nights
after overdosing on marking nut, a potent plant drug valued for its memory-
enhancing properties. As a result of the overdose, boils broke out all over his body,
he was unable to eat or sleep, and he lost significant cognitive power. After recovering from the overdose, he became a leading poet, whose verse is quoted in
A Thousand and One Nights. A letter he wrote to his dear friend Salah al-Din al-
Asyuti (d. 1455) detailed his suffering and social isolation and indicted his fellow

Cairenes, who had shunned him in his illness. He further reacted to his experience of isolation by composing short poems that *eroticized* marked bodies of both men and women. His epigrams praise people who are bald, mentally ill, blind, or deaf, who cast harmful spells with their eyes, who have speech impediments, are one-eyed, bleary-eyed, or feverish, and who have the power to kill others with a glance. All these traits fall under the category of the *'ahat*. Other Arab writers of the fourteenth and fifteenth centuries also wrote to aestheticize the blighted body. Why not view as desirable something that occurs naturally and frequently in medieval urban landscapes? The eroticization of marked bodies is an intriguing strategy, directly addressing the anxiety around bodies that move differently and look different than expected. Beauty is appreciated in their so-called imperfections. They "force us to reconsider fundamental aesthetic assumptions and to embrace another aesthetics."[13]

Al-Hijazi's notion of physical difference accords with what disability theorists Tobin Siebers and Michael Davidson have maintained about the need to reconfigure knowledge about the body. If one can view gender and the body as constructed by culture and social conventions, as modern theorists of gender claim, then one should be comfortably able to regard disability and ability as constructed categories. In this case, "we can no longer conceive of disability as individual physical or mental defect. The defect is located in the environments, institutions, languages, and paradigms of knowledge made inaccessible to people with disabilities, and we have a responsibility to remove it."[14]

By relocating "disability" from the body to society, Siebers and Davidson have de-emphasized the ways that the "disabled" body is normally framed as an object and have instead imagined the body, and its constitutive parts, as historical subjects that have values and narratives attributed to them. This approach also obliges the neutral reader – us – to reconsider his or her place in this complex production of knowledge and social norms.

To study "disability" in the Islamicate middle ages provides ample evidence, therefore, that our notions of physical difference are socially constructed. Through personal letters, poems, chronicles, literary prose and city policies, one sees that individuals in the medieval Middle East continually envisioned physical difference in terms of aesthetics, "social citizenship," professional viability, and standing in the religious community. These texts offer a departure from the modern views categorizing the worth of bodies by their abilities, since medieval Islamicate bodily categories were not tied to modes of production and reproduction. The categories of ability and disability are not "natural" ones, but are rather dependent on a particular worldview that privileges the body as a tool in service of a community and its economic wellbeing. The medieval Islamicate example offers one way, perhaps, for us to re-engage bodily difference, and overcome our society's pervasive tendency to see the "disabled" as exceptions, lying beyond social norms, lacking in physical or mental ability and thus victims and passive recipients of the actions of others rather than agents in their own right. This tendency amounts to a blight on our society.

Notes

1 D. Duncan and J. Wanke, "Afghanistan's Disability Crisis." Produced by E. Butler, *New York Times*, 8 October 2008. Online. Available HTTP: <http://video.nytimes.com/video/2008/10/08/world/1194822634676/afghanistan-s-disability-crisis.html> (accessed 30 January 2011).

2 S.S. Nelson, "Disabled Often Carry Out Afghan Suicide Missions." *National Public Radio*, 15 October 2007. Online. Available HTTP: <www.npr.org/templates/story/story.php?storyId=15276485 > (30 January 2011).

3 R.A. Oppel, Jr., "Files for Suicide Bombers Show No Down Syndrome," *New York Times*, 21 February 2008. Online. Available HTTP: <www.nytimes.com/2008/02/21/world/middleeast/21iraq.html?_r=1> (accessed 30 January 2011).

4 "Minister: Suicide Bomber a Handicapped Child," *Associated Press*, 31 January 2005. Online. Available HTTP: <www.msnbc.msn.com/id/6889106/ns/world_news-mideast/n_africa/> (accessed 30 January 2011).

5 See "Stephanie Sinclair." Online. Available HTTP: <www.stephaniesinclair.com/self immolation/> (accessed 30 January 2011).

6 M. Chulov, "Huge Rise in Birth Defects in Falluja," *Guardian*, 13 November 2009. Online. Available HTTP: <www.guardian.co.uk/world/2009/nov/13/falluja-cancer-children-birth-defects> (accessed 30 January 2011).

7 J. Livingston, "Insights from an African History of Disability," *Radical History Review* 94, 2006, 111–26, at 119.

8 See R. McRuer, "Capitalism and Disabled Identity: Sharon Kowalski, Interdependency, and Queer Domesticity," in his, *Crip Theory: Cultural Signs of Queerness and Disability*, New York: New York University Press, 2006, pp. 77–102.

9 For blindness see e.g. Qur'an 5:71; 6:154; 11:28; 22:46; 27:66; 28:66; 41:17, 44; 47:23. For muteness, 2:17–18; 2:171; 16:76; 6:39; 8:22; 17:97. For lameness, Qur'an 24:61, 48:17. For leprosy, Qur'an 3:49, 5:110.

10 Qur'an 35:19, 40:58.

11 Al-Jahiz, *Al-Bursan wa-al-'urjan wa-al-'umyan wa-al-hulan*, ed. M. Mursi al-Khawli, Cairo: Dar al-I'tisam lil-Tab' wa-al-Nashr, 1972, pp. 139–43, 156.

12 Abu Bakr Taqi al-Din b. 'Abd Allah b. Muhammad b. Ahmad al-Badri al-Dimashqi (d. 1489), *Ghurrat al-sabah fi wasf al-wujuh al-sibah*: London, British Library, Ms. 1423 (add. 23, 445). 25 May 1471, fols 158a-b.

13 T. Siebers, *Disability Aesthetics*, Ann Arbor: University of Michigan Press: 2010, p. 3.

14 M. Davidson and T. Siebers, "Introduction," *Papers from Conference on Disability Studies and the University, Emory University, 5–7 March 2004*, in *Publications of the Modern Language Association of America* 120, 2005, 498–501, at 499.

Suggestions for further reading

Bazna, M.S. and Hatab, T.A., "Disability in the Qur'an: The Islamic Alternative to Defining, Viewing, and Relating to Disability," *Journal of Religion, Disability & Health* 9, 2005, 5–27.

Dols, M., *Majnun: The Madman in Medieval Islamic Society*, Oxford: Oxford University Press, 1992.

Ghaly, M., *Islam and Disability: Perspectives in Theology and Jurisprudence*, London: Routledge, 2010.

Richardson, K., *Blighted Bodies: Difference and Disability in the Medieval Islamicate World*, Manchester: Manchester University Press, forthcoming.

Rispler-Chaim, V., *Disability in Islamic Law*, Dordrecht: Springer, 2006.

Scalenghe, S., *The Body Different: Disability in the Middle East, 1500–1800*. Cambridge: Cambridge University Press, forthcoming.

Schweik, S.M., *Ugly Laws: Disability in Public*, New York: New York University Press, 2009.

10

RACE

What the bookstore hid

Maghan Keita

> A few years ago I was in a major London bookstore trying to find the new-to-print paperback history of black people in Britain, an indispensable and exhaustive study for those like me who work in the field of racial representation across disciplines. Frustrated at not finding it, I finally made my way to a saleswoman, to see if she could locate it. "Madam," she informed me sternly, "there were no black people in England before 1945."
>
> Gretchen Holbrook Gerzina[1]

In much of contemporary Europe, the perception remains that Africans – the most visible target of new immigration policies, the most likely to face discrimination in employment and housing – have no history of which to speak, and to many it therefore seems self-evident they have no history within pre-modern Europe. The imagined history of Britain (a word beneath which always lies the shadow of "England") is emblematic of these misconceptions. The British or English, the so-called Anglo-Saxons, have come to epitomize the "whitest of the whites." Here is the supposed image of unsullied purity: A monolith allegedly unblemished until the recent waves of immigration. This image is untenable. The most basic history of England cannot be told without having that territory intimately related to something larger and more complex. From Roman imperial Britain, through the settlement of Anglo-Saxons and Jutes, Cnut's northern realms of the early eleventh century, the Angevin dynasty's agglomeration of the twelfth century, and beyond, the making of England has always been a deeply transnational affair in which immigration and internationalism have been among the most formative elements. True, to envisage an ancient or medieval African presence in England runs counter to powerful and pernicious myths of racial homogeneity. Yet evidence points increasingly, if fragmentarily, to a long history of diversity. One well-publicized recent instance involved archaeologists participating in a BBC television series, *History Cold Case,* who revealed that a skeleton excavated from a burial ground in Ipswich was that of a thirteenth-century African man: The first scientifically proven case of an African in medieval England. The archaeological team determined that the man was born in the Maghreb, in the modern territory of Tunisia; he may have been captured during a crusading expedition in North Africa, conceivably passing through Muslim Spain before he was transported to England. There, he converted to Christianity and ultimately received a burial in the local friary.

This kind of forensic evidence places in a new light the literary testimony of the medieval authors – such as Geoffrey of Monmouth – who will be the focal point of this essay. Geoffrey's Arthurian tales (stories of King Arthur and his knights of the Round Table) are densely populated by black knights, dark ladies, and swarthy knaves. The probably composite nature of the tales' black characters – the fact they may not have existed as historical individuals – should not preclude a critical and analytical examination of their historical significance, any more than King Arthur's own composite nature has prevented the writing of vast libraries on him. In this essay, I will sketch both the historical presence in early Britain of African people, and responses to that presence in the literary cycle of medieval Arthurian legend known as the "Matter of Britain." But the importance of these considerations goes beyond Britain. As the lead archaeologist on the Ipswich case remarked: "It is fitting that our African man has raised his profile at a time when the issue of immigration has become a central topic of discussion for our modern society." I will conclude by suggesting that it is urgently important we rethink the popular modern view of medieval "Western" culture as a whole as "white," Christian, and European, unmixed with other religions or ethnicities, a view that reinforces current presumptions of a clash of civilizations.

A dark, abiding presence

It is possible to trace an "Afro-Romano British" population in the British Isles from a very early stage in the Roman occupation of Britain. A significant aspect of the presence was service in the Roman military. In the wake of the initial occupation, sources suggest, the strength of the Roman garrison was maintained at roughly 42,000 to 47,000 men-at-arms, and at a conservative estimate, males of African descent made up approximately 10 to 25 percent of those ranks. The military prowess of the North Africans had long been known to the Romans, who aspired to – and eventually succeeded in gaining – control of a large part of the Maghreb; they had encountered fierce resistance from the kings of Numidia, located in modern Algeria and Tunisia, among them Masinissa (c. 240–148 BC) and his grandson Jugurtha (c. 160–104 BC). The experiences of Roman soldiers in the neighboring realm of Carthage recounted by the Roman historian, Livy (d. 17 CE) are thus not the earliest indications, though they are also salient. The evolution of the Roman Empire in the first through fifth centuries CE saw the increasing incorporation of Africans into the empire and its military forces. African strength eventually accounted for almost half of all auxiliary regiments within the Roman army: 21 African regiments out of 44 provincial postings. If we take the two regiments in Mauritania as examples, we find a total of 15,000 men.[2] Many of these would undoubtedly have been relatively light-skinned Amazighen (Berber) people; at the same time, some are explicitly described as dark, even black, a fact made entirely plausible by the existence of a thriving trans-Saharan trade route.[3]

In Britain, the standardization of various Roman military practices insured a continued African presence after the end of the empire. The regularization of length of service; the conferring of citizenship on soldiers who reached the age of retirement; the granting of land at retirement; the legal recognition of marriages to indigenous women; and the privileging of military service to the male children of veterans were essential late imperial policies. We can imagine the types of demographic changes their implementation spurred in the empire and its provinces; the historical record leaves no doubt that at the close of the Roman imperial period, many African soldiers in Britain could have become lords of territories allocated to them. It is important to note, though, that these policies favored the continuation of *de facto* communities with Afro-Roman British populations already in existence before the administrative decisions.

The African soldiers may well have been associated with an emerging horse culture in the ancient British imagination; there is considerable documentation of African horsemen all over the Roman Empire, some of whom held elite status. The great second-century triumphal monument in Rome, Trajan's Column, depicts a number of them on horseback sporting a characteristic African hairstyle – the twists or "dreads" that punctuate much recent "Africanist" culture in the US and Britain. As members of the medium and heavy cavalry, anticipating the medieval knight, they formed a vital arm of the late Roman army. Such men would have been attracted to the cavalry partly by the possibility of promotion through the ranks to commissioned officer. Coupled with the rise of the North African Septimius Severus (Roman emperor from 193 to 211), who had been born in the city of Leptis Magna in the modern territory of Libya, the chances of promotion accelerated African recruitment and admission into imperial service. A witness to the soldiers' exalted status comes from Victor, a young man from Numidia: "My father," he wrote, "was a decurion of Constantina [Cirta], my grandfather a soldier; he had served in the comitatus for our family is of Moorish origin."[4]

In the middle ages, the African men on horseback – men of substance, many of them quite dark – seem to have fueled artistic and literary imaginations across Europe from the British Isles to Russia, imaginations further fed by ongoing contacts between medieval Christians from Europe and Africa. Consider, for instance, the graphic image from the Latin "Book of the Secrets of the Faithful of the Cross" (*Liber secretorum fidelium crucis*; c. 1321) representing the "encirclement of the sultan of Egypt by Crusaders and Christians of Nubia," or the powerful papal appeal of 1300 to "the dear black Christians of Nubia and the other countries of Upper Egypt, 'to join Rome in crusade to recover the Holy Lands'." Clearly, for these medieval writers, African presence in "European" affairs (the Crusades) was no more unimaginable than the legendary letters from the mythical medieval ruler of the "Orient," Prester

John, or than the very real impact of Ethiopian statesmen on church and state in Europe. The eyewitness accounts by the sixteenth-century Portuguese philosopher, Damião de Góis, point to a long-lasting series of relationships between Ethiopia and Europe in which African Christians took the lead. As one modern scholar has put it, Europe was left agog by what the powerful Ethiopian emissaries might have promised.[5]

At least until further archaeological evidence elucidates the obscure history of medieval migration and human trafficking, literary responses must take precedence in suggesting the continued existence of an African presence in Europe, real as well as imagined. At the dawn of the twelfth century, Geoffrey of Monmouth penned what has been referred to as one of the most celebrated "pseudo-histories" of the period, *The History of the Kings of Britain.* Seeking to reveal the "historic" King Arthur and to confer Arthur's legitimacy on all who would follow him (supposedly) as kings of Britain, Geoffrey also bears witness to the existence in medieval Britain of what Toni Morrison – in the US context – has called a "dark, abiding, signing Africanist presence." By this phrase, Morrison means to signal a cultural vein in which the dominant, establishment culture responds to a substantial, and potentially threatening, black "Other," working out its own identity through reference to this "subordinate" population whose skin color is perceived as significant.[6] In an analogous fashion, one key scene of the *History* has Arthur on the European continent, where he has just defeated Rome and its allies; he surveys the battlefield and finds it littered with former comrades-in-arms. Among them are the "kings of the Orient": Mustensar, king of the Africans; Sertorius of Libya; Pandrasus, king of Egypt. Geoffrey is quick to point out that the culture of "farthest Spain" is a mélange of African and Arabic elements.[7] Later he describes the reign of Careticus, king of the Saxons, "hateful unto God and unto the Britons":

> The Saxons having had experience with his shiftiness, went unto Gormund, King of the Africans, in Ireland, wherein, adventuring thither with a vast fleet, he had conquered the folk of the country. Thereupon, by the treachery of the Saxons, he sailed across with a hundred and sixty thousand Africans into Britain … with his countless thousands of Africans, the more part thereof which was called England did he make over unto the Saxons through whose treachery he had come into the land.[8]

Several pages later, Geoffrey has Prince Edwin seek out the future British king, Cadwallo. In their exchange, Edwin laments the fate of Britain from Arthur's betrayal by Mordred up to those who, "belying their fealty unto King Careticus, … brought in upon him Gormund, King of the Africans, by whose invasion hath the country been reft from the people and the King himself driven forth with shame."[9]

The earliest forms of Arthuriana and associated medieval romances are filled with literary expressions of this "dark, abiding, signing, Africanist presence." The works of the twelfth-century French poet, Chrétien de Troyes, have their Africans; the thirteenth-century poem, *Huon de Bourdeaux* presents its Saracens; the fair Nicolette of *Aucassin and Nicolette* hails from a Moorish land (Carthage) in which all the men are black. We might gallop from the *Song of Roland* through Geoffrey Chaucer to the *Morte d'Arthur*, contemplating the dark and lovely ladies of the sixteenth-century romance, *The Seven Champions of Christendom* along the way. But four canonical texts in particular, dating from the thirteenth through fifteenth centuries, illustrate the case: the prose *Romance of Tristan*, composed in roughly 1230–35; Wolfram von Eschenbach's late twelfth-/early thirteenth-century *Parzival*; *Morien*, a fourteenth-century Dutch piece of Arthuriana; and Thomas Malory's fifteenth-century *Morte d'Arthur.*

In the prose version of the *Romance of Tristan*, the convenient modern focus is the triangle between Tristan, Isolde, and King Mark, Tristan's uncle. Nowhere have I seen the pride of place conventionally given to this triangle challenged, though it seems to defy the conventions of medieval literature that Mark never proves himself to be Tristan's worthy adversary. Another knight, however, appears at the court of Isolde's father, King Anguin of Ireland, who proves more worthy than Mark and possibly more than Tristan himself; Tristan describes him as "the best knight I've ever encountered."[10] This knight, resident throughout the text, is a figure of whom Malory would also tell two centuries later, describing him as the "black knight," the "Knight of the Black Laund," and "the knight with the black shield."[11] The earlier work, the prose *Tristan*, refers to him as "the black knight," a man of wondrous martial skills. He is sufficiently full of prowess that he carries not one but two swords – "a sign of his readiness to fight against two opponents: he is Sir Palamedes the Saracen."[12]

Riding with Sir Palamedes

Sir Palamades is possibly the most visible African in all Arthuriana. Readers may justifiably wonder: In what sense is he a "black knight"? In Renee Curtis' translation of the prose *Tristan*, there is enough ambiguity for modern readers to deny both Africa and blackness to Palamedes. Yet a "racial" reading is not implausible. Scholars examining texts rooted in medieval Celtic folklore from the heart of the Celtic lands – Cornwall, Brittany, and Ireland – have noted that black men (the *blamanna*, literally "blue men") were a known quantity with some historical presence and "no doubt were assimilated into the local population."[13] They became essentials of Arthuriana right through Malory, and it might be asked to what degree Malory's depictions are also literary responses to a continued racial coexistence. In the prose *Tristan*, the *Morte d'Arthur*, and other works, Sir Palamedes is first encountered in Ireland in the company of his future comrades, knights of Arthur's Round Table.

In Malory's *Morte d'Arthur*, Sir Palamedes is not the first African knight of Arthur's court, for he has been preceded by the "Saracen" Sir Priamus. Arthur's ventures on the continent, the reader gathers, brought his court into contact with this man, who meets another of Arthur's knights, Gawaine, does battle with him, and forms a pact of mutual admiration. At this juncture, Gawaine asks Priamus who he is; Priamus delivers his genealogy. He is "descended of Alexander and Hector [and] right inheritor of Alexandria and Africa."[14] He is an African, and as such he is joined, in this text, by the "Saracens of the Southland that number sixty thousand of good men at arms." Priamus' service to Arthur's cause was so valuable that "the king let him anon be christened, and did do call his first name Priamus, and made him a duke and knight of the Table Round." It is here that the accolades for African knights begin: With this first black knight of the Round Table, of whom Gawaine opines that there is "not a nobler man nor better knight of his hands." Arthur bequeaths to Priamus the duchy of the defeated duke of Lorraine.[15] Yet it is Palamedes who, from the second quarter of Malory's work to the end, rides, quests, challenges, and battles with the best of the Arthurian elite. The "knight of the black shield ... upon a great black horse" becomes central to what epitomizes chivalry, his African background not-withstanding. He becomes the paragon of knightliness – to such a degree, in fact, that Edmund Spenser would later christen him Sir Courtesie in the epic poem, *The Faerie Queene.*

The sixty thousand "Saracens of the Southland" apart, Malory introduces at least eight definitive characters who might be identified as Africans. The blackness of these characters is confirmed in the fourteenth-century Dutch work, *Morien*, whose protagonist Morien is the son of a knight of Arthur's court, Angloval. Morien's quest is to find his father, so he journeys to his father's land. There, in the reader's first encounter with him, Morien confronts a company of knights led by Lancelot. The description of Morien leaves no doubt as to his ethnic identity:

> On the ninth day there came riding towards them a knight on a goodly steed and well armed withal. He was all black, even as I tell ye: his head, his body, and his hands were all black, saving only his teeth. His shield and his armour were even those of a Moor, and black as a raven. ...
>
> Then was the black blithe, and drew near to Lancelot, and bared his head, which was black as pitch: that was the fashion of his land – Moors are black as burnt brands. But in all that men would praise in a knight was he fair, after his kind. Though he were black, what was he the worse? In him was naught unsightly; he was taller by half a foot than any knight who stood beside him, and as yet he was scarce more than a child.[16]

Ironically, given how racial diversity would be expunged in modern German construc-tions of national identity, the one single piece of Arthuriana that best illustrates the presence of Africa in medieval texts (as well as the subsequent erasure of such readings) is Wolfram von Eschenbach's *Parzival*. This German romance, composed by the early thirteenth century, communicates that presence in ways unnerving to conventional expectations. What can we say, unconventionally, of this tale? Two things: (1) the lands through which the main character, Parzival and his father travel are black lands, epitomized by heroism, honor, wealth, luxury, beauty, and power; and (2) the initial object of his quest is black. *Parzival*, after all, begins with the stay of Parzival's father, Gahmuret, with Queen Belekane in the "Land of the Moors" (Zazamanc). As the text relates: "all those of Zazamanc were people dark as the night." The queen's "appearance was black in color"; as she relates, "black of color as I am, a Moor." The beauty of this "black Moor," the queen of the land, often brought him [Gahmuret] to helplessness."[17] The text, explicitly and by allusion, speaks to Belakane's power. Her wealth is illustrated in her hall and the men she commands. Her comportment and treatment of Gahmuret and the offers her lords are able to make to Gahmuret are also clear signs of her capabilities. Beyond this lies the power of her virtue, symbolized by the ruby of her crown – a power that makes Gahmuret's love "unrequited" for others who seek it.

Von Eschenbach opens the text with a biblical allusion (Proverbs 31:10):

> To the ruby I compare a good woman's behavior: if she is true to her womanhood I shall not inspect the color of her skin, nor her head, the roof of her heart we can see with our eyes. If she is loyal within her breast noble praise will not be given in vain.

He then places the allusion on the head of the Queen of the Moors. In crowning Belakane, he writes that she was "black in color, her crown a shining ruby."[18] It was this woman whom Gahmuret had taken as his wife; their first-born son is not Parzival but Feirefiz ("the checkered-one"). Parzival's initial quest is, in fact, to find his elder brother, Feirefiz, for the sorceress Cundrie, upbraiding Parzival for his self-centeredness, has pointedly told Parzival he has a brother who exemplifies chivalry in the very ways that Parzival is lacking:

> In him the manliness that both your father showed did not go to ruin. Your brother is a great marvel of a man: he is both black and white, the son of the Queen of Zazamanc.[19]

Janfuse, "the heathen lady," supplies the details:

> Cundrie named a man for us who is brother to you, I think. His power rules far and wide. The wealth of two crowns stands fearful in his care, on water and the roads of earth. Azagouc and Zazamanc: The countries are strong, and not weak at all. Nothing compares to his riches, except the Baruc's, when people speak of wealth. ... They worship him like a god. His skin has a very beautiful glow. He is a stranger to the color of all men, since his skin is seen to be both black and white. ... I am the daughter of his mother's sister; he is a high king indeed. I shall tell you more wondrous things: no man ever sat in the saddle after a joust with him. His praise is very highly valued. No lips more generous ever sought the breast, and his virtue is lost to falsehood. He is Feirefiz Anschevin, who knows how to endure pain indeed on a woman's account.[20]

By the time of their meeting, Feirefiz, though a heathen, is possibly the most powerful man in the world. In his company, Parzival continues his quest for the Grail. Feirefiz meets, falls in love with, and then weds Repanse de Schoye, sister of Anfortas, keeper of the Grail; in the meantime, he also converts to Christianity. The union of Feirefiz and Repanse, as André Lefevere puts it, is representative of the union of East and West and the salvation of the crusading Church. Their offspring is the most powerful and mythic of Christian kings, Prester John. In *Parzival*, there is a profound desire to link East and West, black and white, and reconcile with an Islamic world that is "technologically farther advanced and, on the whole, more civilized than its European counterpart."[21]

Carving a new space

Why, given such racial diversity in this literature, do modern readers so systematically underplay or overlook the hybrid dimensions of medieval romance? The answers lie in the intertwining of notions of empire, national identity, and racial construction in the eighteenth and nineteenth centuries that forged the myth of a white Europe. In recent years, historians influenced by postcolonial theory have recognized the multiple ways that, during the eighteenth and nineteenth centuries, the middle ages were envisaged in relation to contemporary imperial designs. The pervasive legend of the medieval era as an irredeemably "dark age" was, not coincidentally, paralleled by growing reference to the "dark continent" of Africa.[22] Yet even though these scholars acknowledge "race" as fundamental to understanding medieval life, they do not go far enough in contending with some obvious attempts to erase the signs of racial diversity in the culture of the period. Few of them have explicitly addressed the ways that representations of the medieval past, and especially of Arthur as an Anglo-Saxon icon, have systemically overlooked Africa and Africans.

In the modern renewal of interest in King Arthur, the eighteenth-/early nineteenth-century Scottish author, Sir Walter Scott, is pivotal. Scott's novel *Waverley*, his collection of poems, *Minstrelsy of the Scottish Border*, and his *Essays on Chivalry, Romance, and Drama* served to subordinate Scottish tradition to Anglo-Saxon hegemony and advanced the continued appropriation of Celtic cultural forms, including Arthurian narratives. In their underlying nationalism and imperialism, Scott's texts are reminiscent of the writings by Geoffrey of Monmouth from seven centuries earlier; but one vital difference is that Scott's instrument for articulating these ideals is the concept of race.

In the novels *Ivanhoe* and *The Talisman*, which are set in the twelfth century, Scott's synecdoche for race and empire is slavery. There are, certainly, Saxon slaves as well as dark-skinned slaves ("Negroes," "Moors," "Saracens," "blacks") in his "twelfth-century" romances, yet no matter how rough and meager the Saxon, no matter how opulently adorned the blacks, they are never equals. Poor English stock is always superior, even when black characters appear in material and cultural splendor. Scott characteristically associates blackness with servitude and evil. His introduction of the chief villain in *Ivanhoe*, Brian Bois-Guilbert, illustrates the way that this association can lead to the corruption and degeneracy of good chivalric stock. Bois-Guilbert is "a man past forty, thin, strong, tall, and muscular; an athletic figure. ... High features, naturally strong and powerfully expressive, had been burnt almost into Negro blackness."[23] His malice is underscored by the physical proximity – behind two youthful pages astride white horses – of true evil in all its splendor, opulence, and modern "other-ness": "two attendants whose dark visages, white turbans, and the Oriental form of their garments showed them to be natives of some distant Eastern country … [H]is Eastern attendants wore silver collars round their throats and bracelets of the same metal upon their swarthy legs and arms."[24] Africa and Africans are thus part of Scott's imagined medieval landscape. Although they are identified with servants, he cannot erase them entirely; and the slaves serve with power, for they are men-at-arms. Africa is still communicated in Scott's Arthuriana; the dark, abiding, presence remains, but in a way befitting a modern, racialized discourse.

Our recognition of and reengagement with that presence needs to be pushed much further. We need new research on the cultural and human presence to which Geoffrey of Monmouth and his medieval successors were responding, and new research, further afield, on the African role in the hybrid Islamic–Jewish–Christian cultures of medieval Spain;[25] for direct and intimate contact with North Africa was a fundamental feature of the medieval Mediterranean. Ultimately, we need to change conventional interpretations of medieval Europe, as a whole, globalizing the African presence within it. We have the opportunity to reimagine the historical fabric of the entire middle ages that has been torn apart as far as Africans are concerned, and in the process, to rethink what the medieval era can say about who and what we wish to be in our own age. "Who *are* we, as a people, as Americans?" the documentary filmmaker Michael Moore asked pointedly after the mid-term US elections of November 2010: A kind of soul-searching likely to become more necessary and pervasive in coming years. "You know, we are responsible at this point for so much death and destruction in certain places in this world … and we just want to try and not think about it, forget about it, stay away from it as far as possible." For many people, the middle ages offer one avenue for this kind of escapism, but we should reconsider its value instead for understanding the context in which we actually live. In an age in which, some have argued, race is the dominant way of knowing how can we – how should we – reimagine ourselves in light of the tales of the Round Table in which black knights appear so pervasively? What rereadings and historical reworkings are possible when these tales are coupled with historical treatments like the work of Geoffrey of Monmouth? What changes in policy might such rethinking suggest in an aging Europe that feels itself besieged by "foreigners"? In particular, what policy changes can be suggested for "African Europe," which has been "European" since the Roman Empire and central to the whole process of defining what it meant and means to be European?

In his book *Ain't No Black in the Union Jack*, Paul Gilroy calls for new histories that engage and dynamize English policy in order to counter racism and the policies it has spawned; the same call should be heeded well beyond the borders of Britain.[26] By reclaiming the people of the middle ages who have been "pushed outside of history," we can carve a new, global space for African agency today. This rethinking of the medieval past will force us to reconsider the modern image of the white West. To realize that Africans are not new people in European culture – to embrace the African within Europe, the African *as* European, and the role of the African in the creation of Europe and the West – is to challenge authority and topple whole systems of knowledge. Perhaps it is one means of moving toward the creation of more equitable societies in the future.

Notes

1 G.H. Gerzina, "The Black Presence in British Cultural History," *Perspectives* 35, 1997, 15–17, at 15.
2 See, e.g., G.L. Cheesman, *The Auxilia of the Roman Imperial Army*, Chicago: Ares, 1975, pp. 31–34, 41, 52–56, 61–62, and 80–81; R.G. Collingwood, *Roman Britain*, London: Oxford University Press, 1923, pp. 13–16 and 20–21; P. Edwards, *The Early African Presence in the British Isles*, Edinburgh: Centre for African Studies, University of Edinburgh, 1990, pp. 1–2; G. Webster, *The Roman Imperial Army of the First and Second Centuries AD*, Norman: University of Oklahoma Press, 1998, pp. 64, 89, and 143.
3 E. Saad has commented on the fiction of the impenetrability of the Sahara Desert and on the modern concoctions of "black" (sub-Saharan) and "white" (northern) Africa, areas supposedly determined by the desert's boundaries. (*Social History of Timbuktu: The Role of Muslim Scholars and Notables, 1400–1900*, Cambridge: Cambridge University Press, 1983, pp. 1–2).
4 A.H.M. Jones, *The Later Roman Empire*, Oxford: Basil Blackwell, 1964, p. 53. Constantina [Cirta] is the modern city of Constantine in Algeria.
5 J. Lawrence, "The Middle Indies: Damião de Góis on Prester John and the Ethiopians," *Renaissance Studies* 6, 1992, 311–12, 313–17.
6 T. Morrison, *Playing in the Dark*, Cambridge, MA: Harvard University Press, 1992, pp. 3–6.
7 Geoffrey of Monmouth, *The History of the Kings of Britain*, Harmondsworth: Penguin, 1966, p. 236.
8 Geoffrey of Monmouth, *History of the Kings of Britain*, pp. 240–41.
9 Geoffrey of Monmouth, *History of the Kings of Britain*, p. 247.
10 *The Romance of Tristan*, trans. R.L. Curtis, Oxford: Oxford University Press, 1994, pp. 47, 116.
11 Thomas Malory, *Le Morte d'Arthur*, New York: Random House, 1993, p. 249.
12 *Romance of Tristan*, pp. 45, 47.
13 P. Edwards, *The Early African Presence in the British Isles*, Edinburgh: Centre for African Studies, University of Edinburgh, 1990, pp. 2–5.
14 Malory, *Morte d'Arthur*, p. 144.
15 Malory, *Morte D'Arthur*, p. 147.
16 *Morien: A Metrical Romance*, trans. J.L. Weston, London: D. Nutt, 1901, pp. 29–30, 39.
17 Wolfram von Eschenbach, *Parzival*, ed. A. Lefevere, New York: Continuum, 1991, pp. 8–11, 12–14.
18 Von Eschenbach, *Parzival*, pp. 4, 8.
19 Von Eschenbach, *Parzival*, pp. 83–84.
20 Von Eschenbach, *Parzival*, p. 86.
21 Von Eschenbach, *Parzival*, p. xiv.
22 J. Dagenais and M. Greer, "Decolonizing the Middle Ages: Introduction," *Journal of Medieval and Early Modern Studies* 30, 2000, 431–48.
23 Sir Walter Scott, *Ivanhoe*, London: Thomas Nelson and Sons, 1832, p. 39.
24 Scott, *Ivanhoe*, pp. 40–41.
25 See M.R. Menocal, *The Ornament of the World: How Muslims, Jews, and Christians Created a Culture of Tolerance in Medieval Spain*, Boston, MA: Little, Brown and Company, 2002.
26 P. Gilroy, *Ain't No Black in the Union Jack: The Cultural Politics of Race and Nation*, Chicago: Chicago University Press, 1991.

Suggestions for further reading

Africans in ancient and medieval Europe

Bernal, M., *Black Athena: The Afroasiatic Roots of Classical Civilization*, New Brunswick, NJ: Rutgers University Press, 1987.
Debrunner, H., *Presence and Prestige, Africans in Europe: A History of Africans in Europe Before 1918*, Basel: Basler Afrika Bibliographien, 1979.

Devisse, J. and Mollat, M. (eds) *The Image of the Black in Western Art, Vol. 2: From the Early Christian Era to the "Age of Discovery,"* Cambridge, MA: Harvard University Press, 1979.

Edwards, P., *The Early African Presence in the British Isles*, Edinburgh: Centre for African Studies, University of Edinburgh, 1990.

Keita, M., "Deconstructing the Classical Age: Africa and the Unity of the Mediterranean World," *Journal of Negro History* 74, 1994, 147–66.

Snowden, F., *Blacks in Antiquity: Ethiopians in the Greco-Roman Experience*, Cambridge, MA: Harvard University Press, 1970.

The Roman Empire and its army

Holder, P.A., *The Roman Army in Britain*, New York: St. Martin's Press, 1982.

Jones, A.H.M., *The Later Roman Empire*, Oxford: Basil Blackwell, 1964.

Keppie, L., *The Making of the Roman Army: From Republic to Empire*, London: B.T. Batsford, 1984.

Watson, G.R., *The Roman Soldier*, Ithaca: Cornell University Press, 1969.

Postcolonial studies of medieval England and Europe

Cohen, J.J., *The Postcolonial Middle Ages*, New York: St. Martin's Press, 2000.

Ingham, P.C., *Sovereign Fantasies: Arthurian Romance and the Making of Britain*, Philadelphia: University of Pennsylvania, 2001.

Warren, M.R., *History on the Edge: Excalibur and the Borders of Britain, 1100–1300*, Minneapolis: University of Minnesota Press, 2000.

11

REFUGEES

Views from thirteenth-century France

Megan Cassidy-Welch

The massive increase in the contemporary global population of displaced people has been expressed by one historian as "a new variety of collective alienation, one of the hallmarks of our time."[1] For most historians and social commentators, the condition of displacement and the categories of "refugee" and "displaced person" are inherently products of modernity, as they rest, for definition and response, on the "modern" conditions of nationality (one must belong to a nation state from which one is then alienated) and internationality (international organizations such as the United Nations are the right agencies to respond to this global issue). The definition of a refugee since the Second World War is, according to the United Nations:

> an individual who … owing to well-founded fear of being persecuted for reasons of race, religion, nationality, membership of a particular social group or political opinion, is outside the country of his nationality and is unable, or owing to such fear, is unwilling to avail himself of the protection of that country; or who, not having a nationality and being outside the country of his former habitual residence as a result of such events, is unable or, owing to such fear, is unwilling to return to it.[2]

The term "refugee" has it origins in the Latin verb *fugere*, to flee, from which terms such as "fugitive" derive. The French word *refugié* (refugee) was first used in France in the late sixteenth century to refer generally to foreigners escaping persecution and needing assistance, and it was this broad term that found its way into the English language. Protestants fleeing persecution in seventeenth-century Catholic France (the so-called Huguenots) were the first large-scale group to whom "refugee" was widely applied: Some 200,000 left France from 1681–1720. The countries that received Huguenot refugees, including the British colonies of North America, understood these people to have suffered religious persecution and the deprivation of other rights and to require protection. Those basic features of the refugee status – persecution, flight, and need for protection – still exist at the heart of the legal and international concept of the refugee.

A "displaced person" is a slightly different sort of individual, according to the UN. This category, too, is a product of the Second World War. Created in 1943 by the UN Relief and Rehabilitation Administration, it accommodates those "refugee-like situations," often again products of war, whereby individuals remain within their national borders but for various reasons cannot return to their homes.[3]

Contemporary studies of the refugee phenomenon thus connect the creation of the modern refugee/displaced person both to political forms of belonging such as citizenship, and increasingly to politicized strategies of exclusion framed around concerns for national security, border protection, and economic protection. At the same time as refugees are seen as a national or domestic "problem," however, twentieth and twenty-first century thinking on refugees contains a number of universal or internationalist strands. As mentioned, the idea that refugees are best dealt with by international or transnational bodies such as the United Nations is one feature of such thinking. Likewise, the idea that refugees and displaced persons should be afforded the supranational protection of universal human rights speaks to the internationalism of contemporary understandings of the refugee; for bodies like Amnesty International, the refugee and the displaced person have become sites for tracking human rights abuses across borders and monitoring human rights practices within nation states. The right of the refugee to the protection offered by human rights principles is understood, at least in international theory, to transcend the specific and subjective concerns of nations. Overall, therefore, contemporary conversations about the status and meaning of the refugee and the displaced person locate these individuals very firmly within the politics and ideologies of modernity.

This modernizing propensity is also to be found in many historical studies of the refugee phenomenon. Indeed, historians have often dismissed premodern varieties of displacement as too small-scale or ill-defined for comparative value. Michael Marrus, whose work on the refugee in twentieth-century society remains a foundational text for the historical study of refugees, notes that medieval refugees, for instance, "seldom appeared different from vagabonds or the itinerant poor who travelled from place to place in every premodern society." For Marrus, the older penalty of exile or physical alienation from a society, which might be politically, socially, or culturally enforced, is essentially different from the situation of refugees today. Marrus agrees that there were certainly people in medieval and early modern times who left their homes for fear or as a result of persecution, but he argues that modern refugees' particularly *acute* state of homelessness "remove[d] them so dramatically and so uniquely from civil society" that they must be distinguished from earlier refugees. Moreover, Marrus contends, the "extraordinary duration" of the modern refugees' displacement – which might be intergenerational – is of a completely different scale than premodern experiences. Premodern refugees, he notes, were not so many that they needed camps to house them, and they "needed no special category to suspend them outside the framework of the civilized community." In fact, he postulates that refugees in premodern times simply died: "winters, generally, would finish them off."[4]

One purpose of this chapter is to counter the notion that the status and experience of the refugee or displaced person are uniquely modern and can only be properly understood as a consequence of modernity. At the outset, it is important to recognize that premodern people did in fact experience the *conditions* understood to mark the "modern" refugee experience. Forced removal from home, forced travel, alienation from culture, community, and family are to be found much earlier than the twentieth century, and for the individuals concerned those experiences were just as acutely disruptive, traumatic, and worrying as for today's displaced people. But there is more than analogy to be derived from a consideration of displacement in a premodern context. Another aim here is to show how records of medieval forms of displacement cast a particularly sharp light on the local and personal dimensions of such experiences, and thus on ways that being a refugee or displaced person involve much more than inhabiting a legal category built on modern concepts of national belonging and international responsibility. The modern criteria of refugee status are not very helpful when trying to come to terms with historical people who lived much more locally than we do, often free of any collective sense of, say, "Frenchness," and as subjects, not citizens. But partly because of how the medieval records therefore focus attention on the local and personal, they can lead us to a more insightful approach to the experiences of displaced people today, if we place greater emphasis on their own particular modes of self-representation and expressions of home, place, and identity.

The Albigensian Crusade

There are many examples of displacement in medieval history, the best known of which are probably the various displacements of Jews that occurred throughout Europe. Expelled at different times from France, England, and Spain and the victims of both sporadic and systemic violence, European Jewish communities were among the most persecuted religious groups of the middle ages. This ongoing diaspora led to the formation of Jewish communities in northern Africa, eastern Europe, and beyond; the literature produced from their exile still resonates today. But smaller-scale episodes of displacement are also valuable for illustrating its nature and meaning for medieval people, and it is one such event that I will consider here: the Albigensian Crusade between 1208 and 1229. This "crusade" provides a good example of how war in the middle ages could precipitate the forced movement of individuals, families, and even communities among and within regions. The episode also had longer repercussions extending well beyond the period of conflict, including for the displaced.

The Albigensian Crusade was one of a number of holy wars involving European armies that took place from the late eleventh century. Mostly, these wars were played out in what is now the Middle East over the city of Jerusalem. The Albigensian Crusade was different, a "war on heresy" conducted from 1208–29 around Albi (hence the name "Albigensian"), a city in the southern French region of the Languedoc or, as it sometimes known, Occitania. In the early thirteenth century, the nation of "France" was still in formation. The patchwork of regions that make up the present day country mostly belonged to the king of France, and his lands were locally governed by lords officially in his service. But there were notable exceptions to actual French royal control. The area known as Aquitaine, which stretched from the southern borders of Brittany, Touraine, and Anjou to the Pyrenee mountains in the southeast, belonged to the English crown. The royal house of Barcelona ruled the southern French region of Provence until 1246. And in much of the Languedoc, the principal aristocrats were the counts of Toulouse, who governed quasi-independently. Grander authorities like those of the papacy and the monarch of France seemed distant and abstract for most residents of the Languedoc. Even the powerful reformist Pope Innocent III (d. 1216), despite his highly interventionist style of administration, had yet, by 1208, to gain the active support of the count of Toulouse, Raymond VI (d. 1222).

Adding to this complexity, the fiefs of the counts of Toulouse (lands granted by the king in return for, in theory, loyalty and military service) were rather loosely spread in Occitania from the southwestern Agenais area to Provence, and from the southern town of Castelnaudary to the northern river Dordogne. In the midst of these swathes of territory were lands belonging to other influential aristocrats as well, most notably the family of the Trencavel, who were quite independent of their overlord, the count of Toulouse, and closely linked to the kings of Aragon (Spain) to the south. Ecclesiastical organization in the region was also fragmented, with four archiepiscopal sees overseeing some 15 bishoprics. Broadly speaking, then, it is important to understand that "there were no black and white borders in Occitania" at this time, but rather variously controlled areas of shifting influence.[5]

Why was a war declared on heretics in this area? Heresy, non-orthodox religious belief seen to undermine Christian doctrine and the Christian community, was an increasingly pressing issue for the papacy in the twelfth and thirteenth centuries. One heretical group reported in the Languedoc by the thirteenth century was the people known as the Cathars. The name seems to have originated with the religious authorities who opposed the movement. Those suspected of Catharism did not call themselves Cathars but instead good men, good women, or Christians; indeed, whether or not Catharism was a coherent religious "movement" at all has recently been contested.[6] Nor were these the only heretics then of concern to the papacy; others, too, such as the Waldensians in southern France and Italy, were also considered serious threats to Christendom. But according to Pope Innocent III, the Cathars benefited from especially widespread support in Occitania, and in particular from the major landholders in the region, the counts of Toulouse. In the eyes of preachers sent by Rome to the region to instruct inhabitants on matters of the faith and debate with suspected heretics, Catharism was an organized and popular religion supported at the top as at lower levels of society, and a potentially grave threat to Christian souls.

The catalyst for the Albigensian Crusade was the murder of a papal legate, Peter of Castelnau, in 1208, who had come to the area to preach against heresy and force Count Raymond VI to act against the supposed heretics in his domains. Peter of Castelnau occasioned the count's excommunication in April 1207, on the grounds that he was a protector of heretics and had failed to defend the Church. When the legate was mysteriously stabbed as he crossed the Rhône river, blame for this act of violence was swiftly attached to Raymond, and the pope secured the agreement of the French king, Philip Augustus, that some of his vassals would participate in a crusade. By June 1209, the crusading army had assembled at Lyon, and the march down the Rhône valley began. The subsequent military events have been described as a war of attrition, since the primary strategy from 1209–18 was siege warfare,[7] though the outset is perhaps better described as a strategy of "shock and awe"; the first major move of the crusaders, in 1209, was to massacre all the inhabitants of the town of Béziers. The city of Carcassonne fell the same year, and a series of some 45 sieges then ensued until 1218. Gradually but firmly, the main besieged towns submitted to the French crown. In 1229, the Treaty of Paris formally ended the crusade, with a number of statutes against heresy passed by the new count of Toulouse, Raymond VII. Carcassonne was formally placed under royal control in 1240; the last Cathar stronghold of Montségur fell in 1244. In the following years, crusading was progressively replaced by teams of "inquisitors" or investigators, who used the Roman law investigative procedure of *inquisitio* or inquiry and were eventually institutionalized as the Inquisition; these inquisitors worked their way through the region in an ongoing mopping-up operation that lasted into the fourteenth century.

This sketch of the trajectory of the crusade is too brief to reveal many of the diverse ideological, political, religious, and personal motivations and actions that propelled it forward. One additional general feature to note, though, is the intense social stress and strain that the singular military tactic of protracted siege warfare caused in the region. The chief aspect of this stress was the experience of displacement for myriad refugees who, beginning immediately after the massacre of Béziers in 1209, fled their homes and in some cases the region altogether. This movement of peoples continued throughout the period of the crusade and well afterwards, as inhabitants also fled inquisitors. We know of the longevity of these population movements from a diverse, illuminating group of thirteenth-century sources.

Sources

Three narrative accounts provide the initial inroads into discovering the displacement of people during the military phase of the conflict: Peter of les Vaux-de-Cernay's *Albigensian History* (*Historia Albigensis*), composed 1212–18 while the crusade was in progress; the *Song of the Albigensian Crusade* or *Song of the Cathar Wars* (*Chanson de la croisade albigeoise*), written by William of Tudela *c.* 1213 and thereafter by an anonymous continuator, which recounts the events of 1208–18; and William of Puylaurens' *Chronicles* (*Chronica*), composed after the crusade was over, between 1250 and 1275. The first and last of these sources are pro-crusade chronicles, and as such, they document the progress of the crusade as a series of victories over heresy. The second source, the *Song*, is more complex as its first composer, William of Tudela, was anti-heretical yet moderately sympathetic to the people of the area, while the anonymous continuator's hostility to the crusaders is transparent. All three sources present a chronological narrative of the crusade punctuated by victories and disasters, and they all focus to greater or lesser degrees on the crusade leaders as the drivers of the narrative action. Supplementing them are more official documents such as papal letters and the reports of the pope's representatives to the region. One example is a report from two of Pope Innocent's legates, Milo and Arnaud Amaric, written during the first few weeks of the crusade.[8]

More insightful in terms of the individual experiences of the region's inhabitants are testimonial sources produced after the crusade was over but within living memory of those who suffered losses. These include a range of testimonies in the registers of Bernard of Caux and Jean of Saint Pierre, two early inquisitors who, from 1245–46, recorded hundreds of depositions given by people in the southwestern French towns of Agen, Cahors, Toulouse, and Pamiers and in the surrounding Lauragais region. The testimonies survive in the inquisitors' original manuscript (handwritten text) now in Toulouse. Other valuable inquisitorial records are found in the trial depositions of Cathars and Waldensians from the Toulouse area dating between 1237 and 1289. Administrative sources for this period also contain testimonial evidence, especially the *enquête* or "inquiry" records of the mid- to late-thirteenth century, from a series of investigations begun by the French king, Louis IX, in 1247. The inquiries by Louis' agents concerned complaints and petitions brought by locals about the activities of royal officials, especially confiscations of property for heresy or rebellion. The documents offer rich insights into the operation of royal government at the local level, and they also reveal the anxieties of ordinary people, particularly about land and property ownership, but about other matters as well.[9]

The refugee experience

What do these sources tell us concerning the experiences of refugees during and after the Albigensian Crusade? The three narrative reports emphasize the initial experience of fear and flight in the context of the many sieges. Peter of les Vaux-de-Cernay mentions a number of times that crusaders arrived in various locations only to discover that people had already fled. At Lavalet in 1212, the crusading army "found no one prepared to await their arrival in any fortified town (*castrum*), however strong, since all the inhabitants of the area had been quite overcome by fear." In the winter of 1210, the notorious crusade leader, Simon de Montfort, found Castres "empty of men but full of supplies." Sometimes the circumstances of flight are more fully described. In December 1211–January 1212, we learn:

> when the townsmen of Saint-Marcel heard that the Count had recovered so many places and was on his way to besiege them, they became afraid; they sent messages to him begging him to make peace with them and offering to submit the town to his will. The Count recalled their crimes and exceptional depravity; he was in no way prepared to treat with them and instead sent messengers to tell them that there was no prayer or payment that would suffice to win his agreement to make peace with them. On this they fled from their town, leaving it empty.[10]

William of Puylaurens echoes such reports of fear and flight. The inhabitants of the neighbouring area, he writes, "were driven by fear to abandon their towns and flee from their towns and fortified places; only three strong towns, Cabaret, Minerve and Termes, continued to resist." The report by the papal legates Milo and Arnauld Amaric to Innocent III, on the early victories of the crusaders after Béziers, narrates that after the massacre: "all were seized with terror; seeking refuge in the mountains and areas where there were no roads, they abandoned more than a hundred notable towns between Béziers and Carcassonne, even though they were all well-furnished with food and equipment which the inhabitants could not carry with them as they fled."[11]

Sometimes, the expulsion of specific groups within defeated communities is described in theatrical terms. According to Peter of les Vaux-de-Cernay, when the clerics were expelled from Toulouse: "they left barefoot, taking with them the Holy Sacrament." *The Song of the Cathar Wars* notes that in the expulsion of notables from the same city, Simon de Montfort "ordered the trumpeters to proclaim that every knight and lady, every man of substance, rank or worth should leave the town ... he ordered them all out ... Out came all the best and the flower of its people, knights, citizens and money-changers, driven out with blows, with threats, abuse and insults, by armed ruffians who hurried them along like running footmen." Writing of the taking of Carcassonne in 1209, not long after the massacre at Béziers, William of Puylaurens reports that "Viscount Roger, stricken with terror, agreed conditions for peace, namely that the citizens should leave the city in their shifts and breeches and allow the crusaders to take possession of it."[12] This disrobing of the inhabitants is also reported by Peter of les Vaux-de-Cernay and in the *Song*. Later French historical sources represent the expelled Carcassonnais pictorially in the same fashion as the expulsion from the garden of Eden. One early fifteenth-century manuscript now in the British Library, for example, includes a poignant depiction of men and women dressed in white underwear being herded out of Carcassonne, the women shielding their bodies modestly from the armed soldiers around them.[13]

Although the narrative sources are not particularly specific about where these victims of war went, it is possible to glean some information. During the siege phase of the crusade, individuals, families, and groups often seem to have first gone to the nearest fortified town for safety, but many soon fled yet further away. The *Song of the Cathar Wars* reports that Carcassonne was "full of suffering people" by 1209 when the city was laid siege; once it fell in August of that year: "out they came, citizens, knights, noblewomen and girls each running as a race until there was no one left in the town. ... This way and that they scattered, some to Toulouse, some to Aragon, others to Spain [presumably meaning the northern Spanish kingdom of Castile]."[14]

Loss and damage to property is also evident in the same writings, particularly from the "scorched-earth" policy of the crusading armies around the city of Toulouse and the lands of the Count of Foix in the Pyrenees. William of Puylaurens reports that at the end of the first siege of Toulouse in 1211, the crusaders "returned to their homes after having done considerable damage to the harvest, vines and other property of the Toulousains." Simon de Montfort directed the destruction of land and property in the summer of 1211 around Foix: "He then entered the territory of the Count of Foix and laid waste numerous fortresses and destroyed the bourg of Foix itself by fire. He spent eight days around Foix destroying woods and uprooting vines and then returned to Pamiers." The *Song*, too, speaks of the desolation: "the crusaders cut down all the vines, corn and trees they could find, everything that grew" at Toulouse; when they came to Foix, the army left "after a long stay in the district of Foix doing all the damage it could, devastating foodstuffs, corn and arable crops."[15]

Property loss was accompanied by the loss of family members. "It was pitiful," writes Peter of les Vaux-de-Cernay, "to see and hear the laments of the people of Toulouse [in September 1213] as they wept for their dead; indeed there was hardly a single house that did not have someone to mourn or a prisoner they believed to be dead." The continuator of the *Song* emphasizes the emotional consequences of forced movement when the citizens of Toulouse were expelled: "Such grief and anger, such heat and dust, distress, anguish, danger, and burning rage brought tears to mingle with their sweat, made hearts and guts ache with a pain that increased their agony and reduced their strength." The inhabitants cried as they were forced to demolish the town themselves; eventually, they were dispersed "to foreign lands. In heavy irons they go, in chains, suffering grief, distress, and pain, the living and the dead all bound together." The aftermath of the war brought new problems. Food was scarce, and even after the Treaty of Paris in 1229, the bishop of Toulouse "did not stop at relieving the distress of the poor beggars who approached him, by a daily distribution of food; he even sought out in their own homes those who were ashamed to acknowledge their hunger and provided food for them."[16]

These narrative sources represent the people of the region as either heretics/supporters of heresy or victims (the continuator of the *Song*). Authors who approved of the Albigensian Crusade described its brutal nature as a marker of its effectiveness. The violent aspects of the conflict and the forced removal or flight of the inhabitants are narrated as evidence of victory and divine will. Their expulsion scourged the land of "that detestable plague, the sin of heresy," as Peter of les Vaux-de-Cernay put it.[17] After the military phase of the crusade ended, the less narrative testimonial sources take over as the major repositories of information on the region's displaced people, and it is in these that we begin to see both the more enduring effects of displacement and some attempts to negotiate those effects. Important in this respect are the records of the inquiries begun under King Louis IX in 1247 concerning complaints about royal officials who took property from alleged heretics and rebels. Many petitioners who came before the investigators told of their experiences of loss and displacement in the crusade and afterwards. The petitions came from both men and women, individuals and groups, but it was the women who mainly complained to the investigators about the damaging effects of war. Some losses, such as domestic objects, were small, while others were more substantial. A frequently expressed concern of the women was the unjust confiscation of their marriage portions. A number of testimonials document forced removal from homes and the loss of homes and land. One woman, Rana, reported that that she had lost all her hereditary rights with the destruction of Carcassonne in 1209; another told of the theft of the family vineyards by Simon de Montfort's men. One man remembered that as a child he had been sent to Narbonne for his safety; when he returned years later, he found that his home and all his property had been taken. Two brothers who had fled in fear of their lives during the uprising around Carcassonne of the early 1240s discovered, when they returned home, that they were paupers and orphans as a result of the war.[18]

The petitions brought before the investigators were intended to narrate specific memories of loss and damage, mostly in order to gain monetary compensation. Those who came before the investigators were not, for the most part, people who had been connected with heretical activity; rather, the majority were tangential victims of the crusade and the ensuing conflicts, the collateral damage, as it were, who brought to the royal inquiries some powerful testimonies of displacement. Many who had fled their homes during the warfare alluded to their fears and worries at being left poor and homeless. Domina Guilellma (Domina, or sometimes simply "Na," was the title given to noble widows in this region) said that Simon de Montfort had taken her inheritance and that after his death it had passed to the count of Foix, Roger Bernard. Guilellma petitioned for an annuity as compensation because, as she told the investigators, she had lived a praiseworthy life but was now decrepit and impoverished.[19] Guilellma's experience illustrates that land ownership changed hands frequently during and after the crusade. By the time she came before the investigators in 1247 to describe her personal loss, she was quite aware that the only possible secure and permanent restitution was monetary, and she did not bother to ask for the land itself.

The final set of sources to discuss telling us something about the experiences of displaced people – in this case people specifically accused of heresy – is the enormous volume of inquisitorial testimonies of the mid-thirteenth century. The Toulouse manuscript of Bernard of Caux and Jean of St Pierre contains many references, again framed as memories, to the effects of the crusade and subsequent upheavals and to the forced movements of people. Some of these memories again go back several decades. One deponent recalled that 20 years earlier he had seen refugees leaving the land for Montségur; the date of his deposition was 14 July 1245, which suggests the flight he witnessed occurred in 1225. Another deponent remembered people fleeing for Montségur 30 years previously (around 1215). Another recalled a woman fleeing in 1209, the very start of the Albigensian Crusade. There are also frequent recollections of supposed heretics living in hiding places in Montségur and Cabaret, which became the refuges of displaced persons from other villages and towns of the region as they fell. They remained there until those places, too, were emptied.[20]

The itinerancy of many who fled is clear in the inquisitorial testimonies, which refer to the existence of networks of support for refugees and communities of exiles as far away as Lombardy in northern Italy. These communities were able to maintain communication with each other, despite the pressures that inquisitors brought to bear. The inquisitors were themselves interested in uncovering networks of heretics, so their questions were designed to encourage that information; nonetheless, it is noteworthy that they used the crusade and its aftermath as temporal markers for flight. Other early inquisitorial testimonies replicate the information in the Toulouse manuscript. A number of people who came before the later thirteenth-century inquisitions at Toulouse, for example, remembered meeting refugees from the region on their way to or returning from Lombardy. Petronilla De Bras of Villefranche reported that she had seen a refugee called Guillaume who had fled his home in fear of the inquisitors and gone to Lombardy. Unfortunately, his experience there was negative and he returned to France. Others said they had provided food and shelter to various fugitives, some of whom then went to Lombardy, in the early 1240s. Still more remembered that their families had broken up as a result of fleeing their homes: Guiraud Hunaud of Lanta asked another fugitive to send words of comfort home to his wife should she be found.[21]

Displaced heretics and other refugees from the crusade also found hiding places closer to home. We hear of one woman who hid in a wood with her daughter; another who left the protection of the fortified towns to live in the woods nearby with her heretical husband; and others who were given shelter by other community members. Lady Biverne Golairan of Avignonet told the inquisitors that she had provided shelter to a homeless Cathar good woman and her female companion in 1230; Arnalda of Lamota told the inquisitors that she and her sister had stayed in a variety of houses – sometimes for a few days, sometimes for a few weeks, sometimes a few months – over a period of some 20 years around 1220–40 before capture. One of the people that Arnalda reported had helped her during these years was Guilhelm Garnier, who built her and her sister temporary dwellings in the woods (cabins or tents) and sometimes led them from one safe place to another. Arnalda's sister died in a dug-out in the woods near Lanta, but Arnalda continued to live in the woods, where she seems to have come into contact with other runaways.[22]

Inquisitorial sources like these reveal the longevity of memories of forced movement and of the attempts in certain communities, despite the turmoil, to maintain social and familial networks. Whether individuals fled the inquisitors because they were associated with heresy or endured years of displacement beginning with the military phase of the war is immaterial. The reality for many was continued movement and relocation over a number of years, and traumatic memories of familial and material loss.

Conclusion

How can these medieval examples help us in thinking about refugees and displaced people today? To offer a few suggestions: As earlier discussed, modern concepts of refugee and displaced person reflect legal distinctions between states of displacement based on nationality and international responsibility. These broad categories were created to provide frameworks of rights for large numbers of people, such as the millions of refugees and displaced persons created by the Second World War. Today, according to the UN High Commission for Refugees (2008 statistics), 42 million people around the world remain uprooted by conflict and persecution.[23] Our understanding of the *individual* refugee experience, however, can be lost amid definitional criteria of this scope and nature. It is hard to get a picture of what displacement might actually mean in a concrete sense to a modern individual when much of the conversation concerning refugee/displaced person status is about categories of legal protection. The medieval records remind us that such categories do not accommodate everyone facing similar upheavals. While these texts tell stories of displacement not fundamentally located in notions of nationality or internationality as the key criteria for belonging, the experiences they refer to – tales of loss, trauma, disruption, and fear – are fully shared by twentieth- and twenty-first century refugees. Thus study of the medieval sources may serve, first of all, as a useful counterweight to our modern legal categories. For both refugees and displaced people in the modern sense of these terms, what makes displacement significant is primarily a particular person's *lived experience* of forced alienation.

Second, in drawing attention to the attachments that people of the Middle Ages felt to kin, local communities, and homes, the medieval accounts remind us of the very personal ways in which all people, past and present, experience belonging or alienation, and of the importance of locality for those forced to flee. Today's displaced people and refugees find themselves part of a global story; their status, movements, and protection are shaped by laws that reach much further than the boundaries of the homes they have lost. In a sense, this means they suffer dislocation not only through the physical experience of flight, but by being thrust into legal categories based on national and international criteria that have little relation to those personal bonds. The individualized, personal tales recorded in the medieval sources, especially the testimonials, can help us recognize and remember the importance of the local and familiar in tying people to places and each other.

Refugees, then, are not products of modernity, nor, as a corollary, are they defined solely by modern legal categories of political or national belonging. This is transparent if we understand the refugee as medieval records assist us to, in terms of individual lived experience. Medieval Europe presents a context in which the definitional paradigms dominant today do not neatly apply, given the looseness of medieval political borders and national identities. Yet if we move from the vexing and contested matter of definitional categorization to how refugees perceived their own experiences – the matter brought to the fore in multiple medieval sources – then we may more easily recognize displacement as a series of actions played out culturally and socially as well as economically and politically. To acknowledge this is to remind ourselves that, although modern international law offers much to instruct national states of their obligation to protect and shelter the displaced, it is the lived experiences of men, women, and children that should guide our understanding of refugees or displaced persons. By taking seriously individual stories and memories today, as well, we may reassure modern victims of war and persecution that the past as they experienced it is important and instructive, and that each individual is more than a category. This is the first step to an empathetic and open understanding of the significance and consequences of displacement.

Notes

1 M. Marrus, *The Unwanted: European Refugees in the Twentieth Century*, New York: Oxford University Press, 1985, p. 13.

2 Office of the UN High Commissioner for Refugees, *Convention and Protocol Relating to the Status of Refugees* (adopted 28 July 1951 by the United Nations Conference of Plenipotentiaries on the Status of Refugees and Stateless Persons convened under General Assembly resolution 429 (V) of 14 December 1950). Online. Available HTTP: <www.unhcr.org/protect/PROTECTION/3b66c2aa10.pdf> (accessed 13 January 2011).

3 See A.R. Zolberg, A. Suhrke, S. Aguayo eds, *Escape from Violence: Conflict and the Refugee Crisis in the Developing World*, Oxford: Oxford University Press, 1989, pp. 3–33; G. Melander, "The Concept of the Term 'Refugee'," in *Refugees in the Age of Total War*, ed. A.C. Bramwell, London: Unwin Hyman, 1988, pp. 7–14.

4 Marrus, *The Unwanted*, pp. 4–5.

5 L.W. Marvin, *The Occitan War: A Military and Political History of the Albigensian Crusade, 1209–1218*, p. 9.

6 B.M. Kienzle, *Cistercians, Heresy, and Crusade in Occitania, 1145–1229: Preaching in the Lord's Vineyard*, Woodbridge: York Medieval Press, 2001; K. Sullivan, *Truth and the Heretic: Crises of Knowledge in Medieval French Literature*, Chicago: University of Chicago Press, 2005.

7 M. Barber, *The Cathars: Dualist Heretics in Languedoc in the High Middle Ages*, New York: Pearson, 2000, p. 122.

8 Peter of les Vaux-de-Cernay, *The History of the Albigensian Crusade*, trans. W.A. and M.D. Sibly, Woodbridge: Boydell Press, 1998; *The Chronicle of William of Puylaurens: The Albigensian Crusade and its Aftermath*, trans. W.A. and M.D. Sibly, Woodbridge: Boydell Press, 2003; William of Tudela and an anonymous successor, *The Song of the Cathar Wars: A History of the Albigensian Crusade*, trans. Janet Shirley, Aldershot: Ashgate, 2000. The report of the papal legates appears in translation as an appendix to *The Chronicle of William of Puylaurens*, pp. 127–29.

9 The registers of Bernard of Caux and Jean of Saint Pierre have not been published and are available only in manuscript: Toulouse, Bibliothèque Municipale (hereafter BM), Ms. 609. Some of the trial depositions have been edited in *Recueil des historiens de Gaules et de la France*, ed. L.V. Delisle, vol. 24, Paris: Aux dépens des librairies, 1904.

10 Peter of Les Vaux de Cernay, *Historia Albigensis*, pp. 157, 101, 151–52.

11 *The Chronicle of William of Puylaurens*, pp. 34–35, 128.

12 Peter of les Vaux-de-Cernay, *Historia Albigensis*, p. 120; *Song of the Cathar Wars*, p. 114, laisse 177; *The Chronicle of William of Puylaurens*, p. 34.

13 London, British Library, Ms. Cotton Nero E. ii, fol. 20v.

14 *Song of the Cathar Wars*, p. 26, laisse 33.

15 *The Chronicle of William of Puylaurens*, pp. 41–42; Peter of Les Vaux de Cernay, *Historia Albigensis*, p. 125; *Song of the Cathar Wars*, p. 46, laisse 80.

16 Peter of les Vaux-de-Cernay, *Historia Albigensis*, pp. 49, 87; *Song of the Cathar Wars*, p. 114, laisse 117, p. 115, laisse 178.

17 Peter of les Vaux-de-Cernay, *Historia Albigensis*, p. 9.

18 *Recueil des historiens de Gaules et de la France*, ed. Delisle, vol. 24, "Querimoniae Carcassonensium," pp. 296–319 [hereafter *Qcar*], case nos. 59, 34, 84, 82.

19 *Qcar*, case no. 42.

20 Toulouse BM, Ms. 609, fols 60b, 52b, 26b, 180b, respectively.

21 Paris, Bibliothèque Nationale de France (hereafter BNF), Collection Doat, vols 25 and 26 contain these later testimonies.

22 Toulouse, BM, Ms. 609, fols 237b–238a, 251a, respectively. Arnalda appeared before the inquisitors twice. Her first deposition is recorded in Paris, BNF, Collection Doat 23, fols 1–49b; the second deposition is recorded in Toulouse, BM MS 609, fols 201b–3b.

23 See UNHCR, The UN Refugee Agency, "UNHCR Annual Report Shows 42 Million People Uprooted Worldwide," Online. Available HTTP: <www.unhcr.org/4a2fd52412d.html> (accessed 13 January 2011).

Suggestions for further reading

Sources in English translation

Peter of les Vaux-de-Cernay, *The History of the Albigensian Crusade*, trans. W.A. and M.D. Sibly, Woodbridge: Boydell Press, 1998.

The Chronicle of William of Puylaurens: the Albigensian Crusade and its Aftermath, trans. W.A. and M.D. Sibly, Woodbridge: Boydell Press, 2003.

William of Tudela and an anonymous successor, *The Song of the Cathar Wars: a History of the Albigensian Crusade*, trans. J. Shirley, Aldershot: Ashgate, 2000.

The Albigensian Crusade and medieval refugees

Bruschi, C., *The Wandering Heretics of Languedoc*, Cambridge: Cambridge University Press, 2009.

Einbinder, S., *No Place of Rest: Jewish Literature, Expulsion and the Memory of Medieval France*, Philadelphia: University of Pennsylvania Press, 2008.

Given, J.B., *Inquisition and Medieval Society: Power, Discipline and Resistance in Languedoc*, Ithaca, NY: Cornell University Press, 1997.

Graham-Leigh, E., *The Southern French Nobility and the Albigensian Crusade*, Woodbridge: The Boydell Press, 2005.

Jordan, W.C., *Louis IX and the Challenge of Crusade: A Study in Rulership*, Princeton, NJ: Princeton University Press, 1979.

Lansing, C., *Power and Purity: Cathar Heresy in Medieval Italy*, Oxford: Oxford University Press, 1998.

Marvin, L.W., *The Occitan War: a Military and Political History of the Albigensian Crusade, 1209–1218*, Cambridge: Cambridge University Press, 2007.

Pegg, M., *A Most Holy War: The Albigensian Crusade and the Battle for Christendom*, Oxford: Oxford University Press, 2008.

Sumption, J., *The Albigensian Crusade*, London: Faber, 1999.

Modern refugees and refugee issues

Burgess, G., *Refuge in the Land of Liberty: France and its Refugees, from the Revolution to the End of Asylum, 1787–1939*, Basingstoke: Palgrave Macmillan, 2008.

Haddad, E., *The Refugee in International Society: Between Sovereigns*, Cambridge: Cambridge University Press, 2008.

Kneebone, S. (ed.) *Refugees, Asylum Seekers and the Rule of Law: Comparative Perspectives*, Cambridge: Cambridge University Press, 2009.

Kushner, T., *Remembering Refugees: Then and Now*, Manchester: Manchester University Press, 2006.

Kusher, T., and Knox, K., *Refugees in an Age of Genocide: Global, National and Local Perspectives during the Twentieth Century*, London: Frank Cass, 1999.

Journal of Refugee Studies, Oxford: Oxford University Press, in association with the Refugee Studies Centre, University of Oxford, 1988.

Marrus, M., *The Unwanted: European Refugees in the Twentieth Century*, New York: Oxford University Press, 1985.

Sassen, S., *Guests and Aliens*, New York: The New Press, 1999.

Tunstall, K.E. (ed.) *Displacement, Asylum, Migration: The Oxford Amnesty Lectures 2004*, Oxford: Oxford University Press, 2006.

United Nations High Commission for Refugees, The UN Refugee Agency. Online. Available HTTP: <http://www.unhcr.org/cgi-bin/texis/vtx/home> (accessed 13 January 2011).

12

TORTURE AND TRUTH

Torquemada's ghost

Amy G. Remensnyder

> Torture means any act by which severe pain or suffering, whether physical or mental, is intentionally inflicted on a person for such purposes as obtaining from him or a third person information or a confession, punishing him for an act he or a third person has committed or is suspected of having committed, or intimidating or coercing him or a third person, or for any reason based on discrimination of any kind, when such pain or suffering is inflicted by or at the instigation of or with the consent or acquiescence of a public official or other person acting in an official capacity.
>
> United Nations Convention Against Torture and Other Cruel, Inhuman or Degrading Treatment or Punishment (ratified by the United States in 1994)

During the heated controversy over the American government's use of torture to extract information from suspected terrorists incarcerated at Guantánamo Bay, Abu Ghraib prison, in Afghanistan, and at black sites around the globe, both sides have summoned the specter of the middle ages and forced it into the role of modernity's evil ancestor. US officials, for example, have sought to exculpate themselves by arguing that their methods of interrogation did not actually constitute torture because these techniques were gentler than those of the Spanish Inquisition. In February 2008, a *Washington Post* article reported Steven J. Bradbury, a Justice Department official, as asserting that the method of "simulated drowning ... used to compel disclosures by prisoners suspected of being al-Qaeda members ... was not ... like the 'water torture' used during the Spanish Inquisition." In his insistence on the difference between medieval practices and those approved by the Bush administration, Bradbury went so far as to declare: "The only thing in common is, I think, the use of water."[1]

Critics were quick to underscore the morally suspect nature of Bradbury's claims. "To invoke the defense that what the Spanish Inquisition did was worse and that we use a benign, non-torture form of waterboarding is obscene," said Martin S. Lederman, a professor of Law at Georgetown University.[2] Yet no one questioned Bradbury's

characterization of the Spanish Inquisition as a negative foil for modern values. The
Black Legend stigmatizing this institution as an agent of exceptional cruelty is still
present in our world, its dark shadow coloring popular views of the middle ages.

For their part, opponents of the United States' use of torture during the "war on
terror" have more than once condemned it as a return to medieval barbarism. They
have, for example, invoked the middle ages in their criticisms of Alan Dershowitz, a
professor at Harvard Law School and a contentious public intellectual who argues for
"a benign use of nonlethal torture to save lives" in extreme circumstances. Courts,
Dershowitz believes, should be authorized to issue "torture warrants" in cases when
the torture of one person might produce the information that would save thousands
of lives from an imminent threat – the so-called "ticking bomb" scenario. Dershowitz
says that when he advocates this policy, "the first question I am often asked is 'Do
you want to take us back to the Middle Ages?'" He has also complained of being
labeled "Torquemada Dershowitz" – a reference to Tomás de Torquemada (d. 1498),
the first inquisitor general of the Spanish Inquisition.[3] In 2008, in fact, one critic of
the Bush administration's torture policy, the prominent British journalist Robert Fisk,
contended that American torturers were doing precisely what Bradbury denied: They
were "just apeing [*sic*] their predecessors in the inquisition," Fisk proclaimed.[4]

Dershowitz's adversaries and Fisk are right to protest the American government's
embrace of interrogation techniques deemed torture by federal law (Title 18, Part I,
Chapter 113 C of the US Code), the Army Field Manual, and international treaties
to which the US is a signatory (the Geneva Conventions and the UN Convention on
Torture). Torture is illegal – and morally unacceptable. Yet in conjuring Torquemada's ghost and labeling torture medieval, these critics join Bradbury in making
important historical errors; not only do they misconceive of the middle ages as an era
of unrelenting and immoral savagery, but they also misunderstand torture itself as
the antithesis of modernity. They ignore a disturbing reality; far from dying with the
middle ages, torture has continued to be employed by modern states.

Torture's use in our own world is not confined to brutal totalitarian dictatorships.
Contemporary democracies – including the United States – have a venerable history
as torturers that long predates the current "war on terror." Not only have US citizens
taught torture techniques to representatives of repressive regimes such as Latin
American dictatorships, but some US soldiers and operatives have stained their own
already bloody wars with the horrors of outlawed physical and psychological torments.
The Philippines during the first decade of the twentieth century and Vietnam during the
1960s and 1970s are only a few of the countries where American combatants have
inflicted torture on their enemies.

Nor is the soil of the United States itself pristine: American jails and prisons
sometimes double as torture chambers. Police interrogations can degenerate into
systematic brutal abuse, as occurred in Chicago between 1968 and the early 1990s.
Tortured by electric shock, by near-suffocation with plastic bags, by suspension in
excruciating positions, or by whipping, dozens of prisoners held in custody by this
city's police force confessed to crimes. This "evidence" was then wielded against
them in court with tragic results: Over eleven men received death sentences based on

the testimony the police had beaten out of them.[5] Infamous as it is, the Chicago case is hardly alone.

Torture also can await US convicts after they pass from the hands of the police to those of the guards in the prisons where they will serve their time, especially if they are incarcerated in a so-called supermax penitentiary. The extreme degree of isolation imposed on prisoners in these latter facilities constitutes such mental cruelty that the UN Human Rights Committee has repeatedly (although to no avail) urged the US government to mitigate the conditions there. Regarding Supermax prisons as equivalent to torture, some European countries are reluctant to allow the extradition of suspected terrorists to the US partly for fear that these people will be sent to such hellholes. In December 2010, for example, "the European Court of Human Rights ... temporarily blocked the extradition of four terrorism suspects from the United Kingdom to the United States on the ground that their confinement in a US 'supermax' prison might violate Article 3 of the European Convention on Human Rights, which prohibits torture and inhuman or degrading treatment or punishment," as the American Civil Liberties Union reported.[6]

Torture then is as modern as it is "medieval." Although contemporary states may hide torture behind the closed doors of prisons or police interrogation rooms and rely on techniques that leave few physical marks on the victim's body, the evidence is there to see if we look closely enough. Yet if during the debate over torture's role in post 9/11 counter-terrorism efforts, some pundits have mistakenly charged the US government with resurrecting the middle ages, American officials themselves have erred in not considering what the medieval past really has to teach us. In making the decision to authorize torture, these officials in fact utterly ignored the long and sordid history of this method of interrogation. "No one involved – not the top two CIA officials pushing the program, not the senior aides to President George W. Bush, not the leaders of the Senate and House Intelligence Committees – investigated the gruesome origins of the techniques they were approving with little debate," reported a *New York Times* article in 2009.

Take what is perhaps the most brutal and notorious method approved by the Bush administration's Department of Justice in a memo of 1 August 2002: Waterboarding, the technique later defended by Bradbury. Deliberately distorting the internationally accepted definition of torture to claim it did not apply to the methods being advocated, the Justice Department memo recommended waterboarding as a "procedure" in which:

> the individual is bound securely to an inclined bench ... the individual's feet are generally elevated. A cloth is placed over the forehead and eyes. Water is then applied to the cloth in a controlled manner. As this is done, the cloth is lowered until it covers both the nose and mouth. Once the cloth is saturated and completely covers the mouth and nose, air flow is slightly restricted for 20 to 40 seconds due to the presence of the cloth. This causes an increase in the carbon dioxide level in the individual's blood. This increase ... stimulates increased efforts to breathe. This effort plus the cloth produces the perception of "suffocation and incipient panic," i.e. the perception of drowning.[7]

According to the *New York Times*, although the then-director of the CIA, George J. Tenet, "insisted the agency had thoroughly researched its proposal" to use this technique, the "top officials he briefed did not learn that waterboarding had been prosecuted by the United States in war-crimes trials after World War II and was a well-documented favorite of despotic governments since the Spanish Inquisition."[8] It apparently took six years for the architects of the Bush administration's torture policy to admit that waterboarding indeed had a history stretching back at least to the middle ages. But once they did, they were quick to disavow any connection to this undesirable past, as Bradbury's statement to *The Washington Post* showed.

Such alleged ignorance of torture's past is typical of modern democratic states. In countries like the United States, the very clandestinity of torture creates a protective shroud that fosters rumor and official amnesia rather than government sponsored research. Yet this obliviousness to the past is utterly inexcusable, for the history of torture offers crucial warnings to those states that would use such techniques for the purposes of interrogation in the present. Several Bush administration officials interviewed by the *New York Times* even admitted as much, saying that "if they had known the full history of the interrogation methods ... they would have advised against using them."[9]

In considerations of how torture's past should influence the shape of counter-terrorism policy today, the much-maligned middle ages deserve a privileged position (although professional medievalists have been slow to point this out in any forum more public than learned journal articles aimed at their peers). The middle ages in fact provide modern day opponents of torture with a valuable weapon that can be wielded even against the utilitarian stance espoused by Dershowitz and his fellows – and against anyone immune to moral arguments condemning torture. As we'll see, Torquemada may not have been the sinister sadist of modern imagination, but he lived in an era when torture was a perfectly legal method of obtaining confessions. During the high middle ages (the twelfth through the fifteenth centuries) and well into the early modern period, secular and ecclesiastical courts all across Europe had the right to employ torture, though they did not exercise this option as often as we assume. By legalizing, regularizing and institutionalizing torture, high medieval and early modern European societies – unlike the modern United States – thus fulfilled many of the conditions spelled out by one expert as those under which torture has the most chance of producing accurate evidence.

"Torture," writes this expert, "would work well when organizations remain coherent and well-integrated, have highly professional interrogators available, receive strong public cooperation and intelligence from multiple independent sources, have no time pressures for information, possess enough resources to verify coerced informa-tion, and release innocents before they are tortured. In short, torture for information works best ... in peacetime nonemergency conditions."[10] The medieval use of tor-ture met these criteria far more fully than does its employment during the United States' current "war on terror." In the middle ages, torture was indeed sometimes an effective means of producing confessions that confirmed the torturers' preconcep-tions. Very frequently, it was also an effective means of intimidation. Yet one has only to glance through the rich records of the institution synonymous in modern popular culture with medieval torment — the Spanish Inquisition — to be convinced that, even under the best of conditions torture is always an extremely ineffective and highly unreliable method of extracting *accurate* information from its victims. As we'll see, inquisitors themselves even sometimes admitted torture's shortcomings as a method of discovering the truth.

Confession, torture, and the Spanish Inquisition

If Torquemada had been asked whether waterboarding constituted torture, he would have answered without hesitation that it did. The inquisitor general would have had no reason to dodge the question, unlike Michael B. Mukasey during his confirmation hearings as Attorney General-elect of the United States in the fall of 2007. In Torquemada's day, torture was recognized by ecclesiastical and secular law alike as an accepted and fully legal method for extracting confessions from people accused of particularly grave offenses — crimes threatening society and God, crimes as feared by some people then as the acts of terrorists are today. In cases where there was not enough evidence for a conviction for such crimes, but reasonable grounds for suspicion existed (at least in theory), medieval judges would order the accused put to the "question," as torture often was called then.

Torture was thus a judicial technique legally available to the inquisitor general and his fellows staffing the Spanish Inquisition when it embarked on its mission in 1480, two years after the pope had authorized its foundation. In its methods and goals, Torquemada's organization in many ways represented a continuation of the inquisition established in the thirteenth century under papal auspices, although the Spanish tribunals were under the direct control not of the pontiff but of the monarchs of Aragon and Castile (kingdoms in the Iberian Peninsula). Modern popular imagination, nourished on such lavishly misleading visions of the middle ages as Mel Brooks' "The Spanish Inquisition: the Musical," remembers Jews as the target of the institution over which Torquemada presided. In reality, the Spanish tribunals directed their considerable zeal toward the same people who had occasioned the papal inquisition's own foundation: heretics, Christian men and women whose orthodoxy had come into question and who were suspected of grave sins against the faith. But although inquisitors possessed no jurisdiction over non-Christian such as Jews, the suspected heretics who most often suffered the Spanish Inquisition's attentions between the 1480s and the 1530s were Jewish converts to Christianity and their descendants, people known as *conversos*. It did not take much for their allegiance to their new faith to seem questionable.

The inquisitors in Spain worked hard to gather evidence against people accused of heresy. They questioned suspects' friends, acquaintances, and family members. Above all, they pressed the presumed heretic for a confession. From the beginning of the trial procedure until its end, inquisitors besieged the accused with demands that he or she admit to having committed errors against the faith. Suspects brought before the Inquisition's tribunals were assumed to be guilty unless proven innocent (the latter a rare occurrence) – a situation unlike that ostensibly prevailing in modern American courts of law but much like that faced by the captives incarcerated at Guantánamo Bay. Even those defendants who obdurately refused to confess but were nonetheless convicted and thus sentenced to the ultimate penalty – death – would be urged to admit their sin, right up until the terrible moment when they were tied to the stake and the bonfire that would consume their bodies began its work.

Like the judges who presided over secular courts, the men who passed sentence on heretics in late medieval and early modern Spain believed that confession was the best possible evidence of guilt. By the thirteenth century, jurists even lauded confession as the "queen of proofs," a phrase that inquisitors themselves fondly quoted. As one wrote in 1583: "Among all forms of evidence, [confession] has dominion as the queen of proofs."[11] Yet the men who ran the Spanish Inquisition had another reason for placing such a premium on a heretic's admission of his or her wrongdoing. They believed that the people tried in their courts were as much sinners as criminals and thus in need of the spiritual remedy of penance. Since there could be no penitence without confession, a defendant's avowal of guilt helped the inquisitors achieve what they saw as their salvific mission of bringing the accused to repentance and to reconciliation with the Church. To be sure, a confession of sins made before an Inquisition tribunal did not have the same spiritual value as an individual's confession to a priest; the former was a judicial act while the latter carried the weight of a holy sacrament. Yet as Henry Charles Lea, the great early twentieth-century historian of the Spanish Inquisition, pointed out, in theory inquisitors accepted as valid confessions only those that expressed "repentance, renunciation of error and prayer for readmission to Catholic unity" – criteria that sacramental confessions were also supposed to meet.[12]

If, as Lea wrote, the inquisitors in Spain had "a two-fold function – to discover and punish the crime and to save the soul of the sinner," torture was an instrument they could wield in the service of both objectives, for it could produce a confession.[13] Like the sometimes painful penances that a priest would prescribe to sinners, torture itself was supposed to benefit heretics spiritually. A inquisitor named Juan de Rojas, who exercised his craft during the late sixteenth century in Valencia (a region on the Mediterranean coast of the Iberian Peninsula), explained: "since it is a matter of the salvation of his soul, [the suspected heretic] is to be tortured so that he should confess under torment and be reconciled [to the Church] and penitence enjoined on him … so that his soul shall be saved."[14]

In Torquemada's lifetime and for several decades after his death, however, the Spanish Inquisition did not use torture very much: Only two of some 400 *conversos* who passed before its tribunals in Ciudad Real between 1483–85 were tortured.[15] Even by the mid-sixteenth century when the inquisitors resorted to torture more often, they still did so far less frequently and with far less severity than did their contemporaries presiding over secular courts. Relatively rare as they are, the transcripts of medieval and early modern torture sessions conducted by the Spanish Inquisition make for wrenching reading. By the early sixteenth century, these meticulous, shockingly detailed documents recorded every word said to the victim and every scream that came from his or her mouth – for truth might lurk in any of the victim's utterances and truth, not punishment, was torture's goal.

As a thirteenth-century Italian professor of law by the name of Azo declared: "torture is the inquiry after truth by means of torment." Azo was paraphrasing his distinguished third-century predecessor, the Roman jurist Ulpian, who had defined torture as "the torment and suffering of the body in order to elicit the truth."[16] Yet by the time Azo began teaching law to students at the University of Bologna, the relationship between torment and truth had grown much more intimate than it had been in Ulpian's day. Medieval Christians had come to see pain not as something to be avoided at all costs but as something potentially meaningful – and, thus, if deciphered correctly, as a privileged vehicle for the articulation of both sacred and secular truths. What one historian has called the increasingly deep "interconnectedness of truth and pain" in the high middle ages manifested itself in many arenas, including the value placed on confessions extracted under torture.[17] Pain was considered so crucial to the expression of truth that some high medieval and early modern jurists even debated whether a confession made without torture (or at least its threat) was valid.

So when in 1490 Pedro de Villada, an episcopal vicar of the Castilian town of Astorga who was soon to be appointed an inquisitor in a trial dear to Torquemada's heart, ordered that waterboarding – or *la toca* as he would have called it – be used against a man in his custody, he did so with the goal of uncovering the truth. Villada suspected that Benito García – a wool carder and a *converso* – was involved in a hideous conspiracy aimed at destroying the Christian way of life. But Villada needed a confession to be sure.

First Villada had Benito whipped –200 lashes, as the wool carder would bitterly remember from the inquisitorial prison in Avila to which he was transferred after Torquemada became interested in his case. Then came the *toca*, the medieval version of waterboarding. Inquisition records and torture manuals composed by high medieval jurists give us a detailed picture of the agony Benito must have suffered in this torture. Despite Steven Bradbury's claims to the contrary, it was much the same torment that some men captured during the "war on terror" have experienced at the hands of US interrogators; the clinical explanation of waterboarding in the Justice Department's memo of August 2002 is disturbingly similar to medieval descriptions of the *toca*.

Benito would have been tied onto a ladder-like structure that was tilted to keep the victim's head lower than his or her feet. An iron band around the forehead or throat would have immobilized his head while another iron device held his mouth open. A piece of cloth, the *toca*, would have been inserted into the wool carder's throat. Then water would have been poured slowly, jar by jar, onto the cloth and into his mouth, giving him the unbearable sensation of drowning. To increase the pain, the torturer also would have wound sharp cords – *garrotes* – around Benito's upper and lower arms, his thighs, and his calves. Sticks slid into these loops would have allowed the torturer to tighten the cords until they bit deep into the wool carder's flesh.

According to medieval manuals of torture, the torturer himself was to remain absolutely silent during the procedure. But the presiding officials, men like Villada, were to constantly exhort the victim to tell the truth. Their voices, incessantly pressing the victim for a confession, form a mind-numbing and repellent litany in the records of inquisitorial torture sessions. Nor did the torture usually cease until the victim either was on the verge of collapse or had confessed. As one set of instructions for inquisitors from early sixteenth-century Valencia baldly states, people may "say they are going to tell the truth, but then when the torture stops, they don't want to tell it and when they start to confess, they can slacken ... Therefore, don't stop [the torture] until they have finished confessing."[18]

Did inquisitors succeed in their quest to produce truth from torture? Undoubtedly sometimes they did. Yet more often than not, such interrogations tore from the victim's lips a farrago of half-truths shading into outright invention and pure fantasy designed to appease the torturers and make the pain stop. Consider the pitiful words wrung by torture in 1568 from Elvira del Campo, a *conversa* woman accused of secretly practicing Judaism despite her professed Christianity. When the inquisitors presiding over her torture ordered that the *garrotes* be tightened, Elvira, according to the official transcript, "screamed and said: 'Tell me what you want me to say, for I don't know what to say.' She was told to tell what she had done, for she was tortured because she had not done so, and another turn of the cord was ordered. She cried, 'Loosen me, Señores, and tell me what I have to say' ... she was told, 'yes, if she would tell the truth.' She said 'Señores, tell me, tell me it.'" Can we really imagine that the inquisitors got the "truth" from this woman, especially when they added the water torture to the *garrotes* and caused her such agony that she eventually could not speak – and then repeated the whole horrific procedure four days later?[19]

Some medieval and early modern jurists and inquisitors themselves did not completely trust the much-vaunted partnership between torment and truth. They saw it instead as a troubled relationship requiring scrutiny. As these men knew, to be valid in the eyes of the law, confessions had to be made of one's free will rather than forced by fear. Yet terror reigned in the torture chamber, potentially tainting the words extracted there. "There are fearful people who would rather lie than endure the torment and so they say false things instead of the truth," wrote Juan de Rojas in the late sixteenth century. Here the inquisitor was quoting a passage from the classical jurist Ulpian often cited by medieval and early modern men writing about torture. Like his fellows, Rojas also repeated his Roman forerunner's description of torture as "a difficult and dangerous business that can cheat truth."[20]

Rojas did not go so far as to renounce torture itself – nor did most authors of the many medieval and early modern legal manuals expressing doubts about the efficacy of torture and the reliability of the confessions it forced from the accused. How could they have done so, given the primacy that confession enjoyed over all other forms of proof? Instead, these men designed procedures they believed would help them sift truth from falsehood in the words uttered under torture – and, quixotic as it seems, ensure that confessions under torture were not coerced. They forbade officials presiding over torture from asking leading questions, although in practice, plenty were asked. Furthermore, no confession made under torture was considered admissible evidence unless the accused ratified it no less than 24 hours later of his or her own free will – not under torture, that is. The transcript of the confession made under torture would be read out loud to the accused, who would then be asked to confirm its veracity. Yet it was a brave person who denied the truth of the words he or she had spoken under torture, for if one did, judges usually decreed that torture be resumed until a satisfactory result was reached – the admission of guilt they expected. Nor did the refusal to confess under torture always constitute evidence of innocence, for it could instead reveal that black magic was helping the accused withstand the pain.

If it seems difficult, impossible even, to reconcile these measures with each other, that is because the entire regimen of torture was riven with inconsistency and paradox. As one historian has commented: "a system that claimed to uncover inner truth and bring it into the daylight yet that was predicated upon coercion, negation of free will, and pain was bound to be self-contradictory."[21] The lethal effects of the internal contradictions fracturing the theory and practice of judicial torment were very much on display during the Spanish Inquisition's trial of Juana González – a woman who actually warned the inquisitors that they would get only lies and not the truth from her under torture.

In 1511, Juana, a maidservant for more than 24 years to a *converso* couple in the Castilian town of Ciudad Real, betrayed her masters by offering "evidence" of their supposed secret practice of Judaism to the Inquisition.[22] She subsequently confessed to a priest that she had lied and that her employers were innocent. The Inquisition arrested Juana and imprisoned her for two years. When the judges admonished her to tell the truth about her earlier testimony, she insisted that she had falsely accused her employers. Asked why she had brought charges against them, Juana said "it was through fear of torture," a reason she gave again and again in response to the inquisitors' questions.

Because of the contradictions in her evidence, the inquisitors then did exactly what Juana so feared: They ordered her put to the question. As they readied the instruments of the water torture – the jar, the cloth – and strapped her down, Juana declared that "if she died in the torment, it would be upon Their Reverences' conscience, and that if she said something through fear of torture, it would not be valid." As the water filled her throat, Juana at first stayed staunch in her defense of her employers' innocence, but when the torturer reached for a second jar she broke down and told the inquisitors what they wanted to hear: That her earlier allegations against her employers had actually been true.

Juana survived her sessions in the inquisition's torture chamber and died in 1516. On her deathbed, she confessed her sins as every good Christian was supposed to. Among the acts for which she needed to repent, she told the priest administering the last rites, was having given false evidence to the inquisitors. She had, she said, lied under torture and had wrongly incriminated her former employers. But it was too late to save them. Partially on the basis of Juana's evidence, tissue of lies though it was, her mistress already had been condemned to life imprisonment and her master to death by fire.

What of Benito García, the *converso* wool-carder tortured in Astorga by Pedro de Villada and then over long months in the inquisitorial prison in Avila? Did torture get the "truth" from him? "Because of the torture," the wool-carder whispered to one of his fellow prisoners in Avila, "[I] said more than [I] knew ... and enough for [the inquisitors] to have [me] burned."[23] In other words, Benito had lied outrageously. And so he did. Under torture, he confessed to having colluded with some other *conversos* and a few Jews in order to obtain a consecrated Eucharistic wafer and the heart of a Christian boy. Benito said that he and his alleged co-conspirators intended to use these objects in a ceremony of sorcery which would cause "all Christians to die ravening ... and the whole Christian religion to die and be subverted and [he and his companions] to possess all the goods belonging to faithful catholic Christians and their own descendents to grow and multiply ... and to extirpate those of faithful Christians."[24] They had torn this heart, declared Benito, from the chest of a Christian boy whom they had lured into a cave outside their hometown of La Guardia, where they proceeded to crucify him, all the while shouting out insults against Christ and Christianity.

The desperate falsity of the wool-carder's confession is patent to modern ears. But to this man's interrogators, his account could not have seemed more true. After all, evidence of just such a heinous plot against Christian society was exactly what Villada and the inquisitors had been looking for when they put Benito to torture. Fantasies about Jewish conspiracies aimed at desecrating Christian symbols, ritually murdering Christian children, and overturning Christianity haunted the imagination of late medieval and early modern Christians. But the inquisitors in Avila had a problem. The confessions they had wrested from the wool-carder and his supposed confederates (who had also been imprisoned) did not quite match. And so over 16 months the inquisitors tortured these men into narrative conformity. Only then were the judges satisfied that they had produced the "truth." In November 1491, Benito and his accomplices were executed for their supposed crimes.

Lessons for the president

There seems little reason to believe that torture procures more trustworthy results today than it did in Torquemada's era. True, modern torturers, aided by new technologies and scientific knowledge of the body, can inflict torments far more hellish than anything their medieval counterparts could have imagined. But more pain does not inevitably produce more truth, as the records of medieval and early modern torture sessions reveal again and again. The opposite is in fact the case: More pain leads to less truth. Repeated torment addles the brain, causing such trauma that, as one modern study has concluded, victims of torture "experience memory loss ... [and] are likely to remember fictions quite vividly ... this is a recipe for retrieving extremely poor information ... [in which] both interrogators and cooperative prisoners have high confidence."[25] By the time Benito García and his companions-in-death caught sight of the bonfires where they would be burned in flames intended to recall those awaiting them in hell, they may then well have believed the wild tales they had been forced to spin under the pressure of torture and repeated interrogation.

If the Spanish Inquisition teaches modern policy makers the negative lesson that torture is an extremely poor method of obtaining accurate information, the era of the past to which this judicial institution belonged also offers a positive example to people in power today: Government officials, from the president on down, would do well to share the skepticism about torture's results that high medieval and early modern judges, lawyers, and legal thinkers themselves occasionally evinced. Admitting that fissures ran through the privileged relationship between pain and truth, these men acknowledged the potential unreliability of confessions extracted under torture – unlike their counterparts in the Bush administration's Department of Justice, who in 2002 assured the CIA that waterboarding was "so successful ... an interrogation technique" that it was "reported to be almost 100 percent effective."[26]

Representatives of the US government should not, however, make the same mistake as those medieval and early modern inquisitors and jurists who overrode their own doubts about torture's efficacy and professed faith in their ability to parse truth from untruth in the words extracted by pain. Such confidence is no more warranted now than it was then. Although medieval and early modern courts weren't supposed to, they all too often sentenced people on the basis of dubious confessions uttered under torture, just as the US government has planned to prosecute suspected terrorists using "evidence" obtained by the same methods.

At least when inquisitors such as Torquemada tortured suspected heretics, they were obeying the laws forged by their culture, according to which confessions were crucial for conviction – and pain was good for the accused's soul. As Juan de Rojas, the Inquisitor of Valencia, wrote in 1583: "A heretic's confession is of great use not only to the state (*reipublicae*) but also to himself ... therefore we can rightly say that the medicine of torture is favorable for the accused, since it is a matter of his ... absolution" from sin.[27] In contrast, when US officials today torture suspected terrorists, they are abrogating federal and international law, and outraging moral standards – and can claim no such spiritually generous excuse for resorting to methods so lacking in ability to produce the truth. The American torturers at Guantánamo Bay could never pretend that they inflicted the pain of waterboarding on their captives for the victims' own benefit. We are then perhaps more "medieval" than Torquemada and his fellows ever dreamed of being.

In an executive order issued the day after he became President of the United States, Barack Obama openly repudiated his predecessor's authorization of torture. Countermanding certain of Bush's own executive orders, Obama reaffirmed the United States' commitment to upholding the provisions of the UN Convention against Torture, the Geneva Conventions and the federal anti-torture statutes. He also commanded US officials to follow the dictates of the Army Field Manual when interrogating suspects. This is a step in the right direction – yet it is not nearly enough. Paradoxically, Obama perhaps has merely driven torture back underground to lurk at the margins of society, the dark place it usually occupies in modern democracies. A close reading of his executive order of 22 January 2009 reveals "loopholes big enough to drive a FEMA camp train through," as one legal expert has concluded.[28] Most strikingly, the protections enunciated by Obama cover only what his order terms "individuals detained in an armed conflict."[29] What then of suspected terrorists apprehended in other contexts? Might torture be used on them?

For several long weeks in the winter of 2010–11, the Obama administration indeed apparently did nothing to protect the human rights of a suspect taken into custody in a non-military situation: the 19-year-old American citizen, Gulet Mohamed, who was detained by local authorities in Kuwait and brutally interrogated about his alleged links to possible terrorists. "I've been beaten and tortured," Mohamed told a *New York Times* reporter.[30] Far from intervening, the US government instead seems to have abetted the Kuwaitis: Mohamed said that FBI agents participated in his questioning. Once the Kuwaitis were through with the teenager and tried to deport him to his own country, Mohamed found that he was literally trapped: He had been placed on the United States' "no-fly" list. Eventually American officials agreed to let him return to his home in Virginia.

Whether Mohamed's claims that he was tortured were true or not, some suspected terrorists in US custody today suffer the same illegal and immoral treatment they received under the Bush administration. Despite Obama's executive order of January 2009, detainees at what appears to be a secret facility associated with the Bagram prison in Afghanistan are still being interrogated with methods outlawed by the US Army Field Manual, including brutal beating and sustained sleep deprivation.[31] It is no wonder then that in January 2011, Dick Cheney, George W. Bush's vice-president who famously termed waterboarding a "no-brainer," praised the Obama administration's counter-terrorism policies.[32] Cheney declared them a pleasing continuation of those implemented under Bush himself.

In contemplating torture's value as a method of interrogation, Obama – and all future presidents of the United States – should heed the simple but stark warning from high medieval and early modern European societies, cultures of the distant past that institutionalized judicial torment yet in which some experts worried over the practice's potential to elicit the truth. As Henry Charles Lea wrote well over a century ago: "it is impossible to read" the records of medieval and early modern torture sessions "without amazement that the incoherent and contradictory admissions through which the victim, in his increasing agonies, sought to devise some statement in satisfaction of the monotonous command to tell the truth, should have been regarded by statesmen and lawgivers as possessed of intrinsic value."[33] Let us hope that no future historian will have cause to say the same thing about the leaders of twenty-first-century America.

Notes

1 D. Eggen, "Justice Official Defends Rough CIA Interrogations: Severe, Lasting Pain is Torture, He Says," *The Washington Post*, 17 February 2008. Online. Available HTTP: <www.washingtonpost.com/wp-dyn/content/article/2008/02/16/AR2008021602634.html> (accessed 11 January 2011).
2 Ibid.
3 A.M. Dershowitz, "Should the Ticking Bomb Terrorist be Tortured? A Case Study in How a Democracy Should Make Tragic Choices," in *Civil Liberties vs. National Security in a Post 9/11 World*, ed. M.K.B. Darmer, R.M. Baird, S.E. Rosenbaum, Amherst, NY:

Prometheus Books, 2004, pp. 198, 203; and his "Tortured Reasoning," in *Torture: A Collection*, ed. S. Levinson, Oxford: Oxford University Press, 2004, p. 265.

4 R. Fisk, "Torture Does Not Work, As History Shows," *Independent*, 2 February 2008. Online. Available HTTP: <www.independent.co.uk/opinion/commentators/fisk/robert-fisk-torture-does-not-work-as-history-shows-777213.html> (accessed 19 September 2010).

5 D. Rejali, *Torture and Democracy*, Princeton, NJ: Princeton University Press, 2007, pp. 240–42. Rejali provides extensive details about the use of torture by the United States both abroad and in domestic contexts.

6 "ACLU comments to European Court of Human Rights in Babar Ahmad and Others v. The United Kingdom," Online. Available HTTP: <www.aclu.org/prisoners-rights/aclu-comments-european-court-human-rights-ibabar-ahmad-and-others-v-united-king-domi> (accessed 28 April 2011). See also G. Pierce, "America's Non-Compliance: The Case against Extradition," *London Review of Books*, 13 May 2010. Online. Available HTTP: <www.lrb.co.uk/v32/n09/gareth-peirce/americas-non-compliance> (accessed 21 February 2011).

7 J.S. Bybee, "Memorandum for John Rizzo, Acting General Counsel of the Central Intelligence Agency," 1 August 2002, pp. 3–4. Online. Available HTTP: <www.aclu.org/accountability/searchdetail.php?r=4610&q=waterboard)> (accessed 11 January 2011).

8 S. Shane and M. Mazzetti, "In Adopting Harsh Tactics, No Look at Past Use," *The New York Times*, 22 April 2009. Online. Available HTTP: <www.nytimes.com/2009/04/22/us/politics/22detain.html?_r=2& hp> (accessed 19 September 2010).

9 Ibid.

10 Rejali, *Torture and Democracy*, p. 478.

11 Juan Rojas, *Singularia iuris in favorem fidei, haeresisque detestationem, tractatus de haereticis*, Part 2.257, Venice: Franciscus Zilettus, 1583, folio 112v.

12 H.C. Lea, *A History of the Inquisition of Spain*, 4 vols., London: Macmillan, 1906–07, Vol. 2, p. 573.

13 Lea, *History*, vol. 2, p. 569.

14 Rojas, *Singularia iuris*, Part 1.374, folio 44r.

15 H. Kamen, *The Spanish Inquisition: A Historical Revision*, New Haven, CT: Yale University Press, 1997, p. 189.

16 For this and the quotation from Azo, see E. Peters, *Torture*, expanded ed., Philadelphia: University of Pennsylvania Press, 1996, p. 1.

17 E. Cohen, *The Modulated Scream: Pain in Late Medieval Culture*, Chicago: Chicago University Press, 2010, p. 85.

18 Quoted in R. García Cárcel, *Orígenes de la inquisición española: el tribunal de Valencia, 1478–1530*, 2nd ed., Barcelona: Ediciones Península, 1985, p. 195.

19 Here I quote from the partial translation of the transcript of this torture session in Lea, *History*, vol. 3, pp. 24–26.

20 Rojas, *Singularia iuris*, Part 2.295, folio 119r.

21 Cohen, *Modulated Scream*, p. 74.

22 In the following, I quote from the record of Juana's trial edited in *Records of the Trials of the Spanish Inquisition in Ciudad Real*, ed. H. Beinart, 4 vols., Jerusalem: Israel National Academy of Sciences and Humanities, 1974–85, Vol. 3, pp. 378–80, 475–78.

23 F. Fita (ed.) "La verdad sobre el martirio del Santo Niño de la Gauardia, ó sea el proceso y quema (16 noviembre, 1491) del judío Jucé Franco en Ávila," *Boletín de la Real Academia de la Historia* 11, 1887, 34–35.

24 Ibid., p. 13.

25 Rejali, *Torture*, p. 469.

26 Bybee, "Memorandum," p. 6.

27 Rojas, *Singularia iuris*, Part 2.296–97, folio 119v.

28 J. Hill, "Obama's Torture Loopholes," *Global Research*, 26 January 2009. Online. Available HTTP: <www.globalresearch.ca/index.php?context=va&aid=12041> (accessed 5 January 2011).

29 "Ensuring Lawful Interrogations," Executive Order 13941 of 22 January 2009. Online. Available HTTP: <www.whitehouse.gov/the_press_office/EnsuringLawfulInterrogations/> (accessed 17 January 2011).
30 M. Mazzetti, "Detained American Says He Was Beaten in Kuwait," *The New York Times*, 5 January 2011. Online. Available HTTP: www.nytimes.com/2011/01/06/world/middleeast/06detain.html?_r=1& hp (accessed 21 January 2011).
31 J. Partlow and J. Tate, "2 Afghans Allege Abuse at U.S. Site," *The Washington Post*, 28 November 2009. Online. Available HTTP: <www.washingtonpost.com/wp-dyn/content/article/2009/11/27/AR2009112703438.html> (accessed 21 January 2011). H. Andersson, "Afghans 'Abused at Secret Prison,'" *BBC News*, 15 April 2010. Online. Available HTTP: <http://news.bbc.co.uk/2/hi/8621973.stm> (accessed 21 January 2011).
32 For Cheney's "no-brainer" statement, see M. Tran, "Cheney Endorses Simulated Drowning," *The Guardian*, 27 October 2006. Online. Available HTTP: <www.guardian.co.uk/world/2006/oct/27/usa.guantanamo> (accessed 20 February 2011). For his praise of Obama's counter-terrorism policies, see G. Greenwald, "The Vindication of Dick Cheney," *Salon.com*, 18 January 2011. Online. Available HTTP: <www.salon.com/news/terrorism/index.html?story=/opinion/greenwald/2011/01/18/cheney> (accessed 20 February 2011).
33 Lea, *History*, vol. 3, p. 27.

Suggestions for further reading

Medieval torture

Asad, T. "Pain and Truth in Medieval Christian Ritual," in his *Genealogies of Religion: Discipline and Reasons of Power in Christianity and Islam*, Baltimore, MD: Johns Hopkins University Press, 1993, pp. 83–124.
Cohen, E., *The Modulated Scream: Pain in Late Medieval Culture*, Chicago: Chicago University Press, 2010.
——, "The Animated Pain of the Body," *American Historical Review* 105 (2000), 36–68.
Pennington, K. "Torture and Fear: Enemies of Justice," *Rivista internazionale di diritto comune* 19 (2008). Online. Available at HTTP: <http://faculty.cua.edu/pennington/PenningtonTortureEssay.htm> (accessed 12 January 2011).
Peters, E., "Destruction of the Flesh – Salvation of the Spirit: The Paradoxes of Torture in Medieval Christian Society," in *The Devil, Heresy and Witchcraft in the Middle Ages: Essays in Honor of Jeffery B. Russell*, ed. Alberto Ferreiro, Leiden: Brill, 1998, pp. 131–48.
——, *Torture*, expanded ed., Philadelphia: University of Pennsylvania Press, 1996.

The Spanish Inquisition

Homza, L.A. (ed.) *The Spanish Inquisition: An Anthology of Sources*, Indianapolis: Hackett Publishing Company, 2006.
Kagan, R.L. and Dyer, A. (eds.) *Inquisitorial Inquiries: Brief Lives of Secret Jews and Other Heretics*, Baltimore, MD: Johns Hopkins University Press, 2004.
Kamen, H. *The Spanish Inquisition: A Historical Revision*, New Haven, CT: Yale University Press, 1997.
Lea, H. C., *A History of the Inquisition of Spain*, 4 vols., London: Macmillan, 1906–7.
——, "El Santo Niño de la Guardia," *The English Historical Review* 4 (1889), 229–50.

Torture in the modern world

Kramer, P., "The Water Cure: Debating Torture and Counterinsurgency – a Century Ago," *The New Yorker*, 25 February 2008, 38–43.

Rejali, D., *Torture and Democracy*, Princeton, NJ: Princeton University Press, 2007.
Strange, C. "The 'Shock' of Torture: A Historiographic Challenge," *History Workshop Journal* 61 (2006), 135–52.
"United Nations Convention Against Torture and other Cruel, Inhuman or Degrading Treatment or Punishment." Online. Available at HTTP: <http://treaties.un.org/Pages/showDetails.aspx?objid=080000028003d679> (accessed 7 January 2011).

The debate over torture and US counterterrorism efforts

Cohn, M. (ed.) *The United States and Torture: Interrogation, Incarceration, and Abuse*, New York: New York University Press, 2011.
Jaffer, J. and Singh, A., *Administration of Torture: A Documentary Record from Washington to Abu Ghraib and Beyond*, New York: Columbia University Press, 2007.
Head, T. (ed.) *Is Torture Ever Justified?* Farmington Hill, MI: Greenhaven Press, 2005.

13

CLASS JUSTICE

Why we need a Wat Tyler Day

Peter Linebaugh

"June 'teenth," or 19 June 1865, was the day when the Emancipation Proclamation was finally read publicly in Texas, two-and-a-half years after the United States President Abraham Lincoln promulgated it. It makes me think about a similar day in English history, 15 June, a temporary emancipation.

It is the anniversary of Magna Carta, the "Great Charter" that baronial rebels forced King John to sign on 15 June 1215. The Magna Carta is considered to be the origin of many rights and liberties now guaranteed by countries in North America, Europe, Africa, the Middle East, Australasia, and the Caribbean, including the right to a trial by one's peers and the writ of *habeas corpus*. At the time, however, such limitations on royal power overwhelmingly protected John's rebellious aristocratic comrades.

But 15 June is also the anniversary of another charter, one proposed by Wat Tyler, a leader of the famous Peasants' Revolt of 1381. In a public referendum, the English people expressed a preference that 15 June be made a national holiday to remember Magna Carta, though some may have also been thinking of Wat Tyler and the great uprising against bondage and the Poll Tax. The 15 June holiday is celebrated for Magna Carta, but it should be named for Wat Tyler. Everyone should know what he fought and died for on that fateful day: The powerful ideal of the commons.

The leaders: Wat Tyler and John Ball

William Langland's *Piers Plowman* may be our guide to some issues at stake in the 1381 Revolt. The poem is an allegorical satire of the 1370s that denounced clerical fraudulence and legal chicanery and took particular aim at the greed-propelled, avarice-prone monetary economy known as "King Penny." Adult head taxes were imposed to finance wars against France, and such a poll tax of one groat per adult (a groat being four pence) began to be collected just before the rising in June 1381. William Langland came to London where he lived in poverty with his wife, Kit.

Educated as a cleric, he made his living by (among other things) saying prayers for rich folks. Otherwise, he held out his begging bowl, unfit for work bending over in the fields on account of his height. Or so he said. "William Langland" was almost certainly not the author's real name, for his excoriation of the clergy would have exposed him to considerable punishment had his identity been known.

Langland's wildly popular poem was meant to be recited. Nevertheless, there are 57 surviving manuscript versions, 17 of them produced before 1400. It was talked about enough that the name, "Piers Plowman," was taken up by the insurgents in 1381. As happened with copies of the English Bible of John Wycliffe, translated at approximately the same time, Christians derisively called "Lollards" (mumblers) by social superiors who could not understand plebeian language passed manuscripts of the poem around, "muttering" the inspirational contents. These included communism, the ideal of "having all things in common." The very phrase appears in Wycliffe's Bible, in Acts 2:44. Wycliffe also argued in favor of such practices in a treatise of 1374:

> [A]ll good things of God ought to be in common. The proof of this is as follows: Every man ought to be in a state of grace; if he is in a state of grace he is lord of the world and all that it contains; therefore every man ought to be lord of the whole world. But, because of the multitudes of men, this will not happen unless they all hold all things in common: therefore all things ought to be in common.[1]

William Langland also spoke with optimistic confidence about the commons:

> For human intelligence is like water, air, and fire — it cannot be bought or sold. These four things the Father of Heaven made to be shared on earth in common. They are Truth's treasures, free for the use of all honest men, and no one can add to them or diminish them without God's will.[2]

This was scary stuff, at a time when work consisted of forms of bondage and the workers were variously named thralls, rustics, churls, villeins, slaves, and serfs. "The rising of the commons is one of the most portentous phenomena to be found in the whole of our history," wrote the Victorian historian, professor, and bishop, William Stubbs, in his *Constitutional History of England*.[3] "Portentous" means both awesome and ominously significant.

England's population was reduced by the plague (Black Death) of 1347–50, when one in three perished. Dramatic demographic decline created a labor shortage and potentially favorable conditions for workers. Preemptively, the Statute of Laborers (1351) obliged workers to work at low wages on pain of imprisonment. The rates were as follows: One penny a day for weeding or hay making, reapers two pence a day, mowers five pence a day, tilers threepence a day and their boys a penny and a half, same for thatchers, and none with food or drink.[4] A fourteenth-century labor statute mandated that all "artificers and craftsmen as well as servants and apprentices who are not of great account" be forced to serve in harvest at cutting, gathering, and bringing in the corn. Imprisonment, likewise, awaited those who "under color of pity or alms" gave anything to "sturdy beggars" or acted "to cherish them in their sloth."[5]

But there was more: Three crippling poll taxes, and continental wars that began to bleed the country white. The combination of military disasters and war taxation converted anxiety to action. Country peasants and town craftsmen rose to defend their commons against tax collectors and cunning lawyers. A tax man molested Wat Tyler's daughter. The people in Tyler's day "certainly were a people who would not be imposed upon," wrote Thomas Paine (1737–1809), an American revolutionary inspired by the portentous phenomenon of fourteenth-century England. The tax-gatherer's indecent examination of Tyler's daughter provided a further example of the unrestrained power of the despotic ruling elites. Tyler lifted his hammer and brought it down upon the tax man's head, bringing all "the neighbourhood discontents to an issue."[6]

Wat Tyler was not the only leader to emerge from the commons in 1381. *Piers Plowman* begins:

> And on a May morning, on Malvern Hills,
> There befell me as by magic a marvelous thing …
> A fair field full of folk I found between them
> Of human beings of all sorts, the high and the low,
> Working and wandering as the world requires.[7]

The tension between "working and wandering," between stability and mobility, was taut. The plowman himself is the figure for stability; his is the hand on the plow, he keeps his eye on the prize, the straight furrow. He follows daily labor; he rolls with the rhythms of the seasons. The figure of mobility is the vagabond, the person who lolls, idles, or loiters, the one who rests at ease. This figure overlaps with the wandering monk, who strolled from monastery to monastery sleeping rough, who brought the religious into everyday life. The fifteenth-century French poet and vagabond, François Villon, honored by hippies and beatniks alike, is perhaps best known of the type. John Ball, Wat's partner in rebellion, was just such a mendicant, a beggar, a lay hermit, part of the ecclesiastical proletariat.

John Ball, the vagrant priest, and Wat Tyler, a tile-maker, were the leaders of the revolt. John Ball's letters were broadsides, attached to public places. The surviving letters were found in the garment of a man about to be hanged. Public hangings were frequent, "one might almost say uninterrupted."[8] The established Christian religion of the era exalted as Son of God and Savior of Mankind a man who had been crucified – hung – between common thieves. The comparison was noticed in *Piers Plowman*, which quotes Jesus in hell dialoguing with Lucifer: "And as a tree caused Adam and all mankind to die, so my gallows-tree shall bring them back to life."[9]

And what was mankind? What was a person? This question was at the center of the revolt. The notion that "Lordship over men, as all thinkers agreed, was of divine origin," was undermined by the very posing of the question.[10] John Ball preached on riddles, sometimes rather menacing ones. Some have been recited down the centuries, and are (perhaps unsurprisingly) amenable to being rapped. This first riddle is quite well known:

> John the Miller hath ground small, small, small;
> The King's son of heaven shall pay for all.
> Beware or ye be woe,
> Know your friend from your foe,
> Have enough, and say ho![11]

This second one, cunning in its avowal of equality and its subtle subversion of hierarchy, is as famous as it is powerful:

> When Adam delved and Eve span
> Who was then the gentleman?[12]

This was a revolutionary question capable of turning the world upside down.

The commons: kindness and the collective

The fourteenth century was the period of stabilization of the English surname in its modern form, as a heritable paternal addition. Surnames were introduced for purposes of taxation and of patrilinear inheritance. Through surnames, the rights of tenants were claimed through time; through tenancies of individual plots, came access to common rights over related lands, such as pasturage for animals. People were named most frequently for occupations. The way the rebels treated surnames reveals much.

John Ball sent a letter to the commons of Essex, followed by a poem. The letter exhorts the craftsmen to stand united with the plowmen, to rebuke ruling class thieves, and to follow the lead of the true man:

> John Schep ... priest ... greeteth well John Nameless, and John the Miller, and John Carter, and biddeth them that they ... stand together in God's name, and biddeth Piers Plowman go to his work, and chastise well Hob the Robber, and take with you John Trueman, and all his fellows, and no more.

The poem ends with a revolutionary prayer: "And pray for John Trueman and all his fellows." Shepherd, carter, miller, plowman are joined by John Nameless and John Trueman. Anonymity was politically essential, as it certainly was to "William Langland." What is expressed is also a collectivity opposed to the process of individuation and rampant individualism (the pursuit of selfish interest). Another revolutionary, "Jack the Miller," said:

> Look thy mill go aright,
> with the four sails,
> and the post stand in steadfastness.

With right and with might,
with skill and with will,
let might keep right,
and skill go before will
and right before might,
then goeth our mill aright.
And if might go before right,
and will before skill,
then is our mill mis-adight [unprepared].[13]

The miller operated the most advanced machine of the day, the watermill or the windmill. Here, the machine is taken as the force of the collective.

A new identity emerges in the struggle for social justice. The victory of the commons must bring with it a new kind of human being. John the Miller, John Carter, John Trueman, Piers Plowman – these figures are all of indeterminate historical status between fictive and actual. They bear confected names and improvised identities.[14] There have been many such "confected" figures in English social history, perhaps including Wat Tyler. In the sixteenth century, Lord Pity, Lord Poverty, and Captain Charity led risings of the commons. Lady Skimmington did so in the seventeenth century, as did Captain Ludd and Captain Swing in the nineteenth. Hovering over the arch of all these centuries like a green arbor is the equally confected person of Robin Hood – elusive, ecological, avenging, beautiful, and just.

This new kind of leader, this new kind of human being, fought for the collective. The true man. Everyman. Like its modern equivalent, the Middle English word "kynde" denotes both benevolence and the nature of something. To be unkind is to be unnatural, cruel, and devoid of the company of others of your class. To be kind is to live in benevolent solidarity with those of your class. The notion of "commoning" may rest neither on the natural law many associate with the eighteenth-century Enlightenment, nor on pragmatic agrarian customs, but on a third ground, namely, the law of "kynde." The early fourteenth-century *Dialogue of the Rich Man with the Pauper* declares "by the lawe of kynde and by Goddes lawe all thynge is common."[15] The simple virtue of kindness is the essence of the social relations of the commons.

The Revolt: 1381

In 1381, country people marched on London, one contingent from Essex and another from Kent. The city workers enabled the country people to enter by opening the gates and clearing the bridge. There was sympathy between the apprentices and trained crafts people of London on the one hand, and the incoming insurgents on the other. The latter had slept for days in the open, they were hungry and thirsty, and they were ready for hospitality. Among their first deeds, comparable to the liberation of defendants in American fugitive slave cases, was the opening of the prisons. The Kentish commons opened the Marshalsea prison in Southwark on Wednesday. On Thursday they freed the prisoners of the Fleet. Then they broke open Westminster prison and freed the prisoners, and proceeded by way of Holborn to break open Newgate prison. This was *habeas corpus* in action, the promise of the Magna Carta made good. Often the crowds also searched out the legal documentation justifying oppressions and destroyed it in the bonfires of the rising.

The Kentish and Essex rebels met in London on Thursday, 13 June 1381, the Feast of Corpus Christi. Corpus Christi, a veneration of the Eucharist as the body of Christ, was a new feast, proclaimed by the pope in 1317. With the formation of Corpus Christi fraternities in 1350s came elaborate outdoor processions. "The element of disorder, the excitement of a populous event, percolated and erupted in a variety of ways."[16] And no wonder. Midsummer is also the beginning of harvest time, the most labor intensive time of year.

Keeping body and soul together was a cooperative labor and visible to all. Strip-farming in open-field agriculture required intensive *ad hoc* cooperation, to share the plow, coordinate grazing, distribute wastes, and glean. Customary bylaws were by common consent. When the communities brought out from the fields by the tocsin marched along highways and by-ways they elevated the bread high, stuck on the trines of a long-handled pitch fork. Reaping the last of the ripened grain, bringing in the last load to the barn, was ritualized in folkish but not churchy ways. The lead reaper was lord of the harvest, and was accompanied by the harvest queen. The wagons were bedecked with flowers. All was accompanied by shout and song. Harvest-home was a solemn, sacred moment of triumph – or in bad years, of defeat. The lord of the manor, or employing farmer, was expected to display generosity at the harvest-home feast by roasting a goose, opening a barrel of ale, and so forth. It was the most important rural holiday in England, as the wellbeing, if not the life, of the community depended on the size and security of the harvest.

The Feast of Corpus Christi was therefore a time when the central Christian ritual of the miracle of the Mass would have had a particular inflection. The Eucharist celebrated the last supper of Jesus with his disciples, when he held up bread saying, eat this as a symbol/as remembrance/as my body. A year before the revolt, John Wycliffe had lectured, and authored a book, on this central Christian sacrament. He was thrown out of Oxford as a heretic in the winter of 1380–81 for objecting to the doctrine of transubstantiation on the grounds that it over-emphasized the miraculous power of the priest. Likewise, the peasantry of Essex and Kent might easily construe this mystery, not as a priestly mystery of *consumption* (transubstantiating bread into body), but as a collective action of *production* when plowing, sowing, mowing, weeding, harrowing, reaping, harvesting, binding, threshing, carting, milling, and kneading works (transubstantiates) seeds into grain into bread. It did not take much imagination to find a celebration of labor (the work of the body) at the heart of the sacrament.

So, the Kent and Essex rebels gathered on Corpus Christi Thursday and called for "a charter to free them from all manner of serfdom." On Friday, the commons met just outside the city walls at Mile End, a location between city and country where sports and games were commonly held. Henry Knighton, an early chronicler, wrote of the Friday gathering:

The king, for the sake of peace and because of the circumstances at the time, granted the commons, at their petition, a charter under his great seal – declaring that all men in the realm of England should be free and of free condition; they and their heirs should be forever released from the yoke of servitude and villeinage.

The king ordered 30 clerks to start writing in preparation for royal sigillation, the sealing that would render the documents official. Parchment charters were drawn up for Essex, Kent, Norfolk, Suffolk, and Hertford on this pattern:

Richard, by the grace of God, king of England and France, and lord of Ireland, to all his bailiffs and faithful men to whom these present letters come, greetings. Know that by our special grace we have manumitted all our liegemen, subjects, and others of the country of Hertford; and we have freed and quitted each of them from bondage by the present letters.[17]

Simple legal emancipation was not enough. The chronicler, Thomas Walsingham of St Albans explains that the charters were unacceptable to Wat Tyler. On Saturday, 15 June 1381, when Tyler, Jack Straw, and John Ball "had assembled their company to common together in a place called Smithfield," Tyler separated himself from his "kynde" and approached the king.

[Tyler] half bent his knee and took the king by the hand, shaking his arm forcefully and roughly, saying to him "Brother, be of good comfort and joyful, for you shall have, in the fortnight that is to come, forty thousand more commons than you have at present, and we shall be good companions." And the king said, "Why will you not go back to your own country?" But the other answered, with a great oath, that neither he nor his fellows would leave until they had got their charter as they wished to have it with the inclusion of certain points.[18]

Two accounts of the Smithfield meeting describe Tyler's specific demands. The *Anonimalle Chronicle* says that Wat asked that there be no law except for the law of Winchester. This substituted mutilation for hanging as punishment for felonies, and asserted rights for sokemen (an intermediate status between serfs and the fully free) including exemption from military service. He also demanded that henceforward there be no outlawry in any process of law. Most spectacularly, he called for the abolition of lordship, which should be divided among all men, except for the king's own lordship. He also asked that ecclesiastical property be divided among the people of the parish, saving only the need for sustenance of the clergy.

And he demanded that there should be no more villeins in England but that all men should be free and of one condition. To this the king gave an easy answer, and said that Wat should have all that he could fairly grant, reserving only for himself the regality of his crown.[19]

The *Anonimalle Chronicle* attributes to Tyler the principle of redistribution of wealth as well as the principle of restorative justice, but not of commons. Henry Knighton supplies a second account which refers specifically to the rural commons:

> The rebels petitioned the king that all preserves of water, parks, and woods should be made common to all: so that throughout the kingdom the poor as well as the rich should be free to take game in water, fish ponds, woods and forests as well as to hunt hares in the fields – and to do these and many other things without impediment.[20]

This is the key. Hearing this demand, the lord mayor of London, William Walworth, knocked Wat Tyler in the gutter, stabbing him in the throat.

Wat Tyler perished "while his hands and feet quivered for some time. Thereupon an enormous wailing broke out. ... "[21]

John Ball was drawn, hanged, and quartered at St Alban's on 13 July 1381, his body parts sent for exhibition to four towns of the kingdom. Two days later, John Shirle of Nottinghamshire was tried in Cambridge as a vagabond who carried "lies as well as silly and worthless talk from district to district," and who was overheard to have said in a tavern:

> that the stewards of the lord the king as well as the justices and many other officers and ministers of the king were more deserving to be drawn and hanged and to suffer other lawful pains and torments than John Ball, ... a true and worthy man, prophesying things useful to the commons of the kingdom and telling of wrongs and oppressions done to the people by the king and aforesaid ministers.

Shirle was hanged.[22]

Lordship depended on extraction of surplus from the peasantry. The serf was obliged to give boons (in cash or kind), corvées (specific labor services), or full days of labor to the lord. The abolition of lordship would have entailed the abolition of surplus labor, and of surplus value. Not only would feudalism have fallen, but capitalism would have had no basis. That is the significance of the charter proposed by Tyler.

Posterity

In *Piers Plowman*, the Tower on the hill represents Truth who:

> commanded the earth to provide wool and linen and food, enough for everyone to live in comfort and moderation. And of his goodness he ordained three things in common, which are all that your body requires: clothing to protect you from cold, food to keep you from want, and drink when you are thirsty.[23]

We may therefore distinguish three meanings of "the commons" as this bountiful concept was used at the time of the Peasants' Revolt. There is a religious meaning, which Wycliffe expressed in his translation of the Bible, "to have all things in common." There is a natural meaning, which Langland expressed as food, clothing, and drink. Finally, there is the economic meaning employed by Wat Tyler: customary access to woods, waters, and field.

What about all that scribbling at Mile End and Smithfield, all those charters, all that emancipation? The king's fingers were crossed:

> Miserable and detested men, who have sought to be your lord's equals, you are not worthy to live. You were and are serfs, and you will remain in bondage not as before, but incomparably viler. For as long as we live, we shall do our utmost with all faculties at our disposal to suppress you, so that the rigor of your servitude will serve as an example to posterity. Both now and in the future people like yourselves will always have your misery before your eyes like a mirror, so that you will be cursed by them and they will fear to do as you have done.[24]

Certainly that is part of the story. Yet posterity has not been unanimous in condemnation, nor in fear. Future workers also struggled, and many looked backwards to 1381.

The manuscript versions of *Piers Plowman* appeared during the first great peasants' revolt in defense of their commons. The printed version of the poem appeared in 1550, at the time of the huge revolts of the commons against enclosure (the fencing in of formerly common areas, deeding them to the exclusive control of a limited beneficiary) known as Kett's Rebellion in the east and the Prayer Book Rebellion in the west. It was published by Robert Crowley, whose diatribes against greed, enclosure, and egotism retain their force even into the twenty-first century. Crowley was surely pleased to be able to publish some of Langland's forceful, and scarcely outdated, arguments:

> Need, who knows no law and is indebted to no one. For to keep alive, there are three things which Need takes without asking. The first is food; for if men refuse to give him any, and he has no money, nothing to pawn, and no one to guarantee him, then he seizes it for himself. And there he commits no sin, even if he uses deceit to get it. He can take clothing in the same way, provided he has no better payment to offer; Need is always ready to bail a man out of prison for that. And thirdly, if his tongue is parched, the law of his nature compels him to drink at every ditch rather than die of thirst. So in great necessity, Need may help himself, without consulting Conscience or the Cardinal Virtues – provided he keep the Spirit of Moderation.[25]

The project of equality and the concept of the commons have continued to arise together. The fourteenth-century historian, Jean Froissart put into John Ball's preaching the doctrine "that matters goeth not well to pass in England nor shall do till everything be common and that there be no villeins nor gentlemen but that we may be all united together and that the lords be no greater masters than we be. ... "[26]

Wat Tyler has had an afterlife that is hardly uniform in its vilification. A play about the revolt, *Jack Straw* (one of Tyler's aliases), was performed in 1593 and included the following lines:

> England is growne to such a passe of late,
> That rich men triumph to see the poore beg at their gate.
> But I am able by good scripture before you to prove,
> That God doth not this dealing allow nor love,
> But when Adam delved and Eve span,
> Who was then a Gentleman.[27]

Thomas Paine praised Tyler in his *Rights of Man* (published in February 1792) as a successful rebel against taxes. Paine was answered by an English royal proclamation banning the book as subversive and banning its author as an outlaw. As for "the people," answered Edmund Burke, Paine's antagonist, they were "wild beasts," "a disbanded race of deserters and vagabonds," and John Ball was a "patriarch of sedition."[28] Paine called William Walworth "a cowardly assassin," while Burke praised Walworth's "spirited exertion."[29]

The split opinion of posterity concerning the rebel leaders is also reflected in the visual arts. James Northcote (1746–1831) exhibited a huge canvas (nine feet tall and more than 12 feet wide) of the death of Wat Tyler at the Royal Academy in London in 1787, representing the violence at the Smithfield meeting.[30] Commissioned by a London alderman, it was displayed while the memory was still fresh of the Gordon riots of 1780 which opened the London prisons, threatened the Bank of England, and destroyed property. The inverted pose of Tyler and the rearing horses depict the upside down, unnatural world of the rebel. The title expressed the municipal priorities: "Sir William Walworth, mayor of London, A.D. 1381, in the presence of Richard II then 15 years old, kills Wat Tyler, at the head of the insurgents, who are appeased by the heroic speech of the king." The better to permanently enshrine those priorities, in 1794 the painting was put on permanent display in the Council Chamber of Guildhall, where it remained until destroyed by bombs in the Second World War. In contrast, William Blake (1757–1827) depicted Wat Tyler (twice) in a more heroic vein. His first portrait was commissioned to accompany *A New and Improved History of England* (1798). Entitled "Wat Tyler and the Tax-gatherer," it shows the tax man dead on the ground, Tyler's daughter fleeing the scene in horror, and a young athletic Wat Tyler straddling the corpse, with a hammer in his hand, looking stunned at his deed. The second depiction of Wat Tyler was one of Blake's "Visionary Heads," the result of a séance with an astrologer that also conjured Socrates, Mohammed, and Voltaire. The pencil drawing of Tyler's neck and head is entitled "Wat Tyler by Wm. Blake from his spectre as in the act of striking the Tax Gatherer on the head, October 1819." Tyler is clear-eyed and focused, his mouth in articulate anger, his brows elegant, his neck strong, his hair curling like flames. The image is powerful and expressive, but – unlike Northcote's Royal Academy canvas – it is private and commemorative rather than public and instructional.[31]

Alliance with public authority has thus entailed taking the side of the double-crossing king over the commoner. In 1794 Robert Southey (1774–1843), believing that Tyler was one of his ancestors, wrote a dramatic poem called *Wat Tyler*, a work suffused with language Wat would have understood:

> … all mankind are equal, is most true;
> Ye came as helpless infants to the world:
> Ye feel alike the infirmities of nature;
> And at last moulder into common clay.
> Why then these vain distinctions! – bears not the earth
> Food in abundance? – must your granaries
> O'erflow with plenty, while the poor man starves?[32]

Southey didn't publish the play. He later rejected his revolutionary belief in equality and was rewarded as poet laureate. In 1817 his enemies published *Wat Tyler*, to Southey's acute embarrassment.

The persistence of the old regime: what is to be done?

Half a millennium after the Peasants' Rebellion, social inequality and economic injustice still marked the English scene. William Morris's (1834–96) *A Dream of John Ball* was published in a year that began with "Black Monday," when "an immense mass of poverty stricken humanity" marched through the genteel club land of Pall Mall smashing shop windows. *A Dream of John Ball* appeared between November 1886 and February 1887 in *Commonweal*, the newspaper of Morris' Socialist League. It was an extraordinarily creative time for Morris, who had just founded the League. He was also developing the Arts and Crafts Movement, a style that depended upon the handiwork of the individual artisan, rather than on industrial production.[33]

Morris himself desired a socialist transformation of labor. He could often be found wandering the streets of the East End, an habitué of its International Club where he held forth with fiery invective, eyes shining, head back. He aspired to an expression of ideas that could actually *move* people, as John Ball had done. In the *Dream*, Morris is transported back to June 1381 and the company of the Kentish rebels, a few days after they had delivered John Ball from the archbishop's prison in Canterbury, and a few weeks before the rebel's execution. Morris is privileged to hear Ball preach upon the famous couplet about Adam and Eve, and sees how he rouses the people to action. But Morris is also vouchsafed a poignant realization:

> I pondered all these things, and how men fight and lose the battle, and the thing that they fought for comes about in spite of their defeat, and when it comes turns out not to be what they meant, and other men have to fight for what they meant under another name.[34]

Friedrich Engels, in his *The Peasant War in Germany* (1850), had already concluded of medieval peasant wars generally that their "anticipation of communism nurtured by fantasy became in reality an anticipation of modern bourgeois conditions."[35] From this perspective, all the attempts of men such as Tyler and Ball were worse than failures. Intra-ruling-class resolution, repeatedly invigorated by the absorption of newly ascendant classes, perpetually blocks an equitable access to and distribution of the commons. Even Magna Carta can hardly be called a resounding success, while the Peasants' Revolt is certainly a portent whose promise is unfulfilled, as certain sectors of society become ever more affluent, and the gap between rich and poor grows dramatically.

Wat Tyler was assassinated by a man, namely the lord mayor of London, who made his money from the Flemish sex workers in the Southwark brothels.[36] The coat of arms of the City of London includes a red sword, commonly understood to commemorate the killing of Tyler by Walworth. The blade that attempted to silence the commons is a symbol of the urban bourgeoisie coming to power on the backs of the Peasants' Revolt. The City of London, that vibrant center of international capitalism, celebrates on its crest a panderer, an assassin, a sex-trafficker whose victim spoke for kindness, for emancipation, and for the commons. This should be known.[37]

The person Wat Tyler might be slain, but the ideas he spoke of were not. Above all, there is the importance of the commons. Thomas Paine concluded his concise account of the rising: "If the Barons merited a monument to be erected in Runny-mede [to commemorate the Great Charter], Tyler merits one in Smithfield."[38] Since 1866, the authorities in London have commemorated certain houses with a blue plaque where historically significant people once lived. In London today, there is no blue plaque attached at Smithfield, or at Mile End, or Southwark to remember this medieval worker who called the King "brother" and called for emancipation from serfdom. There should be. This popular rebellion raised issues that are by no means dead. The opening of the prisons, the emancipation from serfdom, the resumption of commoning (actual and ideal), the search for "kynde," all went hand in hand.

Notes

1 N. Cohn, *The Pursuit of the Millennium: Revolutionary Millenarians and Mystical Anarchists of the Middle Ages*, rev. edn, Oxford: Oxford University Press, 1970, p. 200.
2 W. Langland, *Piers the Ploughman*, trans. J.F. Goodridge, London: Penguin, 1959, p. 93.
3 W. Stubbs, *The Constitutional History of England in its Origin and Development*, 3rd edn, 3 vols, vol. 2, Oxford: Clarendon Press, 1887, p. 471.
4 R.B. Dobson (ed.) *The Peasants' Revolt of 1381*, London: Macmillan and Co, 1970, pp. 63–68.
5 A.E. Bland, P.A. Brown, and R.H. Tawney (eds) *English Economic History: Select Documents*, 3rd ed, New York: Macmillan, 1919, pp. 171–73.
6 T. Paine, *Rights of Man, Common Sense and Other Political Writings*, ed. M. Philip, New York: Oxford University Press, 2009, pp. 283–84.
7 W. Langland, *Will's Vision of Piers Plowman: An Alliterative Verse Translation*, trans. E.T. Donaldson, ed. E.D. Kirk and J.H. Anderson, New York: W.W. Norton, 1990, pp. 1–2.
8 J. Huizinga, *The Waning of the Middle Ages*, New York: Doubleday, 1954, p. 11.
9 Langland, *Piers the Ploughman*, trans. Goodridge, p. 227.
10 K.B. McFarlane, *John Wycliffe and the Beginnings of English Nonconformity*, London: Macmillan, 1952, p. 67.

11 T. Walsingham, *The Chronica Maiora of Thomas Walsingham (1376–1422)*, trans. D. Preest, Hambledon: Boydell Press, 2005, p. 163.
12 For the centrality of this popular quotation, see the *Wikipedia* article, "John Ball." Online. Available HTTP: <http://en.wikipedia.org/wiki/John_Ball_(priest)> (accessed 17 December 2010).
13 Dobson (ed.) *The Peasants' Revolt of 1381*, pp. 380, 382.
14 A. Middleton, "William Langland's 'Kynde Name': Authorial Signature and Social Identity in Late Fourteenth Century England," in *Literary Practice and Social Change in Britain, 1380–1530*, ed. L. Patterson, Berkeley: University of California Press, 1989, pp. 15–82.
15 Cohn, *The Pursuit of the Millennium*, p. 200.
16 M. Rubin, *Corpus Christi: The Eucharist in Late Medieval Culture*, Cambridge: Cambridge University Press, 1991, p. 263.
17 Dobson (ed.) *The Peasants' Revolt of 1381*, pp. 183, 180.
18 Dobson (ed.) *The Peasants' Revolt of 1381*, p. 164.
19 Dobson (ed.) *The Peasants' Revolt of 1381*, p. 164.
20 Dobson (ed.) *The Peasants' Revolt of 1381*, p. 186.
21 Dobson (ed.) *The Peasants' Revolt of 1381*, p. 186.
22 R. Hanna, *Pursuing History: Middle English Manuscripts and their Texts*, Stanford, CA: Stanford University Press, 1996, p. 268.
23 Langland, *Piers the Ploughman*, trans. Goodridge, p.32.
24 Dobson (ed.) *The Peasants' Revolt of 1381*, p. 311.
25 Langland, *Piers the Ploughman*, trans. Goodridge, p. 246.
26 R. Hilton, *Bond Men Made Free: Medieval Peasant Movements and the English Rising of 1381*, New York: Viking, 1973, p. 222.
27 Dobson (ed.) *The Peasants' Revolt of 1381*, p. 390.
28 Dobson (ed.) *The Peasants' Revolt of 1381*, p. 393.
29 Paine, *Rights of Man*, p. 284.
30 R. Dias, "Loyal Subjects? Exhibiting the Hero of James Northcote's *Death of Wat Tyler*," Visual Culture in Britain 8, 2007, 21–43.
31 P. Ackroyd, *Blake*, New York: Knopf, 1996, pp. 328–30.
32 Dobson (ed.) *The Peasants' Revolt of 1381*, pp. 397–98.
33 F. MacCarthy, *William Morris: A Life for Our Time*, New York: Knopf, 1995.
34 W. Morris, "A Dream of John Ball and a King's Lesson," *The Commonweal*, November 1886. Online. Available HTTP: <http://etext.virginia.edu/etcbin/toccer-new2?id=MorDrea.sgm&images=images/modeng&data=/texts/english/modeng/parsed&tag=public&part=4&division=div1> (accessed 19 December 2010).
35 Dobson (ed.) *The Peasants' Revolt of 1381*, p. 402.
36 Dobson (ed.) *The Peasants' Revolt of 1381*, p. 156.
37 "Coat of Arms of the City of London," Wikipedia. Online. Available HTTP: <http://en.wikipedia.org/wiki/File:Coat_of_Arms_of_The_City_of_London.svg> (accessed 21 January 2011).
38 Dobson (ed.) *The Peasants' Revolt of 1381*, p. 396.

Suggestions for further reading

Medieval sources in English translation

Dobson, R.B., *The Peasants' Revolt of 1381*, London: Macmillan and Co, 1970, available as an American Council of Learned Societies History E-Book Project Reprint.
Langland, W., *Piers the Ploughman*, trans. J.F. Goodridge, London: Penguin, 1959.
——, *Will's Vision of Piers Plowman: An Alliterative Verse Translation*, trans. E.T. Donaldson, ed. E.D. Kirk and J.H. Anderson, New York: W.W. Norton, 1990.

Medieval social and political history

Ault, W.O., "By-Laws by Common Consent," *Speculum* 29, 1954, 378–94.

Hilton, R., *Bond Men Made Free: Medieval Peasant Movements and the English Rising of 1381*, New York: Viking, 1973.

Hutton, R., *The Rise and Fall of Merry England: The Ritual Year, 1400–1700*, Oxford: Oxford University Press, 1994.

Justice, S., *Writing and Rebellion: England in 1381*, Berkeley: University of California Press, 1994.

Linebaugh, P., *The Magna Carta Manifesto: Liberties and Commons for All*, Berkeley: University of California Press, 2008.

Middleton, A., "Acts of Vagrancy: The C Version 'Autobiography' and the Statute of 1388," in *Written Work: Langland, Labor, and Authorship*, ed. S. Justice and K. Kerby-Fulton, Philadelphia: University of Pennsylvania Press, 1997, pp. 208–318.

Strohm, P., "A 'Peasants' Revolt'?," in *Misconceptions about the Middle Ages*, ed. S.J. Harris and B.L. Grigsby, New York: Routledge, 2008, pp. 197–203.

Modern conditions

De Angelis, M., *The Beginning of History: Value Struggles and Global Capital*, London: Pluto Press, 2007.

Gooch, S., *Will Wat? If Not What Will?* London: Pluto Press, 1973.

Hyde, L., *The Gift: Creativity and the Artist in the Modern World*, New York: Vintage, 2007.

Savage, C., *Takeover: The Return of the Imperial Presidency and the Subversion of American Democracy*, New York: Little, Brown and Company, 2008.

14

LEADERSHIP

Why we have mirrors for princes but none for presidents

Geoffrey Koziol

One of the things that struck me during the run-up to the war in Iraq was that so few asked the simplest of all possible questions: Was it wise? As a medieval historian I could not help but notice the omission and think about it, because in medieval writings on rulership – principally the writings we call mirrors for princes – wisdom was consistently regarded as the crowning virtue of rulers. Well into the seventeenth century, it was next to impossible to talk about political power without insisting on the need for leaders to make decisions based on virtues like wisdom and moderation. This does not mean that leaders were wise in judgments and moderate in actions. It does mean that political policy was discussed in such terms. At some point this stopped being true – at least it stopped being true in the liberal tradition of political philosophy that is one of our most important intellectual inheritances. Especially as it developed in England, Scotland, and the United States, classical liberal theory tended to banish ethics from public political discourse, relegating it to a private sphere of religion and belief. As a result, modern liberal theorists rarely look at premodern political theory, and never at early medieval political theory. There is, I think, a cost. Our understanding of the historical antecedents of liberalism is historically simplistic, and our understanding of political society is incomplete.

Mirrors for princes are treatises written to advise rulers on the principles of good and bad governance. Their antecedents lie in late antiquity. By the seventh century, the Irish had begun to turn the antecedents into something like a genre. But the genre itself was largely created on the continent in the eighth and ninth centuries, during the zenith of the Carolingian dynasty that established an empire encompassing much of modern Western Europe.[1] Written by church leaders, the treatises take their name from one of their recurring metaphors; the author claimed to be presenting a distillation of scriptural and patristic teachings on virtue and vice, good and bad rulership, that might serve as a "mirror" in which a king could examine himself and the quality of his actions. They accordingly discuss a wide range of issues, including the purposes of kingship, the governance of the royal court and household, the nature of justice, the goals and limits of warfare, the appointment of counselors and administrative agents, and the principles that determine reward and punishment.

If a modern political philosopher did happen to look at the mirrors, he would likely find them uninspiring. To begin with, they can be enormously repetitive. Granted, specialists can easily recognize shifts of emphasis according to whatever problem seemed to be most acute at the time. Over the course of the dynasty's history, mirrors tended to become more concerned to protect the church's prerogatives, more subtly critical of royal policies, above all more rhetorically involuted. Nevertheless, most non-specialists who read the mirrors will be more impressed by their dulling sameness, as identical points are made over and over, backed up by the same scriptural and patristic citations.

Carolingian mirrors can also seem simplistic to the point of being vapid. For what is their advice? That good kings rule long and leave a happy memory, whereas evil kings invite insurrection and failure. A king should therefore be pious, just, merciful, and wise. He should show mercy to the weak and unfortunate, severity to the wicked. He should always take counsel, but only from those who are upright, honest, and God-fearing. Posing as just such counselors, the mirrorists offer advice that is upright and godly but utterly unrealistic, consisting mostly of platitudes. Take the well-known axiom of kingship that appears in them almost without fail: "Rex a regendo vocatur" or "Rex a recte agendo uocatur." The statements cannot be translated without losing an essential pun, but the former might be approximated as "a ruler is called 'ruler' from ruling." Quite apart from the fact that this seems like an obvious tautology, what possible practical significance does it have for politics? Generally, the statement leads to an argument that in order to rule a kingdom a king must be able to rule first himself, then his family, then his household or palace: "For how will he be able to correct others if he cannot correct his own behavior?"[2] Yet this, too, seems an empty abstraction, illustrating the mirrorists' desire for symmetry between microcosm and macrocosm. What it does not show is a willingness to grapple with the hard issues of power.

The statement also illustrates a third reason the mirrors might seem irrelevant: their teachings are embedded in an ideology that is thoroughly hierarchical, the product of a social reality foreign to us. As the principle that rulership comes from ruling is expanded upon, it is explained as meaning that a king should rule over himself by subjecting his passions to his reason. But this argument is simply the application of a principle of subjection that is thought to run throughout Creation. That is, reason should rule over passions as a king should rule over the subordinate members of his household, husbands over wives, fathers over children, leaders over subjects, and God over the universe. These are hardly principles compatible with the complex pluralism of our own industrial and post-industrial democracies.

Equally incompatible is the mirrors' assumption that learned churchmen have the right and duty to rule on issues of political morality. From a cynical perspective, their advice boils down to this: If a king wants to become a good and successful ruler, he should uphold the prerogatives of churchmen, always heed their counsel, always maintain their churches' rights. The basic rule seems to be, "Do what we say." Whatever this is, it is not political theory. Theory is by definition critical: That is, theorists engage in a dialogue not only with those who agree with them but also with those who do not. In justifying their own positions, they make arguments against opposing positions. But Carolingian mirrorists do not argue; they admonish. They adopt the role of Old Testament prophets, rebuking and correcting kings as Samuel rebuked Saul and Nathan corrected David (I Samuel 13, 15; II Samuel 12). They adopt not just the role but the very words of the prophets, quoting them so extensively that ultimately it is not a ninth-century bishop who speaks but the prophets themselves. How could one possibly do the same today? A "mirror" for presidents or prime ministers would be laughable in its simplicity: Be just, listen only to the advice of the ethically upright, do not be either too angry or too mild. It would be laughable in its political naïveté, for the ability to admonish presumes a position of recognized moral authority, and we do not grant such authority to any person or group.

Yet the people who wrote the mirrors were not naïve at all. They were among the most active and influential leaders of their society, and very experienced in matters of government. Mirrors were also an immensely popular genre in the ninth century, and they remained so throughout the middle ages and even beyond. In fact, the two most famous mirrors for princes are from the later middle ages: The twelfth-century John of Salisbury's *Policraticus* and – written *c.* 1300 by a disciple of Thomas Aquinas – *On the Government of Rulers (De regimine principum)*. In the fourteenth century, the Renaissance humanist, Francesco Petrarch, wrote a mirror for the prince of an Italian city-state. Constructed almost entirely from citations of classical, pre-Christian authors, it barely mentions God and quotes hardly any passages from the Bible. Yet it is recognizably a descendant of the ninth-century mirrors, treating many of the same topics in much the same order, and giving much the same advice. As late as 1641, Cardinal Richelieu wrote a mirror for the king of France, Louis XIII, and Richelieu was a legend for his political cunning.

For nearly a thousand years, sophisticated people judged mirrors for princes a useful genre for making important points about power and politics. Given this fact, if we dismiss them because we find them naïve, we are clearly misunderstanding them. In such situations, it is often helpful to ground an analysis on the very qualities one finds most confounding, meaning, in this case, the mirrors' apparently simplistic advice, their moralizing, and their posture of admonition. If we take these seriously – if, that is, we take these characteristics not as weaknesses of the mirrors but as reasons they were thought important – then we end up at an interesting place. For these characteristics point to a fundamental difference between medieval and modern liberal political theory. The difference is quite simple: Classical liberalism holds that politics and morality have nothing to do with each other and that political power cannot usefully be discussed in terms of ethics. The mirrorists demand precisely the opposite beliefs.

Private interest and common good

It is often assumed that modern liberalism is built upon a theory of rights. In other words, the core beliefs of liberalism are that all individuals have rights with which government cannot interfere and that government exists to protect these rights. However, both logically and chronologically prior to the liberal theory of rights was a liberal theory of interests. This theory first fully emerged in the eighteenth century; but a key ingredient appeared quite suddenly in the sixteenth century with the Italian political philosopher, Niccolò Machiavelli (1469–1527). Before Machiavelli, interests – meaning private interests – were bad for society. Interests were what political leaders were supposed to restrain, not countenance, still less promote. For interests were motivated by the worst of the human vices (such as greed, envy, and pride) and worked against the common good of the society as a whole. Everyone assumed that the two primary purposes of government were to promote the virtue of individuals and to promote the common good. The ideal may have rarely motivated decisions of political leaders, but it was still the only ideal thought possible to justify the coercive powers of governments. Machiavelli created a revolution in political theory by conducting a simple thought-experiment; instead of judging political decisions according to their morality and their promotion of the common good, what would happen if we judged them according to the private interest of the ruler? The result was his most famous treatise, *The Prince*, which was quite intentionally a mirror for princes turned inside-out. Where mirrors insisted that a ruler should choose counselors for their virtue and sense of justice, Machiaevelli said they should be chosen for their loyalty. Where mirrors advised rulers to avoid unnecessary wars, Machiavelli claimed to esteem rulers who successfully engaged in wars of pure expansion. We may dislike the moral implications of Machiavelli's suggestion that a ruler might be guided only by what promotes his own advantage; but like it or not, the future of European political theory lay in working out those implications. The domain of political inquiry was no longer what rulers *should* do by virtue of moral imperatives. Political inquiry concerned what rulers actually did to promote their interests.

By the eighteenth century, many political theorists had come to apply a model of interests to the entire society, analyzing political communities as the product of complex negotiations between the private interests of all individuals within it. In the beginning, they argued that if individuals were left free to pursue their own self-interests, then the extremes would cancel each other out, leaving something like a virtuous mean. Thus, an individual's desire for wealth or power would be counterbalanced by a desire for good reputation, leading to greed that was productive but restrained. Eventually, this led to a second theoretical revolution. What eighteenth-century theorists did that no one had done before was to transform the very principles of political ethics by arguing that, if a government allowed free rein to the pursuit of private interests, then everyone's individual pursuit of private interest would positively benefit society as a whole, by creating a greater sum total of goods for all individuals. The common good became the product of private interests, not its contrary. This was the axiom of liberalism as it developed in the late eighteenth and early nineteenth centuries, especially in Britain and the United States.

This underlying theory of interests is the fundamental reason the mirrors seem foreign to us. The entire stance of the mirrors is predicated on two exactly opposite assumptions: That the moral behavior of individuals is important to the proper political functioning of a society, and that the common good is an end in itself, different from and opposed to private interests. All liberal political theory begins with the assumption that individuals in society are pursuing their interests. By embracing this, Machiavelli seems modern to us. In contrast, by insisting on the ethical behavior expected of rulers and on the common good that rulers must protect, the mirrors come across as simplistic and impractical, and therefore un-modern and irrelevant.

Setting up the problem in this way allows us to read the mirrors more generously, by identifying important principles within them that can contrast with modern liberalism. For example, as is well known, classic liberal theory is very good at stating what individuals should be protected from but not particularly helpful at saying what individuals should do – essentially allowing them to do anything they want short of murder, rape, robbery, and arson. In contrast, pick up any Carolingian mirror for princes and read it in light of either classical liberal theory or its descendants, and one may be struck by an immediate and overwhelming contrast; it proudly states a political morality – goals and imperatives that stand apart from all private interests. The injunction that recurs most frequently is that a ruler must protect widows, orphans, and the poor – that is, the powerless. But there are others. Appoint upright individuals as officials. Listen to a wide array of counsel from good men. Punish the wicked, support the upright. Be humble, because power that goes up will someday come down, and in the ultimate scheme of things, rulers are worth no more than those they rule. Punish, but do not just punish: Be moderate in your punishments, and merciful, not because it is ultimately advantageous but because everyone sins, and all punishment must take account of context and capacity. Eventually the author will state that the good of society is oriented to a final goal and principle, which is God. Accordingly, he will argue that a ruler must always act knowing that at the end of time he will be judged by God according to his actions. Yet for the most part, in the practical injunctions, and despite the frequent recourse to scripture and patristic texts, God does not come into it. This is why Petrarch could write a mirror that enunciated the traditional political morality with only the most fleeting references to God and scriptures. The injunctions of the mirrors are inherently moral (in the sense of being categorical imperatives, meaning intuitively good in themselves, and incumbent on us simply by virtue of being good); they are religious only by historical circumstance. The difference between the mirrors' political ethics and modern liberalism is only circumstantially a matter of Christianity. The more fundamental differences are the oppositions between ethics and advantage, common good and private interest.

The point, then, is that Carolingian mirrors strongly assert a political morality. In contrast, the best classical liberalism can do is justify decisions based on utility, which is not a moral injunction at all, or evacuate any kind of moral injunction from the public sphere, leaving morality to be defined as an entirely private concern, liberty to be defined only negatively – freedom *from*, as it is often described. But the Carolingian mirrors do have a social morality, a morality that binds individuals within a society. In effect, it is an ecclesial morality. That is, all of society was seen as a church (*ecclesia*). Seen as a church, society as a whole became a moral entity. Within such an ecclesial society, individuals had positive moral and ethical obligations to themselves, to others, and to the society as a whole.

This interpretation goes against a strongly hierarchical reading of Carolingian mirrors, but such a reading is possible only if the mirrors are read as a specialized genre aimed solely at kings and analyzed in isolation from other genres characteristic of the Carolingian reform program in its totality. That is not how they should be read. To be sure, being written for kings, the mirrors dwell on aspects of royal governance. Above all, they tend to insist on the king's duty of correction (*correctio*) or discipline (*disciplina*): That is, his obligation to punish what should be punished, to defend those who need protection, to lead the cause of reform in order to obtain God's blessings for God's people. And of course, they are shot through with the belief that kings are owed unquestioned obedience, unquestioned because rooted in the commands of Apostles Peter and Paul to subject oneself to the proper authorities (Romans 13; I Peter 2). Yet the mirrors do not just celebrate royal authority and demand obedience to it. On the contrary, their primary concern was to lay out the virtues required of rulers. One cannot separate their insistence on royal authority from that on royal ethics. Given the first, the second is logically necessary. If kings are to be obeyed because they rule in the image of God, then kings must rule ethically because ruling ethically is part of God's image. More important, if kings are to be unquestioningly obeyed, then the only safeguard against royal tyranny is a king's own ethical conscience. Since there was no "constitutional" mechanism that could hold kings to justice – no model of separation of powers, no theory of latent popular sovereignty that might justify rebellion against an unjust king – the only possibility for ensuring ethical authority was ethical education – that is, admonition.

In linking rulership and ethics, Carolingian political thought was not all that different from much ancient political thought, notably Stoicism. Stoicism's influence on Christianity is well known and came very early: Paul's treatment of the fellowship of Christians as a kind of body politic is already extremely Stoic (I Corinthians 12). Carolingian mirrorists were beneficiaries of this influence. Thus, their insistence that rulers cultivate the four cardinal virtues (justice, prudence, fortitude, and temperance) was a Stoic commonplace, transmitted partly through the Roman philosopher Cicero (d. 43 BCE), partly through Pope Gregory the Great (d. 604). The very axiom of Carolingian political theory – that a ruler must know how to rule himself in order to rule others – was taken over from the Stoics (again partly through Gregory). Mirrorists do not give the idea's underlying logic, so it comes across as simplistic. Though simple, the idea is not simplistic at all: A ruler must cultivate reason so that he might learn how to rule his passions, for ungoverned passions lead to false judgments. Nevertheless, there are important differences between Stoic and Carolingian ethical writings that underscore the Carolingians' innovation. To the

Stoics, the ideal of *apathēia* (not "apathy" but "dispassion") was attainable only by the sage who had trained arduously to discipline himself. Being so difficult, it lay beyond the capacity of most human beings – which is precisely why ordinary men and women needed to be governed by those superior in rational self-control. In contrast, the Carolingians universalized ethics both politically and socially. That is, Carolingian ethics were not the preserve of an intellectual or political elite. Carolingian ethical behavior was asserted to be a requirement of all people in their ordinary social existence, in everyday social interactions, as a condition of being members of society.

Here again, one cannot escape the influence of Gregory the Great. Those who do not know the period often assume that Augustine of Hippo (354–430) was the most important patristic author for the formation of early medieval Christianity. Augustine was important, but not as important as Gregory, and the reasons are paramount for understanding the development of European political ethics. More than any other early Christian author, Gregory repackaged and transmitted the basics of Stoic ethical teachings in a way that could be adopted in fully Christian societies. He also couched his teachings on Christian leadership in a way that applied to all leaders of society – not just bishops but abbots, not just prelates but kings, not just kings but all who held positions of power. Yet at the same time, he insisted on the underlying equality of all human beings: rulers and ruled, free and slaves, men and women. As a result, he made the same ethics an imperative of behavior for all Christians, regardless of their status or authority.

Gregory's way of commenting on the scriptures accordingly tended to draw out moral lessons relevant to the behavior of individuals, and again not just leaders but every Christian.[3] In adopting Gregory, the Carolingian mirrors ended up absorbing all these traits. They reveal Gregory's Stoic legacy not only in their insistence on the tempering qualities of the four cardinal virtues, but even more in their tendency to believe that extremes of behavior and ethical absolutism lead to poor decisions. While insisting that bishops and kings belong to different orders within the church and therefore have separate responsibilities, they apply Gregory's standards of pastoral care to all those they call prelates (*praelati*) – which includes not only kings, bishops, and abbots but also counts, counselors, and judges.[4] While assuming a division of society between rulers and ruled, like Gregory the mirrors still insist on an underlying human equality, further arguing that this equality is the reason any tyranny is evil. But the basic equality of men and women, free and slaves, rulers and ruled is also the reason that Gregory's ethics can be, in some sense, universalized to apply equally to all people. If all people have the same rights by virtue of being the children of God, all also have the same obligations to each other.

These became the crucial innovatory principles of the Carolingians' great transformation of political discourse. For the Carolingians created an empire that stretched across the European subcontinent, from the Pyrenees to the Elbe and from Italy to the English Channel. If one were not a Jew, one was a member of this empire as both a subject and a baptized Christian. Church and empire became different aspects of a single Christian society. To reform the church was therefore to reform the empire, and vice-versa. To be a good subject was to be a good Christian, and vice-versa. As a result, the same ethics that applied to Christian believers automatically applied to citizens of the empire. An ethics that had been distinctly Christian now became indistinctly political.

In this new political and religious context, though a king ruled his subjects, he was no longer ethically superior to them. Rather, he ruled the people by setting them an example. The mirrorists say this quite explicitly: "Ruler" comes from "ruling," and therefore a ruler must first strive to rule himself and his household and "abound in good works" so that his subjects may "take a good example" from his actions. As he establishes precepts for others, so he must follow the precepts of Christ "obediently and faithfully, and by acting rightly show good works in peace, concord, and charity, providing an example of justice and mercy."[5]

Carolingian ethics and education

In this way, the mirrorists' expectations for kings cannot be separated from their expectations for all individuals in Christian society. One must therefore recognize that the ethical admonitions enunciated in mirrors for kings were not addressed only to kings. Alcuin (d. 804) – probably the empire's single most influential teacher – wrote a treatise on the virtues and vices for a member of the high Carolingian aristocracy named Wido.[6] It is essentially a mirror for princes; it simply applies injunctions normally made for kings to royal ministers, simplifying them a bit in the process but also generalizing them. Besides writing a mirror for the young king of Aquitaine, Bishop Jonas of Orléans (d. 840/1) wrote a treatise for another high-ranking Frankish aristocrat. The first two books concern Christianity and marriage, but the entire third book is a tutorial on ethics.[7] In the 840s, the high-born, highly educated Dhuoda wrote a fascinating handbook for her son. It, too, is a mirror (she explicitly speaks of it as such), woven from ethical injunctions taken from scriptures and Gregory the Great.[8] Yet one does not find this concern for ethics only in mirrors for kings and the noble elite. Quite the contrary, ethics was the core of the great reform legislation (or "capitularies") produced under the Carolingian emperors Charlemagne (747–814) and his son Louis the Pious (781–840).[9] These documents include the "General Admonition" of 789 (much of it written by Alcuin) and the acts of the Council of Paris of 829, largely written by Jonas of Orléans.

Looking at the Carolingian reform capitularies, historians have often emphasized the expectation of obedience and the division of Christian society into distinct social orders. Certainly these traits are hard to ignore. For example, a capitulary issued around 811 urges children to love and honor parents, wives to be subject to husbands, and clerics to obey bishops, and much is made of the power of nobles to judge and punish. But the full context of such statements gives a somewhat different impression. Let a wife be subject to her husband "in all goodness and purity," but let a husband love his wife. If kings rule in the image of God, counts and judges are "sharers in the royal ministry" and must therefore exercise their ministries according to the same ethical standards that apply to kings.[10] They must judge righteously, with compassion for the poor and shunning bribery, and they must not use their power to punish or oppress the innocent.

In any case, the vast bulk of this and other legislation has nothing to do with enforcing respect for authority. The vast bulk is ethical and applies to every subject of the empire. Love your neighbor as yourself. Live in peace with each other. Help the oppressed. Care for strangers and give alms to the poor as you are able. Visit the sick and be merciful to prisoners. Do not commit theft, do not commit murder, do not fornicate. Avoid perjury, drunkenness, adultery, usury, all excessive profiteering in selling food and drink, and any lawsuits motivated solely by gain. Above all and summarizing all, we should live knowing that this life is short, the time of our death uncertain, and that at the end of all time we will be judged according to what we have done. If we want to obtain the mercy of God, we should be merciful to others.

Emphasizing the Carolingians' demand for order and obedience can therefore blind us to something more interesting – and in the long run, more important. The Carolingians did not simply create a specialized genre known as mirrors for princes that imposed moral obligations on kings and society's other leaders. Nor did their legislation only demand that subjects obey leaders. The Carolingians created a wide array of moral exhortations applicable to all individuals, whatever their status or office. By virtue of membership in a Christian society, every single individual had moral responsibilities – and not just moral responsibilities but essentially the same moral responsibilities. Whether they addressed kings or aristocrats, leaders or subjects, ordinary lay persons or monks, Carolingian moralists applied the same ethics to all. The common identity of Christians as equally children of God was so deeply axiomatic that in profoundly important ways, not even slavery and gender stood in its way. The ethical measures of behavior and the moral imperatives that applied to kings therefore applied to all men and women, of all social classes and orders. There was a single Carolingian ethics, a single Carolingian political morality. If kings were emblematic of ordinary individuals, the flipside was that ordinary individuals were kings of themselves.

This is utterly different from the writings of the great classical Greek philosophers, Plato and Aristotle. Although one can find antecedents in Stoicism and the Old Testament, in Paul and the early Christian text known as the *Didache*, in Augustine and Gregory the Great, the Carolingians were the ones who wove these antecedents into a coherent political ethics applicable to ordinary members of society in their daily existence. The full force of such expectations can be seen in one of Charlemagne's most famous capitularies, one that followed his imperial coronation in 800, in which he required all free males over the age of 12 to swear a new oath of loyalty to him. There had been previous demands for such oaths, but those had been sworn to him as king. This oath would be sworn to him as emperor, but that was a minor change due to the new title. The real innovation was of far greater importance: Where earlier oaths had been sworn in terms of not doing harm to the ruler, this oath was explained in terms of its positive injunctions. Those injunctions are yet another résumé of the Carolingians' moral and ethical program, and the very first stipulation is this one:

> That each and every person strive to fully keep his own person in the holy service of God according to the precept of God and according to his promise, according to the capacity of his understanding and his ability, because the lord emperor cannot himself show the necessary concern and disciplining in every single thing.[11]

This startling statement goes to the very heart of the Carolingian reforms. Quite simply, what it says is that a government cannot do it all. We are each individually responsible, for ourselves and for others. We are individually responsible for our own ethical behavior. We are each king of ourselves. We must each govern ourselves.

Just as the autonomy of kings required them to be educated about their moral responsibilities, so it was for all members of a society in which kingship was exemplary of the self-rule of individuals. This, I think, is the real reason for the Carolingians' well known attention to education – or better, as French and German have it, "formation." Because ethics requires reason, understanding, and an individual's active commitment, ethics cannot be legislated; it can only be taught. And it was taught, across an astonishingly wide array of platforms: In mirrors for kings and nobles, in capitularies both royal and episcopal, in synods and assemblies, in prayers and sermons. In all these texts one finds the same exhortations to the same ethical behavior. Capitularies and conciliar decrees repeatedly insist that bishops preach in churches, that royal legates teach in local public assemblies. They are to teach not simply that usury is wrong but exactly what it is and why it is wrong (because it is associated with greed, which is the "root of all evil"); not just that homicide is wrong but why (because we are all children of God, so that any homicide is a kind of fratricide); that all should avoid drunkenness but leaders especially, so that their followers may learn from their example. In both royal and episcopal capitularies, local priests are told to instruct their parishioners – about the essentials of the Christian faith, to be sure, but also about the essentials of Christian ethics: To provide for guests without demanding compensation; to avoid perjury, lying, drunkenness, and profiteering; to practice true charity in everything. All this priests should teach as best they are able, and if they know nothing else they can at least teach the people this: "That they shall renounce evil and do good, seek peace and follow it."[12] The same legislation insists that godparents have a duty to educate their godchildren in the fundamentals of faith, which is to say the fundamentals of Christian ethics. Then there are the sermons, the best known being those of Alcuin's student Hrabanus Maurus (d. 856). Though many of them were written for monks and clerics, a surprisingly large number were addressed to laypeople of all statuses. These, too, are exhortations to ethical behavior: To practice justice and mercy; to avoid drunkenness, covetousness, fraud, theft, and lying; to care for widows, pilgrims, and the poor; to remember that even a serf is one's brother, "because we are all descended from one man … and all alike we are born, die, and decay."[13] Finally, there are the prayers written for daily use by ordinary Christians (Alcuin again began the trend) which largely resume the same ethical injunctions found in mirrors, royal and episcopal capitularies, and sermons:

Give me prudence, courage, justice, and temperance. Give me the discernment to distinguish good from evil. … Keep the spirit of pride away from me. Grant me humility of heart. …

Or again:

Keep my mouth from vain speech, let me not engage in idle talk, let me not disparage my neighbor. … Guard my ears so that I hear no criticism or lies or useless words. … [14]

If individuals are individually responsible for the good of society, then individuals must be educated to know what their ethical expectations are. The Carolingian leadership worked to foster this kind of education in schools and families, assemblies and courts, in books of law to be read and books of prayers to be learned by heart and daily recited.

The legacy of the mirrors

In learning to appreciate mirrors for princes, one does not want to make the Carolingians paragons of virtue. In particular, one needs to recognize how problematic their understanding of virtue is for us. Carolingian rulers could be cunning and cruel. They humiliated enemies in show trials whose outcomes were foregone conclusions. They blinded their opponents for treason, even when the opponent was a son or nephew. In the course of a 30-year-long war against the Saxons, Charlemagne had 4,500 Saxon prisoners of war executed. When unrest continued, he declared the harshest imaginable martial law against the "rebels" (who, however, never asked to be conquered or converted), punishing every conceivable offense with death, from conspiracy against the king to refusal to pay tithes or observe Lent. To break continuing resistance, he finally began the wholesale deportation of the most hostile Saxons, removing them from their villages and transporting them to settlements within Frankish territories, while a friendly Slavic tribe was called in to colonize the deserted lands. All such actions could be justified according to contemporary understandings of Christian imperial authority. In fact, they illustrated, if at an extreme, the same duty of a ruler to correct and discipline that the mirrors championed. Nevertheless, they are not the whole story. Though Louis the Pious had his nephew blinded, criticism of his action was so severe that five years later he did public penance for his sin. Alcuin spoke out respectfully but firmly against the harshness with which Charlemagne required the Saxons to pay tithes, arguing that it was entirely counterproductive, that teaching made better converts than force.[15] Nor can one read Hrabanus Maurus' sermons and not have a sense that here was a bishop who tried to live up to his calling as he had learned it from Gregory the Great and Alcuin, his own teacher.

Although ideas of virtue may be specific to different societies, perhaps if a society espouses virtue it creates standards that can lead, in fact, to virtue. Perhaps exemplars of virtue really do serve as a mirror in which we can examine our own actions. This is one reason to appreciate the mirrors, but there is also another: The effect they had on European political discourse. Historians have often not perceived it, for it operated over a glacially long period of time – not years or decades but centuries – and was accompanied by angrier revolutions, more destructive wars, and equal if not greater social injustices. Yet an effect there was. Though the Carolingian empire was already falling apart by the middle of the ninth century, its ideal of ecclesial community endured. It was received in new settings, adapted to new circumstances, and transformed in its underlying political ideology, but it endured. Throughout the middle ages, the Carolingian ideal of society as a moral community continued to inform learned justifications of government, as with later mirrors for princes. It remained the dominant ideal of governance, never more so than in the French king, Louis IX's great reform ordinance of 1254, in both style and substance much like a Carolingian capitulary.[16] It continued to shape European understandings of the individual, as in the strangely captivating treatise known as *The Goodman of Paris*, written by an elderly Parisian burgher for his young wife. Counseling her to avoid anger, he quotes what he calls "a rustic proverb": "None is worthy to have rule or lordship over any other who cannot rule himself." Even in the fourteenth century, the old axiom of Carolingian kingship still applied to the ethical behavior of ordinary Christians.[17]

More important, the Carolingian idea of individual ethical responsibility and the common good penetrated deep into counties and castellanies and towns and villages – even in England, thanks to the kingdom's conquest by princes from once Carolingian lands. A village community or an urban community was very much conceived of as a moral community, defined by parish boundaries, knit together by Christian rituals, and saturated with Christian moral and ethical teachings now less an ideology of authority than of social uprightness. In France and England called *le commun*, in Germany *Gemain*, "community" became the rallying cry for reform movements led by elites, but also the watchword of peasants and artisans in their rebellions. It later infused the ideal of the total Christian community in radical Protestantism (Anabaptist Münster and Calvinist Geneva, for example). But it also remained the ideal of local communities of villagers, artisans, and workers – what the British historian E.P. Thompson (d. 1993) called the "moral economy of the crowd"[18] – to be re-Christianized and re-universalized in early nineteenth-century Britain by Methodists who preached the need of a Christian society to protect widows, orphans, and the poor. Then something very interesting happened.

By the 1830s and 1840s, unrestrained industrialization in England had created social injustices and environmental degradation hardly rivaled even in today's most rapidly expanding industrial economies. Economic liberalism – the un-tempered, immoderate pursuit of private interests – justified these excesses. The first effective, organized movement against liberal theory and its real world effects came in a movement known as Chartism, so-called because it promoted the adoption of a "National Charter" that would protect the rights of workers. But Chartists did not limit themselves to an economic platform. They demanded, for example, the vote for all adult males, regardless of class or property qualifications, on the grounds that only political representation would lead to significant economic and social reform. Given this democratic program, one might think Chartism had nothing in common with the Carolingian reform. Yet Chartism's program grew out of the "moral economy" of local communities, and one of its most important influences was Methodism. In the case of both Chartism and Methodism, if one pares away their democratic goals, one finds at the core a recognizably ecclesial ideal of the common social good and a social ethic recognizably descending from the Carolingian reform. There is the same emphasis on the social obligations of individuals; the same understanding that in a just society the powerful must help the poor; the same insistence on upright living as a condition of participation in the political community; even the same vices the upright are to shun (gambling, drunkenness, and sexual promiscuity). One also finds the same understanding that the key to instilling ethical awareness in the individual is education. Similar correspondences hold true for social democracy on the European continent, especially as it developed after the Second World War. They are easily overlooked because of the movement's originally strong class analysis, its demand for universal suffrage, and its insistence on the separation of church and state – traits obviously opposed to Carolingian principles. Yet look more deeply and one finds principles that are fundamentally ecclesial and ultimately Carolingian: A strong insistence that justice is a matter of equity and not law; a commitment to the belief that government should not simply protect individual interests but also promote the common good; the belief that a common social bond requires an awareness that individuals in society have mutual obligations towards each other; an understanding that those obligations are intrinsically ethical rather than legal, and that the key to instilling ethical values is, again, education. In 1959, the entirety of the program was summarized in two virtues: "responsibility for self and social obligation" (*freier Selbst-verantwortung und gesellschaftlicher Verpflichtung*).[19] Are these not the very virtues promoted by the leaders of the Carolingian reform? Much changed in the thousand years between the collapse of the Carolingian Empire and the emergence of social democracy. But without the Carolingian reform, there would be no "social" in European social democracy.

It goes without saying that liberals have good reason to work to exclude moralities from the public sphere; that way lies the tyranny of the majority. Yet in concentrating so exclusively on liberalism, with its theory of individual interests and rights, political philosophers and historians of political philosophy ignore the roots of a quite different set of principles that have been equally important in shaping Western politics. In ignoring them, defenders of liberalism overlook a basic truth that the Carolingian mirrorists saw with a simple clarity and that we ourselves confront in every weekly scandal: The more a political system empowers individuals, the more those individuals must exercise their power with moderation, wisdom, and consideration for the needs of society as a whole. More than any other political philosophy, liberalism demands ethics, because in a society whose individuals are held to be their own rulers, only ethics can temper their actions. And ethics cannot be legislated. As Alcuin and Hrabanus knew, it can only be taught.

Notes

1 J.M. Wallace-Hadrill, "The *Via Regia* of the Carolingian Age," in *Trends in Medieval Political Thought*, ed. B. Smalley, Oxford: Blackwell, 1965. The most important, foundational study of the Carolingian mirrors is in German; there is no English translation: H.H. Anton, *Fürstenspiegel und Herrscherethos in der Karolingerzeit Bonner historische Forschungen*, 32, Bonn: L. Röhrscheid, 1968.

2 Hincmar of Reims, *De regis persona et regio ministerio ad Carolum Calvum regem* 2, *Patrologia Latina* (hereafter PL) 125, cols 833–56 at cols 835–36, quoting from the seventh-century Irish tract, *De duodecim abusivis saeculi*. Similarly Sedulius Scottus, *De rectoribus christianis* 2, 5, trans. E.G. Doyle, *On Christian Rulers and The Poems*, Medieval and Renaissance Texts and Studies 17, Binghamton, NY: State University of New York at Binghamton Press, 1983, pp. 54, 59; Jonas of Orléans, *De institutione regia/Le métier du roi* 3, ed. and trans. A. Dubreucq, Paris: Editions du Cerf, pp. 184–85.

3 The major example is Gregory the Great's commentary on the Old Testament Book of Job; unfortunately there is no English translation: *Moralia in Job*, ed. M. Adriaen, Corpus Christianorum Series Latina, vols 143A–B, Turnhout: Brepols, 1979.

4 Compare Gregory the Great, *Pastoral Care*, trans. H. Davis, Westminster, MD: Newman Press, 1950.

5 Jonas of Orléans, *De institutione regia* 3, pp. 184–85.

6 Alcuin, *De virtutibus et vitiis liber ad Widonem comitem*, PL 101, cols 613–38.

7 Written for Count Matfrid of Orléans: Jonas of Orléans, *De institutione laicali libri tres*, PL 106, cols 121–278.

8 Dhuoda's mirror is one of the few available in a modern English translation: *Handbook for William: A Carolingian Woman's Counsel for Her Son*, trans. C. Neel, Lincoln, NE: University of Nebraska Press, 1991; paperback rpt. Washington, DC: Catholic University of America, 1999.

9 *Capitularia regum Francorum*, Monumenta Germaniae Historica (hereafter MGH), *Legum* 2, ed. A. Boretius and V. Kraus, 2 vols, Hanover: Impensis Bibliopolii Hahniani, 1883–89; *Capitula episcoporum*, MGH, ed. P. Brommer, R. Pokorny, and M. Stratmann, 3 vols, Hanover: Impensis Bibliopolii Hahniani, 1984–95.

10 *121. Missi cuiusdam admonitio*, in *Capitularia*, 1, MGH, *Legum* 2, pp. 238–40; trans. P.E. Dutton, *Carolingian Civilization: A Reader*, Peterborough, ON: Broadview Press, 1993, pp. 81–83.

11 *33. Capitulare missorum generale* c. 3, *Capitularia*, 1, MGH, *Legum* 2, p. 92.

12 Theodulf of Orléans, *Erstes Kapitular*, esp. 28, *Capitula Episcoporum*, 1, pp. 73–142, at pp. 125–26; largely taken over by Radulf of Bourges: see Radulf von Bourges, *Capitula Episcoporum*, 1, pp. 227–68.

13 Hrabanus *Maurus, Homilia* 11, PL 110, col. 26.

14 *Precum libelli quattuor aevi Karolini cum aliorum indicibus* 2–3, ed. A. Wilmart, Rome: Ephemerides liturgicae, 1940, pp. 37–38.

15 Alcuin, *Epistola* 110, MGH, *Epistolae Karolini aevi*, 2, ed. E. Dümmler, Berlin: Weidmann, 1895, pp. 157–59.

16 See M.C. Gaposchkin, "Louis IX, Crusade, and the Promise of Joshua," *Journal of Medieval History* 34, 2008, 245–74; W.C. Jordan, *Louis IX and the Challenge of the Crusade: A Study in Rulership*, Princeton, NJ: Princeton University Press, 1979, pp. 135–81.

17 *The Goodman of Paris (Le ménagier de Paris): A Treatise on Moral and Domestic Economy by a Citizen of Paris, c. 1393*, trans. E. Power, London, 1928; rpt. Woodbridge: The Folio Society, 2006, p. 118.

18 E.P. Thompson, "The Moral Economy of the English Crowd in the Eighteenth Century," *Past and Present* 50, 1971, 76–136.

19 *Programmatische Dokumente der deutschen Sozialdemokratie*, ed. D. Dowe and K. Klotzbach, Bad Godesberg: Dietz, 1959, p. 353.

Suggestions for further reading

Carolingian sources in English translation

Alcuin, *The Rhetoric of Alcuin and Charlemagne*, ed. and trans. W.S. Howell, New York: Russell and Russell, 1965.

Dhuoda, *Handbook for William: A Carolingian Woman's Counsel for Her Son*, trans. C. Neel, Lincoln, NE: University of Nebraska Press, 1991; paperback rpt. Washington, DC: Catholic University of America, 1999.

Dutton, P.E., *Carolingian Civilization: A Reader*, Peterborough, ON: Broadview Press, 1993.

Sedulius Scottus, *On Christian Rulers and The Poems*, trans. E.G. Doyle, Medieval and Renaissance Texts and Studies 17, Binghamton, NY: State University of New York at Binghamton Press, 1983.

The Reign of Charlemagne: Documents on Carolingian Government and Administration, trans. H.R. Loyn and J. Percival, London: St. Martin's Press, 1975.

Medieval developments and thought

Amos, T.L., "Preaching and the Sermon in the Carolingian World," in *De ore domini: Preacher and Word in the Middle Ages*, ed. T.L. Amos, E.A. Green, and B.M. Kienzle, Kalamazoo, MI: Medieval Institute Publications, 1989, pp. 41–60.

De Jong, M., *The Penitential State: Authority and Atonement in the Age of Louis the Pious, 814–840*, Cambridge: Cambridge University Press, 2009.

Harding, A., *Medieval Law and the Foundations of the State*, Oxford: Oxford University Press, 2002.

Justice, S., *Writing and Rebellion: England in 1381*, Berkeley: University of California Press, 1994.

Leyser, C., *Authority and Asceticism from Augustine to Gregory the Great*, Oxford: Oxford University Press, 2000.

Lynch, J., *Godparents and Kinship in Early Medieval Europe*, Princeton, NJ: Princeton University Press, 1986.

Moorehead, J., *Gregory the Great*, London: Routledge, 2005.

McKitterick, R., *The Frankish Church and the Carolingian Reforms, 789–895*, London: Royal Historical Society, 1977.

Wallace-Hadrill, J.M., "The *Via Regia* of the Carolingian Age," in *Trends in Medieval Political Thought*, ed. B. Smalley, Oxford: Blackwell, 1965.

Wormald, P. and Nelson, J.L. (eds) *Lay Intellectuals in the Carolingian World*, Cambridge: Cambridge University Press, 2007.

Ancient, early modern, and modern developments and thought

Blickle, P., *The Revolution of 1525: The German Peasants' War from a New Perspective*, trans. T.A. Brady, Jr. and H.C.E. Midelfort, Baltimore, MD: Johns Hopkins University Press, 1981.

Dunn, J., *Western Political Theory in the Face of the Future*, Cambridge: Cambridge University Press, 1979.

Gueye, C.M., *Late Stoic Cosmopolitanism: Foundations and Relevance*, Heidelberg: Winter, 2006.

Habermas, J., *The Structural Transformation of the Public Sphere: An Inquiry into Bourgeois Society*, trans. T. Burger and F. Lawrence, Cambridge, MA: MIT Press, 1991.

Hirschmann, A.O., *The Passions and the Interests: Political Arguments for Capitalism before Its Triumph*. Princeton, NJ: Princeton University Press, 1977.

MacIntyre, A., *After Virtue: A Study in Moral Theory*, 2nd ed., Notre Dame, IN: University of Notre Dame Press, 1984.

Pococke, J.G.A., *The Machiavellian Moment: Florentine Political Thought and the Atlantic Republican Tradition*, Princeton, NJ: Princeton University Press, 1975.

Sandel, M.J., *Liberalism and the Limits of Justice*, 2nd ed., Cambridge: Cambridge University Press, 1998.

Sharples, R.W., *Stoics, Epicureans and Sceptics: An Introduction to Hellenistic Philosophy*, London: Routledge, 1996.

Stephens, J.R., *Chartism and Christianity*, London: Garland Publishing, 1986.

Thompson, D. (ed.) *The Early Chartists*, London: Macmillan, 1971.

Thompson, E.P., *The Making of the English Working Class*, London: V. Gollancz, 1963.

——, "The Moral Economy of the English Crowd in the Eighteenth Century," *Past and Present* 50, 1971, 76–136.

Vogt, K.M., *Law, Reason, and the Cosmic City: Political Philosophy in the Early Stoa*, Oxford: Oxford University Press, 2008.

INDEX

Abelard, Peter 102; *Sic et Non [Yes and No]* 102
abortion 101
abstinence: *see* celibacy
Adam, biblical figure 54, 79, 86, 110–11, 116, 171–72, 178–79
Adeodatus, 80
Aeneid 82
Aethelbert, prince of Kent 20
Aethelred, prince of Kent 20
Afghanistan 7, 121, 122–23, 129, 154, 165
Africa and Africans 7, 10, 79, 124, 130–38, 140, 169; *see also* North Africa
African-Americans 15–16, 21–23, 36
agriculture 12, 19, 21, 108–18, 125, 147, 148, 170–71, 174
Albi 143
Alcuin 190, 192–93, 195
Alexander II, pope 95
Alexander, hermit 93–94, 97
Alexander the Great 82
Alexandria 126, 134
alms and alms-houses 20, 31–32, 34, 171, 191; *see also* charity and charities
Alypius 80–81, 85
Ambrose, Saint, bishop of Milan 80
American Civil Liberties Union 156
American Historical Association 4, 14
Amnesty International 142
Amsterdam 37
Anderson, Patrick 68
angels 74, 86, 90
Anglicanism: *see* Episcopalian Church

animals and insects 57–58, 84–85, 123–26, 132, 137, 172
Annunciation, Feast of the 74
Anonimalle Chronicle 175–76
Antinoüs 82
antiquity 5–6, 11, 50, 55, 80–82, 84, 108, 110, 125, 161, 183, 185, 187, 191; *see also* Greek culture, Roman Empire
Antoninus of Florence 97
Apocrypha 72, 90
apostles 70–73, 102, 110, 188; *see also* individual names
Aragon 8, 144, 147, 158
arbitration: *see* dispute settlement
archaeology: 6, 16, 130–31, 133
archbishops: *see* bishops
Ariès, Philippe 41
Arthur, king and Arthurian literature 131, 133–38
Assumption of Mary, Feast of 74
al-Asyuti, Salah al-Din, 127
Augustine, Saint, bishop of Canterbury 73
Augustine, Saint, bishop of Hippo 11, 60, 77–88, 92, 98, 189, 191; *Confessions*, 78, 80, 82, 85; *City of God* 85, 86
Augustinian rule 98
Australia 45
Ávila 160, 162–63

Ball, John 169, 171–72, 175, 175–80
baptism 44, 92, 189
Barcelona 37, 144
Barnard College 74
Basques 9

Thanatos, Greek god 42
theology and theological writings 57, 60,
    69–70, 74, 78–79, 83, 86, 91–92, 100–
    102, 108, 110–13, 116, 125, 127
Thessalonians, Second Letter to the 110
Thomas Aquinas, Saint 92, 185
Thompson, E.P. 194
Time Magazine 70
Timothy, First Letter to 56
Torquemada, Tomás de, 155, 157–60, 164
torture (physical and mental) 1, 5, 11, 17,
    19, 83, 86, 154–65; waterboarding 154,
    156–58, 160–61, 164–65
Toulouse, city of 146–50; counts of 144–45
Tourin, Christina 47
trauma 122–23, 143, 150–51, 163
trials and tribunals: *see* law
Trinity Broadcasting Network 77
Tubal-Cain 110
Tunisia 131
Tyler, Wat 12, 169–80
Tyndale, William 59

Ulpian 160–61
unemployment 21–22, 107; *see also* labor
    and laborers
UNESCO 71
United Nations 141–22, 150, 155–56, 164
United States of America 2, 4–5, 10–11,
    15–16, 18, 21–24, 35–37, 45, 54–55,
    60–62, 68, 75, 77, 101, 121–24, 132–33,
    138, 154–58, 160, 164–66, 169, 183, 186
universities 96–97; Oxford University 96–97;
    Regis College and Regis University
    (Denver) 46; University of California,
    Berkeley 44; University of Washington
    44; University of Paris 1, 97–98
urban centers 15, 21–25, 29–38, 61, 81,
    84, 93, 108, 123, 126–28, 132, 143, 145,
    155, 173–76, 180, 185, 194;
    urbanization 34, 38; *see also* individual
    names; Augustine, *City of God*

vagabonds and wanderers 127, 142, 171,
    176, 178
Valerian of Cimelium 81
Valla, Lorenzo 8
Vatican: *see* Roman Christianity, Church
    of Rome
vengeance 18, 22, 47, 58, 82, 98
Venice 33
Vergil 82

Vermont 58
Vézélay, monastery of 71
Vienna, archbishop of 77
Vietnam 155
vigils 43, 93, 112
Villon, François 171
virtues 11, 86, 111, 117, 136, 173, 177,
    184–95
Visigoths 9; *see also* Sisebut; Suinthila

Wall-E, film 12
Walsingham, Thomas 175
Walworth, William, mayor of London
    176, 178, 180
war and warfare 1, 9, 101, 109, 110, 121–28,
    123, 131–32, 142, 144–45, 147–48, 151,
    155, 170, 171; *see also* crusades and
    crusading; terrorism and suicide
    bombing; World War II
Ward-Perkins, Brian 12
Washington Post, The 68, 154, 157
Weber, Max 108
Wergeld 19
Westboro Baptist Church 58
White, Lawrence (Jr.) 42
Wikipedia 70
Wills, Garry 91
wisdom (political) 11, 183, 195
witches and witch hunts 57–59
women 6, 7, 18, 20, 22–23, 34, 54–62,
    66–75, 79–80, 85, 90, 92, 94, 97–99,
    102, 108–14, 121, 123–24, 126, 128,
    130, 132, 136, 144, 147–50, 161–62,
    189, 191; *see also* feminism and anti-
    feminism; gender
work and workers: *see* labor and laborers
World Heritage sites 71
World Trade Center 7
World War II (including Holocaust) 1, 10,
    21, 32, 34, 141, 142, 150, 157, 178, 195
Wycliffe, John 170, 174, 177; *see also*
    Lollards
Wyschogrod, Edith 74

Yadgari, Yusef 122
Young Men's Christian Association
    (YMCA) 77

al-Zahir Barquq, sultan 127
al-Zahir Baybars I, sultan 127
Zechariah, biblical figure 56
Zinn, Howard 4, 5